The Russian Labour Market

The Russian Labour Market

Between Transition and Turmoil

Vladimir Gimpelson and Douglas Lippoldt

ROWMAN & LITTLEFIELD PUBLISHERS, INC.
Lanham • Boulder • New York • Oxford

ROWMAN & LITTLEFIELD PUBLISHERS, INC.

Published in the United States of America
by Rowman & Littlefield Publishers, Inc.
4720 Boston Way, Lanham, Maryland 20706
http://www.rowmanlittlefield.com

12 Hid's Copse Road
Cumnor Hill, Oxford OX2 9JJ, England

British Library Cataloguing in Publication Information Available

Library of Congress Cataloging-in-Publication Data

Gimpelson, Vladimir.
  The Russian labour market : between transition and turmoil / Vladimir Gimpelson and
Douglas Lippoldt.
    p. cm.
  Includes bibliographical references (p.) and index.
  ISBN 0-7425-0911-7 (alk. paper)—ISBN 0-7425-0912-5 (pbk. : alk. paper)
    1. Labor market—Russia (Federation) 2. Russia (Federation)—Economic
conditions—1991- I. Lippoldt, Douglas. II. Title.

HD5797.2.A6 G56 2000
331.12'0947—dc21

                                                                    00-059060

⊗™ The paper used in this publication meets the minimum requirements of American
National Standard for Information Sciences—Permanence of Paper for Printed Library
Materials, ANSI/NISO Z39.48-1992.

Contents

List of Abbreviations

CEE	Central and Eastern Europe
EAP	Economically active population
EWT	Excess Wage Tax
FNPR	Federation of Independent Trade Unions of Russia
Goskomstat	State Committee of the Russian Federation on Statistics
ILO	International Labour Organisation
JSC	Joint stock companies
LFS	Labour force survey
OECD	Organisation for Economic Co-Operation and Development
REB	Russian Economic Barometer
RET	*Russian Economic Trends*
RF	Russian Federation
RLMS	Russian Longitudinal Monitoring Survey
SES	State Employment Service
ULC	Unit labour costs
UTS	Uniform Tariff Scale
VCIOM	All-Russian Centre for Public Opinion Research

Tables

Charts and Figures

Preface

For millions of Russians, the year 1992 offered the first real prospect of deep, market-oriented economic reform and restructuring. Price liberalisation, decreased regulation in the labour market, partial privatisation, introduction of an expanded social safety net, and many other changes seemed to create tremendous new economic potential for Russian workers and employers. Yet years later the economy remained mired, having undergone substantial adjustment but with much less deep restructuring than was initially expected. Unlike some transition countries such as Poland, several years into the transition Russia still had not resumed growth in a sustained fashion. Succinctly put: the full potential of economic reform was not realised and the consequences could be clearly seen in the labour market.

The early years of the economic transition were a critical period for Russia when the preconditions for the subsequent economic malaise were laid out. Instead of a process of constant, credible, and viable reform, this period was characterised by uncertainty and inconsistency in policy. Policy-making sometimes deadlocked. Where reforms were implemented, many came with built-in bugs. For example, poorly structured institutional reforms left control of funds for labour market programmes in a grey area with overlapping claims from competing local, regional, and national interests. Privatisation left insiders in a position to dominate firms, sometimes shutting out infusions of outside management talent that were needed for restructuring. Federal fiscal and monetary policies subjected firms to waves of inflation and to government payment arrears that echoed through the whole economy. These arrears returned to haunt the government in the form of enterprise tax arrears. Employment tax revenue shortfalls led to arrears in unemployment benefit payments in many regions. A weak bankruptcy law enabled many firms to avoid pressures to restructure. And so on.

From a labour market perspective, the first years of economic transition merit a careful study. Policy-makers seeking to exit from the current situation face a difficult starting point. Unemployment is relatively high. Distressed enterprises have already suffered loss and devaluation of their human capital. Many households have drawn down their assets in an effort to maintain living standards. Restarting the economy will probably involve further dislocation and economic hardship as existing enterprises are forced to restructure. Yet the picture is not entirely negative. Some enterprise restructuring has already taken place and elements of the initial reforms have laid down a portion of the foundation for a sound labour market policy in the future. For example, a network of local employment centres has been established with the potential to facilitate part of the reallocation of labour through its system for matching job-seekers and vacancies.

While labour market policies cannot be expected to resolve the full range of problems facing the Russian labour market, they can contribute to a partial solution. These policies, for example, could be centred on a credible social safety net for workers that supports the reallocation of labour, promotes job matching, and—to some extent—contributes to the development of human capital. With such policy goals in mind, this book takes a detailed look at the Russian labour market during the first years of transition, which are defined here as beginning with the institution of wide-ranging labour market reforms in 1992 and ending with the fallout from the financial crisis of 1998. The choice of starting point to mark the beginning of transition might be contested in that some experimentation with labour market reform had already begun in the 1980s. Nevertheless, the authors decided to choose 1992 because it was then that the scale of economic reform was greatly expanded in the aftermath of the break-up of the Soviet Union.

The book begins with an overview of the Russian labour market in transition. Within this framework, it then moves on to present a review of the labour market dynamics during the initial years of the transition. This look at the dynamic processes is complemented by an assessment of the destinations of those who moved into "new" jobs or unemployment, as well as the situation of those who remained in "old" jobs. Subsequent chapters are devoted to an examination of wage developments and social protection for labour market participants. A special thematic chapter assesses the association between the unsettled political situation and the evolution of labour market policy. The conclusions synthesise an integrated picture of the Russian labour market in the aftermath of the early transition period and highlight the implications of the experience for future policy action.

The authors have prepared the main text using generally nontechnical language. Where necessary, explanatory notes and references are provided. Data on the main labour market trends are presented in charts that capture and present the information in a clear fashion. For those desiring more details, we have included ample and detailed tables containing a large volume of descriptive and analytical information.

The authors have had a unique position from which to study Russian labour market development, combining the advantages of being insiders and outside observers simultaneously. The book was drafted during 1999 and early 2000, but it was not done from scratch. The writing was heavily based on field work carried out from 1993 to 1998. The project was an exciting example of cooperation, despite spells of geographical separation between the authors. Technology (especially electronic communication) and friendship helped make its completion possible.

Vladimir Gimpelson is a scholar of the Russian transition and is affiliated with the Institute of World Economy and International Relations (IMEMO) of the Russian Academy of Sciences. However, his tenure there was interrupted several times during recent years. First, he had short-term stays at the London School of Economics (1997) and at CREES, University of Birmingham (1997). Second, he participated during 1997–1998 as a member of a focus group on the political economy of the transition, convened by Janos Kornai at the Collegium Budapest. Third, during 1998–1999 he had the happy chance to lecture on the economics of transition at the Faculty of Economics of the University of Tokyo. All of these contributed to his understanding of the emerging market economy in Russia and its particular problems of transition.

Douglas Lippoldt has long taken an active interest in Eastern Europe. From his time as a Fulbright Scholar in Germany (1979–1980) through his current tenure as a labour economist at the Organisation for Economic Co-Operation and Development (OECD), he has pursued studies and work related to the region. During 1992–1998, within the framework of the OECD's Centre for Co-Operation with Economies in Transition, he managed several projects focusing on the Russian labour market—an assignment that provided many opportunities for in-country work. He continues to be actively involved in study of economic transition and labour market adjustment.

A number of research papers were produced based on the field work and these papers form the original core of the present book.[1] Preliminary results were also presented at a number of lectures, seminars, and conferences at the Institute for Advanced Studies, Vienna (1994 and 1998); London School of Economics (1997); CREES, University of Birmingham (1997); LICOS, Catholic University, Leuven (1997); the Collegium Budapest (1998); Central European University, Budapest (1998); DELTA-ENS, Paris (1998); University of Kyoto (1999); SRC, Sapporo (1999); IZA, Bonn (2000); and at several OECD Workshops in Moscow and Paris (1993–1999). Various sections were presented to participants of the permanent seminar held at the Center for Comparative Economic and Social Studies, IMEMO. The authors are grateful for the critique and comments received on these occasions.

Directly and indirectly, the authors have benefited from the support and assistance of numerous institutions and individuals. Particular thanks are due to the representatives of the State Employment Service, the State Committee of the Russian Federation on Statistics, the erstwhile Ministries of Labour and of Social Protection, and regional and local authorities in Astrakhan, Kaluga, Krasnoyarsk, Moscow region, Novosibirsk, St. Petersburg, Samara, and Tomsk.

The research efforts were bolstered through cooperation with two TACIS project teams directed by H. Lehmann (Projects nos. T94-1073-R and T95-4099-R). Vladimir Gimpelson would like to acknowledge the support over the years from IMEMO, University of Tokyo (1998–1999), Collegium Budapest (1997–1998), and NATO Democratic Institutions Fellowship programme (1996–1998). Douglas Lippoldt would like to acknowledge the support of his colleagues at the OECD.

The authors would like to express their gratitude for comments on their earlier papers provided by T. Boeri, S. Clarke, J. Earle, R. Fay, Ye. Gontmakher, T. Gorbacheva, L. Gordon, J. Hellman, V. Kabalina, R. Kapeliushnikov, E. Kapstein, E. Klopov, J. Kollo, J. Konings, J. Kornai, R. Koumakhov, M. Kramer, H. Lehmann, J. Litwack, V. Magun, J. Martin, V. Mikhalev, M. Moskvina, B. Najman, S. Ohtsu, V. Radayev, A. Reuterswärd, M. Schaffer, G. Standing, D. Treisman, M. Williamson, and several anonymous referees. The suggestions of these scholars helped to improve the quality of the present text. The authors are also grateful to the many enterprise managers, government officials, and workers in Russia who shared their views and insights with us.

G. Monusova and N. Vishnevskaya ably contributed to the field work and data collection and their assistance is gratefully acknowledged. The authors would also like to thank A. Johnston for her detailed editorial suggestions on the initial draft. The authors remain accountable for any remaining errors or omissions. And, in particular, the opinions expressed do not necessarily reflect the views of the Russian Academy of Sciences or the OECD.

This book stakes out a position in the radical middle of the range of opinion on the Russian transition. While many Russian scholars tend to focus on the extremes, citing a lack of adjustment or the initial successes with macroeconomic stabilisation (sometimes side-stepping micro issues), the arguments presented here suggest that despite many impediments, there was adjustment in the labour market. However, this adjustment sometimes took on grotesque forms due to a combination of micro- and macro-distortions. In short, the labour market adjustment path was not smooth and there were many reversals; nowhere was it well advanced. Its evolution could not be separated from the larger economic, social, and political environment. These are some of the elements contributing to the turmoil and to the evolution of a peculiar Russian model for labour market adjustment. This is the story laid out in the following chapters.

*

This book is dedicated to our families who endured our many absences on mission and our long hours of toil. Their support was essential to the success of this multiyear project.

NOTE

1. The authors' most referenced papers and volumes are cited in the References. The authors are grateful to Blackwell Publishers, Cambridge University Press, and the OECD for granting permission to republish materials from these earlier works, albeit updated and revised for information that has since become available.

1

Key Factors Shaping the Transition

TRANSITION AND THE LABOUR MARKET

Labour markets "mediate the transition" by channelling outcomes of macro- and microeconomic reforms into the everyday life of households, contributing directly to the evolution of economic and social well-being. The effects are multiple and complex, direct and indirect, with both positive and negative consequences. For example, the redeployment of labour during the transition is linked to changes in earnings opportunities across various segments of the population that, in turn, are associated with shifts in incentives and that influence living standards, patterns of social hardship, and other socioeconomic variables even inflation. The labour market situation—through availability of jobs and level of wages—strongly affects perceptions of the transition. Popular support for reforms and, ultimately, the sustainability of the transition depend, therefore, partly on labour market outcomes as well.

The messy Russian transition of the 1990s provides quite a peculiar manifestation of transition, one that perhaps stretches the notion as to what transition entails. This book is about the change in system as seen from the perspective of labour market participants during the critical first six years of the post-Soviet era. The introductory chapter provides a short overview of the transition and then moves on to highlight major labour market developments and key aspects of the context in which they occurred. Subsequent chapters each present a core element of the transition in the labour market. The analysis seeks to explore the puzzling turns in the evolution of the main dimensions of the labour market, essentially in labour demand, supply, and price. The answers lie not only in the labour market per se, but are also embedded in the political, economic, and social landscape of the country. The concluding chapter underscores the interrelationships between the factors shaping the labour market and outlines the main policy implications.

What Is Meant by "Transition"?

In the context of the former socialist countries, "transition" refers to a change in system. The World Bank's *World Development Report* (1996) defines it as a movement "from plan to market." Similarly, Blanchard and Kremer (1997) describe it as a shift "from plan and plan institutions to market and market institutions." But, in fact, the transition was even broader.

The former socialist system was characterised by the absolute power of the Marxist-Leninist party, state and quasi-state ownership of resources, and bureaucratic co-ordination of economic activity. These three key systemic features resulted in many of the familiar characteristics of the old system: soft budget constraints, weak market signals, emphasis on quantity over quality of goods produced, inefficient use of resources, chronic shortages, and limited freedom, among many others. In order to complete the shift toward a capitalist system, reforms were needed to change the political basis of state power, increase the share of property held privately, and expose most economic activity to market forces.[1] Such reforms might have been expected to result in the strengthening of budget constraints, reallocation of resources, increased efficiency, higher quality, and better responsiveness to consumers, along with many other important outcomes.

The transition was more than just a "bigger" role for the market and a "smaller" one for government. It involved a complete systemic overhaul, whereby almost all socialist-type institutions needed to be rapidly dismantled and new ones—market-compatible—were to be created and empowered. Historically, capitalist institutions evolved over a period of centuries, but the transition in Central and Eastern Europe was intended to compress institutional development into a few years by relying on designs adapted from other countries. The same generation of individuals was to observe the decay of socialism, the chaos of transition, and the emergence of mature capitalism.

While market reforms were intended to raise economic efficiency, in the early stages they often resulted in some degree of disorganisation. Indeed, a measure of turmoil seems to be a systemic feature of the transition.[2] Such disorganisation contributed to output decline, increased transaction costs, and caused various economic and social disruptions such as growth of unemployment, inequality, and poverty. It is not by chance that all post-communist countries have experienced or are still mired in economic and political turmoil. Multiple reasons exist for large-scale disorganisation. One of them was the collapse of bureaucratic coordination while market signals were still weak and imperfect. Firms were left to face great uncertainty regarding prices and wages, distribution networks, and resource availability, among other aspects of doing business. The scale of disruption depended on many noneconomic factors as well, such as history, geography, and culture. Thus Central Europe, which experienced communist rule for a shorter time than Russia, had a real comparative advantage. It retained some institutional memory or even experience of capitalism. (Its geographical position—being closer to the European Union—might be another advantage.) In general, initial conditions such as the extent of prior socialist domination of the economy had an influence on the transition that could not be ignored.[3]

In Russia, where the socialist system was deeply embedded in all aspects of social and economic life, the transition meant a radical break with the past. So it is not surprising that such deep and complex change should be associated with great disorganisation or turmoil, particularly during the early years of transition. Russia faced a triple transition. Besides the economic transformation, there was a complex political transition and the building of a new nation state on the ruins of the Soviet empire. These simultaneous transitions were interrelated, each one making the others more difficult and costly and feeding the turmoil, particularly during the early transition years considered here.

How Did the Transition Affect the Labour Market?

As one of the factor markets, the labour market was freed in the early stages of reform and developed in the course of the transition process. The "quasi" labour market that existed prior to the transition operated with many distortions and was shaped and managed institutionally in a completely different way from a capitalist labour market.[4] Employment targets and wage rates were set centrally and imposed on enterprises from above. Wages had nothing to do with the marginal productivity of labour. Officially, unemployment did not exist, and labour was a cheap and chronically scarce input. Institutional and legal arrangements were deliberately designed to limit uncontrolled labour mobility. Barriers included residence permits (*propiska*), tenure-related benefits, enterprise-tied social benefits, and moral condemnation of active job-shopping, among others. Nevertheless, ongoing and widespread turnover occurred as workers sought to improve their terms of employment, and, consequently, enterprises continually sought to hire more labour. Among the population, attitudes to work were captured by references to "unemployment while on a job" or jokes that "the government pretends to pay us and we pretend to work." At the same time, the official labour market co-existed with an informal or shadow market where supply met demand.

The transition brought a radical change in the way the labour market operated. Most of the major reforms influenced its functioning: monetary and fiscal policies, privatisation and small business development, foreign trade, and the conversion of military-industrial assets, among others. In addition, the institutional mechanisms of the labour market itself were completely reshaped. These reform-oriented changes, as well as the inability of the government to stick to sound and consistent policies, all fuelled the turmoil.

The present volume, in examining the Russian labour market developments from 1992 to 1998, highlights the interrelationship between the transition and turmoil. This interrelationship is evident in each area considered in subsequent chapters: employment, wages, labour mobility, social protection, and the political economy. Everywhere, reforms and disorganisation went hand in hand; transition and turmoil became two sides of the same coin. They were influenced by a variety of factors.

SHAPING THE POST-SOCIALIST LABOUR MARKET: ECONOMIC REFORMS, POLITICS, AND SOCIETY

The socialist legacy was one factor shaping and complicating the transition. It was reflected in well-entrenched socialist-type institutions, policies, and mentalities. As De Melo et al. argue, adverse initial conditions were associated with suboptimal policy choices, leading to inferior policy outcomes.[5] The legacy inherited by Russia from the Soviet Union included severe structural and macroeconomic distortions, lack of non-socialist institutional memory, low living standards, and absence of a common vision for the political system, among many other disadvantages. Any one of these constituted a strong challenge to the smooth functioning of the labour markets.

An Economy in Turmoil

The transition period brought great economic and social distress to Russia. The transformational recession in Russia was much longer and deeper than was initially expected by most observers. Muddling through with stop-and-go reforms in the early years of transition, the country saw its industrial production contract by half and its GDP by about 40 percent.[6] An OECD survey of the Russian Federation notes, "The sheer scale of what could be called the Great Contraction is such that some observers simply refuse to believe the data published by the national statistical office."[7] In 1997, the first signs of renewed growth were seen, but by 1998 the economy was shrinking again (by an additional 5 percent). Throughout this period, reform-minded economic policy-makers sought to chart a course focusing, in particular, on macroeconomic stabilisation (i.e., containing inflation and fiscal shortfalls) and privatisation. Institutional development, human capital issues, and improvement of the social safety net were generally viewed as secondary.

The struggle to implement a macroeconomic policy aimed at slowing inflation was the major headache for the government. The first years of transition were marked by very high and variable inflation. Periods of fiscal restraint were followed by periods of lax monetary policy with corresponding jumps in inflation. Then, in 1995, a more consistent and tighter monetary policy brought inflation down from 17 percent per month early in the year to about 3 percent per month. During the following period, from 1996 through the first half of 1998, inflation was kept at a relatively low pace. At the same time the exchange rate effectively lagged behind the Consumer Price Index (CPI) with a corresponding appreciation of the national currency, the ruble. The government and the central bank defended the increasingly overvalued ruble. This had adverse effects on the competitiveness of Russian firms, promoted massive import penetration, eroded export revenues, and contributed to a worsening of fiscal problems.

The fiscal deficit remained rather large throughout these years, imposing terrible pressures on public finance. The "Great Contraction" in output and the growth in barter and nontransparency in inter- and intrafirm transactions undermined the effective tax base. Tax collection rates were generally poor and very sensitive to any signs of political instability (which were plentiful). The relatively low rate of price increase in the 2½ years from 1996 reduced the inflation tax as a means of governmental financing.[8] Export revenues (mostly from oil, gas, and other commodities) were constrained by pressures linked to the terms of trade. Meanwhile, there was a political deadlock in moves to pursue crucial structural reforms (e.g., those concerning taxes, the military, housing, social security, regulation of natural monopolies, and introduction of a sound bankruptcy regulation, among many others).

Various types of short-term state bonds (abbreviated as "GKO" in Russian) and external borrowing (largely, the IMF/World Bank loans and Eurobonds) became major sources of deficit financing. The use of borrowing to cover budget gaps (as opposed to simply expanding the money supply) led to steady disinflation but exposed the government to the harsh judgement of the domestic and later international financial markets. As long as investors believed that government debt would be serviced, they were willing to roll over these loans. As dependence on short-term borrowing rose, the general fiscal situation became increasingly fragile and dangerous. Eventually, the share of debt servicing in total budgetary spending rose sharply. In 1995, 19 percent of all federal expenditures went for debt service, in 1996 about 26 percent, in 1997 about 24 percent, and then during the period January–July 1998 interest payments totalled about 37 percent of all expenditures.[9]

While more transparent and legitimate fiscal adjustment was stalled in the State Duma (the lower house of the Russian legislature), the government effectively relied on sequestration to control budgetary expenditures. This caused persistent underfinancing of the army and the public sector and generated mass budgetary arrears and late wages and pensions. In 1996–1997, the arrears grew rapidly, damaging the credibility of the government and undermining political and social stability; they also contributed to further erosion of public finances and to increasingly politicised claims for public funds. The economy entered a vicious circle. The Asian financial crisis and falling commodity prices also heightened concerns. Finally, in mid-1998, the Russian financial system collapsed, overburdened by fiscal and debt pressures.

Mass privatisation was another key element of the early transition policies. The Federal Privatisation Programme, launched in 1992, offered three different options that varied in terms of the privileges for insiders.[10] Already by mid-1994, some 15,000 enterprises had been privatised under this programme, encompassing 17 million employees or nearly one-fourth of the economically active population. In most cases, privatisation resulted in insiders dominating firms. Often the state was the largest outside shareholder, but it played a relatively passive role in enterprise management. Meanwhile, in the face of uncertainty, insider coalitions became a brake on restructuring firms. Ultimately, some positive restructuring was accomplished during the first five years of transition, but it remained fairly modest in scope, a point documented by a number of studies.[11]

Still, enterprises no longer acted as they had under the system of economic planning. Facing conflicting or unclear market signals, managers often adopted what was referred to as a "survival-oriented strategy."[12] Among other features, this strategy emphasised addressing short-term cash flow problems in part through barter and arrears; a conservative and ad hoc, but not intransigent, approach to restructuring; and some striving to minimise open conflict, at least with respect to essential operations. This not only differed from what was expected in a market economy, but also effectively undermined the credibility of reform efforts and perpetuated inefficiencies.

The last but not the least important feature of the Russian economy in the 1990s was in its institutional weakness. Macroeconomic reforms enjoyed priority over institution building (in line with the priorities of the so-called "Washington consensus" among the analysts in key international organisations), leaving the country with an unreformed or semi-reformed set of institutions. In turn, numerous institutional loopholes created opportunities for corruption, poor enforcement of laws and contracts, and violation of shareholders rights. As a result, businesses and governments (both federal and local) engaged in predatory rent-seeking. Public money was diverted to other uses (including, apparently, personal offshore accounts), leaving the military, schools, and hospitals without sufficient operating funds. Flourishing corruption and tax evasion were accompanied by massive capital flight and a shift toward barter and in-kind exchanges. This state of affairs seriously damaged incentives and opportunities for enterprise restructuring and job creation. As one might expect, this also affected the "real" sector, causing more decay and less liquidity.

The labour market was not insulated from this disruption, which left its mark on the life and work of households. Employment adjustment lagged output declines, leading to falls in labour productivity. Unemployment grew gradually but steadily. Large enterprises—often unwilling to restructure deeply—kept hoarding labour while avoiding lay-offs and creating few jobs. Underemployment spread and was accompanied by large-scale churning in the labour market and growing wage differentiation. Inequality increased dramatically. Claims for money wages in overvalued rubles became less and less sustainable and led to the accumulation of arrears. Wages and pensions lost a significant portion of their real value, having failed to keep up. While a handful of people made huge fortunes, rising poverty affected about a third of the population. Overall life expectancy at birth fell and male life expectancy dropped under 60 years—a development that would be unthinkable in any other industrial country.

Russia's Messy Politics

Purely economic factors explain only a portion of the policies and outcomes of the transition. Political considerations also play an important role. As Alesina and Rodrik note, "Economics is concerned with expanding the pie while politics is about distributing it."[13] Indeed, the transition is largely about redistribution and reallocation. While a detailed discussion of Russian politics goes beyond the scope of this book, it is important to note that the political scene was messy, with many contradictory tendencies.[14] Unsettled political institutions and general political uncertainty took their toll on the labour market. For example, political instability discouraged long-term investment; this in turn inhibited job creation. It also shortened the horizons for both policy-makers and managers; it paid to seek short-term rents rather than long-term returns. A further political complication was the failure of the Russian Constitution (adopted in 1993) to provide the basis for a transparent and constructive budget process—a point linked to bloated spending plans and subsequent arrears.

Society Taken by Surprise

Generally, the people of the former Soviet Union had little experience in dealing with the workings of markets. Their knowledge of labour markets was no exception, as life-long employment was practically guaranteed and wages across all jobs were fixed from above. Tenure and loyalty were rewarded more highly than were achievements. Jobs and "workers' collectives" formed a framework for socialist society, with numerous benefits and social activities dependent on the workplace. Company-towns and enterprise-linked residential areas in large cities were striking examples of this social and territorial organisation of society. As a result, many households found it extremely difficult to accept any disruption to these ties.

All of this meant that the general public saw unemployment as a major threat. For many people, a feeling of "enterprise dependence" contributed to a strong and adverse attitude to changes that might result in job loss. From the outset of the reforms in the late 1980s, people perceived unemployment to be much higher than it was. This mass fear of unemployment—whether indigenous or deliberately generated by politicians—was among the factors that paralysed Gorbachev's will to undertake reform and it was bound to affect the transition in the 1990s. Fear of unemployment became a factor actively used by critics to slow down the transition, and it may have contributed to widespread acceptance of the trade-off between wage arrears and employment in the mid-1990s.

As is well known, human capital is a crucial factor for economic growth. At the same time, in a market economy, up-to-date human capital tends to provide one of the best protections against unemployment while facilitating labour realloca- tion. In all transition countries, people with higher education and modern skills were the least exposed to the hazards of unemployment and were among the win- ners under the reforms. Russia inherited a huge stock of human capital, with al- most 100 percent literacy, an extensive educational system, and large research and development sector. This legacy might be thought to be an asset, but it is not entirely so. In Russia, the structure of human capital stock appeared to be skewed to emphasise technical expertise. During the transition period, a shrinking indus- trial base needed far fewer engineers and technicians, while market-oriented lawyers, economists, and certain other occupational groups were in great demand under the new economic system. Needless to say, entrepreneurial skills and mod- ern managerial expertise were practically absent in the Russian human capital stock at the beginning of the 1990s.

WHAT MAKES THE RUSSIAN CASE SPECIAL?

Though all the post-communist economies have experienced what Kornai called "a transformational recession,"[15] the Russian recession was deeper and longer than those in most Central and East European (CEE) countries. The loss in output everywhere in the region was accompanied by a steep rise in non- employment.[16] Relatively large declines in employment and corresponding in- creases in unemployment were elements of a fairly "standard" response to the demand shock that hit CEE countries.[17] Real wages declined as well, but in most countries the brunt of labour market adjustment was borne largely through shrinking employment and growing unemployment (i.e., quantity ad- justments). This was the case in the CEE countries, and it was widely expected to happen in Russia as well.

In its response to the economic shocks, however, Russia differed from most transition nations in Central and Eastern Europe. There, the labour market tended to adjust largely through extreme downward wage flexibility, while declines in employment played a secondary role—the growth in short-time working notwith- standing. The particular dynamics and flexibility of the Russian labour market prompted Layard and Richter to refer to "the Russian way" of adjustment. They wrote that "Russia has in effect had much more real wage flexibility than many other countries, due to more factors than solely hyperinflation."[18] This extreme flexibility was achieved by various means but generally worked through informal institutions. While formal laws and rules governing wage formation obviously existed in Russia, they were often poorly enforced and tended to be of lesser importance than the informal relationships between actors. The particular pattern of labour market adjustment in this de-institutionalised economy may have had lower social and political costs in the short run. However, it also entailed substantial economic costs since it stalled restructuring; ultimately, it became politically costly as well. This response to economic shock through wage flexibility rather than a far-reaching reallocation of labour resources was characterised by Kapeliushnikov as "adjustment without restructuring."[19]

The general picture of "the Russian Way" includes the following key features:

Declines in employment and increases in unemployment were relatively small and developed slowly against the large falls in output. In 1991, the Russian economy employed about 74 million individuals. By the end of 1998, this figure amounted to 63.2 million, a decline of about 15 percent. At the same time, the falls in GDP and industrial output were much larger (over 40 and 50 percent, respectively). Gradual and relatively small declines in employment translated into a gradual but steady rise in unemployment. This rise was not as much as one might expect, given the "Great Contraction" in output. Unemployment began to reach substantial levels only in the second half of the decade. On the other hand, employment in many transition countries—particularly in Central Europe—tended to be more responsive to declines in output. In Hungary and Poland, for example, each 1 percent decline in output was associated with an employment decline of 0.6 and 1.1 percent, respectively.[20] In Russia, the ratio was about –1.0 to –0.4.[21]

The labour market remained dynamic throughout the transition period, with relatively high turnover and large flows between jobs. In the CEE countries, state-owned and recently privatised enterprises facing hardening budget constraints stopped or minimised new hiring and increased lay-offs. Reallocation of labour across sectors accelerated. Flows out of employment were larger than those into jobs. Though the private sector intensified job creation, it was not enough to offset the increase in unemployment.

The dynamics of the labour market in Russia—as measured by labour and job turnover—functioned differently, in part as a result of the continuation of relatively soft budget constraints, particularly for firms with state or mixed ownership. Having lost soft direct credits in 1993–1994, many of these older enterprises began to resort to various barter schemes, mutual nonpayments, and arrears to stay afloat. Lack of liquidity became the price for this approach to survival, which in turn was associated with a deterioration in employment conditions that led many of the best workers to quit. Enterprises used lay-offs sparingly.

The fairly high incidence of separations was accompanied by a substantial rate of hiring, which constituted a perplexing phenomenon in light of the need to downsize. Slowing the rate of new hires could have greatly cut excess labour in a short period. Nevertheless, this did not happen. Various arguments have been put forward, but no single explanation seems satisfactory, a point explored in more detail in the following chapters.

Compared with the fairly substantial overall labour turnover in Russia, outflows into unemployment remained relatively modest. Instead, substantial movement of labour occurred between enterprises but with limited reallocation across regions or between sectors. Recorded job creation remained quite low. Under these circumstances, mobile workers moved primarily into ongoing jobs, the grey economy, or secondary employment in small enterprises, with relatively little new primary job creation. Often this job-to-job movement amounted to little more than churning.

Significant labour market flexibility was achieved through a combination of underemployment and wage arrears. Labour market flexibility in Russia was based on a few key mechanisms, which included working hour cuts, flexibility in compensation (in terms of overall levels, structure, and relative levels within the enterprise), wage arrears, and fixed-term contracts (instead of indefinite-term contracts). Withdrawals from the labour market and failures to compensate wage losses due to inflation also helped to contain labour costs. Enterprises resorted to these devices in various combinations, depending on their individual circumstances.

Initially, flexible working hours and lack of compensation for inflation were probably among the most widely used. In the years after 1993–1994, wage arrears played an increasingly important role in limiting labour costs. This became especially evident in the period from 1996 through the first half of 1998. The development of wage arrears might seem an unusual or even illegal form of flexibility, but the Russian legal system appeared to be unable to combat it. In addition, the least competitive part of the Russian labour force (which apparently suffered most from wage arrears) implicitly accepted delayed payments as a trade-off against potential job losses. Decentralised wage-setting with little trade union influence also facilitated wage flexibility. Also, although the Russian labour code technically permitted only very limited use of fixed-term contracts, this limitation was increasingly abused.

Institutions functioned poorly and a high degree of informalisation characterised the labour market. A "de-institutionalised labour market is a component of [the] de-institutionalised Russian economy," concludes Kapeliushnikov.[22] Even where institutions (including laws and regulations) existed, they were often enforced in a very selective or arbitrary way. Instead, informal agreements and informal transactions took on growing importance in the economy. This de-institutionalisation was associated with the rise in semiformal or informal employment, hidden unemployment, late pay, and violations of labour standards, among other aspects of worsening employment conditions. Employees whose labour rights were violated were often reluctant to resist publicly. They feared being fired, lacked knowledge of laws or viewed courts as ineffectual, and/or had little faith in trade unions, which in turn were often too weak to defend their members. Such flexibility helped firms to reduce labour costs in the near term but with uncertain longer-term implications.

KEY LABOUR MARKET INSTITUTIONS

Prior to 1992, there were severe impediments to the functioning of the labour market in Russia, where—among other distortions—the state limited labour mobility, centrally determined wage rates, and impeded administratively the free choice of career. The passage of the Employment Law in 1991 and the introduction of a wide-ranging reform programme in early 1992 dramatically changed conditions. The new law acknowledged the right of workers to make their own choices in the labour market and granted unemployed persons a measure of social protection. Employer rights to freedom in making recruitment decisions were also stated. As a consequence of this liberalisation and various economic shocks, open unemployment—which previously had hardly existed—began to grow. New labour market institutions were needed to deal with these new conditions in the labour market.

Employment Service and Ministry of Labour

In order to back up the guarantees laid out in the Employment Law and to facilitate the functioning of the labour market, the State Employment Service (SES) was established as an independent agency by presidential decree in June 1992. Built upon an existing system of labour offices, the SES was expanded and developed into the primary vehicle for implementing labour market policy targeting the unemployed. In the years that followed, the combination of basic employment protection legislation and SES measures provided the first line of social protection for workers at risk of becoming unemployed. The SES was the main state institution implementing active and passive labour market policies. Throughout the initial transition period it operated more or less independently, but in 1998 it was incorporated into a new Ministry of Labour and Social Development.[23]

The SES offices played a much different role than those that existed in the USSR under the State Committee for Labour and Social Questions. Although its predecessor served primarily to recruit workers for priority areas of the economy suffering from labour shortages, the SES focused much of its resources on counselling, matching of job-seekers and vacancies, and payment of unemployment benefits. The activities of the SES were bolstered by a new source of dedicated funding in the form of the Employment Fund, which was financed through an employer-paid tax on wages.[24]

The social protection provided to the unemployed through the SES was intended to mesh with a set of redundancy regulations that offered workers certain guarantees. Under the labour code, firms were required to offer redundant workers alternative employment if possible, to secure trade union approval for redundancies, to notify the SES, and to provide up to three months of severance pay. However, this social safety net fell short of offering broad protection. Collection of unemployment benefits was effectively discouraged by bureaucratic hurdles for registration with the SES and by the low real value of benefits. The redundancy regulations provided an incentive to employers to avoid lay-offs or, alternatively, for them to encourage voluntary quitting, which was not protected by some of the guarantees. Instead, a situation arose that pushed less competitive workers to stay at their current jobs, despite deteriorating conditions and pay.

The Ministry of Labour (MOL), lacking access to the resources of the Employment Fund, was much less involved in direct policy implementation. It continued to retain responsibility for certain administrative functions such as calculating the "minimum subsistence income" indicator and regulating health and safety, workers' rights, and other labour code issues. It also conducted policy analysis for the government and participated in the Russian Tripartite Commission. The MOL enjoyed higher formal status than the SES but lost almost all of its former financial and administrative leverage. This fuelled tension between the two institutions and effectively undermined the ability of the federal government to establish a clear and integrated labour market policy throughout the early transition years.

During the first four years of the transition, government policy also included an excess-wage tax, which encouraged employers to limit the growth in wages as part of an ostensibly anti-inflation policy. The tax was levied on the portion of average wages exceeding a threshold set at six times the official minimum wage; wages above this amount were called "profits" and taxed at a 35 percent rate. Since adjustments in the minimum wage did not keep up with inflation, the volume of wages exposed to this tax increased rapidly. Many enterprises reportedly evaded their liabilities by understating their wage bills or overstating their employment (the tax was based on wages per employee, so retention of excess low-paid workers could bring down the liability). Although the wage controls may have been relatively ineffective, they still may have contributed to labour hoarding or at least to statistical distortions (e.g., through misreporting of employment) until their abolition in early 1996.

Trade Unions and Collective Bargaining

As in other transition countries, independent trade unions, collective bargaining, and the right to strike became legal in Russia with the collapse of central planning. The old trade unions, which previously had nearly universal membership but no bargaining role, began to take on an independent but conservative posture. They remained grouped in an association—renamed the Federation of Independent Trade Unions (FNPR)—and continued to dominate organised labour. In the mid-1990s, FNPR claimed some 60 million nominal members but the active membership was much smaller.

Independent trade unions had begun to develop even before the 1992 labour market reforms. However, their influence and membership remained modest. The most powerful of these included the Independent Trade Union of Miners, which successfully struck for improvement of employment conditions on several occasions. A number of other occupational unions and nonconventional groupings and strike committees also were formed. Overall, however, the rate of unionisation was lower in the transition period than in the Soviet past, when almost 100 percent of employees were unionised. According to one survey, the unionisation rate in the Russian economy fell in 1993–1995 by about 7 percent.[25]

The 1992 Law on Collective Bargaining and Agreements provided a framework for a bargaining mechanism at the establishment level, but the impact of collective bargaining on the wage-setting process was weak.[26] Enterprises could opt out of new agreements by not signing on, and firms experiencing financial difficulties routinely broke existing agreements. Although wages were discussed in the Russian Tripartite Commission, this body remained ineffectual and wage formation was guided primarily by enterprise-level processes. However, at the same time, formal intrafirm labour institutions offered only weak bargaining power for rank-and-file employees. As a result, employers dominated the wage-setting process.

BASIC LABOUR MARKET TRENDS

Labour Force

As in any country, the working-age population in Russia can be divided into three groups, according to labour market status: employed, unemployed, or inactive (not in the labour force). Russian adults continued to exhibit relatively strong attachment to the labour force, but the tendency was for this to decline during the transition period. Table 1.1 and chart 1.1 present labour force participation rates, taking into account the relatively low retirement ages that were applicable in East European nations: generally fifty-five years of age for women and sixty for men.[27] (Box 1.1 provides an overview of the main data sources used in this volume.) Russia had a higher participation rate than such transition countries as Bulgaria, Hungary, and Poland, but a portion of this difference was accounted for by higher retirement ages in the latter two countries.[28] However, by 1996 in Russia the rates had declined to a point where they were not dramatically higher than those in the Czech or Slovak Republics. Between 1992 and 1998, the overall activity rate among the working age population in Russia had declined by over 8 percentage points. Disaggregating by gender indicates that the participation rate for Russian women remained higher than in other countries shown in the table. A closer look at unemployment and employment also reveals a unique Russian pattern.

Unemployment

Table 1.1 and chart 1.2 present an international comparison of unemployment rates based on labour force survey data. Unemployment is defined here using the ILO/OECD definition (whereby an unemployed person is defined as someone without work, currently available for work, and actively seeking work).[29] The tendency in Russia for unemployment to rise gradually but continuously contrasts with the patterns in many CEE countries, which experienced substantial surges early in the economic transition, followed by gradual declines.[30]

Table 1.1 Structure of the Labour Market[a]

	Russia							Q1 1996				
	Q4 92	Q4 93	Q4 94	Q4 95	Q1 96	Q4 97	Q4 98	Bulgaria	Czech Republic	Hungary	Poland	Slovakia
Labour Force participation rate[b] (WA)												
Men and women	84.2	82.2	81.1	80.3	79.0	77.2	76.0	70.4	77.3	64.7	68.7	75.0
Men	86.6	84.7	83.6	82.8	81.4	79.8	78.5	71.6	83.0	69.6	73.7	79.8
Women	81.6	79.4	78.3	77.6	76.3	74.5	73.3	69.1	70.9	59.3	63.5	69.9
Employment/population ratio (WA)	79.9	77.3	74.4	72.5	71.2	67.9	65.7	59.5	74.3	57.7	58.8	65.9
LFS unemployment rate (15–72)												
Men and women	5.2	5.9	8.1	9.5	9.7	11.8	13.3	15.3	3.8	10.6	14.0	12.1
Men	5.2	5.9	8.3	9.7	10.0	12.2	13.6	15.4	3.2	11.9	13.4	10.9
Women	5.2	5.8	7.9	9.2	9.3	11.5	13.0	15.1	4.5	9.0	14.6	13.4
Youth (16–29)	9.5	10.6	13.0	15.4	15.2	18.3	20.7	36.9	7.3	20.5	33.9	22.6
Prime-age (30–49)	3.6	4.4	6.7	7.7	8.1	10.1	11.3	13.2	3.3	9.4	12.5	10.6
Older (50–54 women, 50–59 men)	3.7	3.5	5.2	5.7	6.2	7.7	8.8	10.4	2.1	6.4	8.3	6.5
Higher education	3.3	3.5	4.8	5.0	4.5	5.7	7.1	5.2	0.6	3.2	3.7	2.2
Secondary education	5.2	6.0	8.4	10.0	10.2	12.4	14.0	13.2	3.1	10.1	15.2	11.0
Primary or less	4.0	4.1	6.4	7.3	7.7	15.9	17.5	26.4	11.2	16.3	16.4	27.5
Long-term unemployment	0.6	1.1	2.0	3.0	3.3	4.7	5.7	9.5	1.2	5.5	5.5	6.1

Note: Age ranges shown in parentheses; "WA" stands for "working age."
(a) Definitions may vary across countries. See *OECD-CCET Labour Market Database 1990–1997*, no. 2 (Paris: OECD, 1997) for detailed information.
(b) Labour force as a percentage of the working age population (women aged 15 to 54 years and men aged 15 to 59).
Sources: Authors' estimates based on Goskomstat data from *Statistichesky bulleten* (*Statistical Bulletin*) 53, no. 3 (May 1999), and OECD/CEET labour market data base.

Chart 1.1   Labour Force Participation Rates, Percentage of Working Age Population

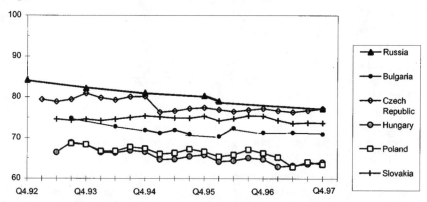

Sources: Authors' estimates based on *Statistichesky bulleten,* no. 3 (53), May 1999, Goskomstat, Moscow, *OEC Short-term Economic Indicators: Transition Economies* 3/1995 and 1/1997; and OECD-OCET labour market data.

Box 1.1   Overview of Sources and Caveats

Main data sources used in the book—An in-depth study of labour market developments over time requires comprehensive and consistent data.[37] Statistics in the transition countries are usually also in transition. As a result, data produced by official statistical agencies are often not up to the required standard. The data are often incomplete and are not always consistent over time. Some data are not available at all; others become outdated even before they are made public. In some cases, there is an insufficient level of detail.[38] This book is based on a range of data sources for which a more detailed account is given in the Data Sources Annex. Here we mention just a few of the most important sources.

The Russian State Statistical Committee (Goskomstat) was the main data source. It collects and publishes a number of data series on the labour market, drawn from mandatory administrative reporting by enterprises and various surveys. The official labour force survey (LFS) is a household survey providing the most representative coverage of individuals in relation to their labour market participation and household circumstances. It includes breakdowns by demographic characteristics and by regions. However, during the period from 1992 to 1998 the survey was conducted on a relatively infrequent basis due to budget problems. Also, since 1994, Goskomstat surveys (annually) labour costs across major sectors of the economy.

Box 1.1 *Continued*

The State Employment Service was another important source of data. It collects administrative data on the registered unemployed and other registered job seekers. Despite many caveats, these data are useful for characterising the stocks and flows of individuals that have applied for SES services. They must be used with caution because of inconsistencies due to changes in the administrative procedures over time and across regions. The most notable case occurred in May 1996 when changes in the Employment Law were instituted that resulted in a reduction of registered unemployment.

There are also a few nonofficial survey sources that provided us with important insights into labour market developments. These include the Russian Longitudinal Monitoring Survey (RLMS—a household survey), the Russian Economic Barometer (REB—an enterprise survey), and the Russian Centre for Public Opinion Research (VCIOM—ad hoc surveys).

Qualitative information sources were used to complement the quantitative administrative and survey sources. Formal case studies and less formal field visits enabled the authors to interview numerous government officials, managers, professionals, workers, trade union activists, and others in order to collect evidence not readily available from other sources.

Methodological caveats apply—Official data sources in Russia provide only an approximate—and in some aspects incomplete—story. Despite the progress in restructuring the Russian statistical system, substantial limitations in the coverage and availability of data remain. Therefore, sources beyond the official Goskomstat data—in particular, data from RLMS, REB, and VCIOM—can be very useful. Although these sources are subject to limitations as well (e.g., limited coverage and sampling problems), they complement and confirm the official figures. They are especially important in dealing with the substantial portion of the economy outside the large and medium enterprise sector (which is relatively well-covered by Goskomstat). Still, these data sources together provide only a rough indication of the full range of economic activity; a gap remains between the recorded developments and the actual situation.

Case studies can help to close part of this gap. Although case studies are not a representative basis for research, they are useful in gaining insights in the Russian context. First, case studies can be used to gather data that are not fully available otherwise (e.g., on enterprise staffing patterns). Second, they can provide institutional and environmental details, which continue to influence the enterprise behaviour. Third, case studies offer an additional check on survey data. Fourth, they help in development of hypotheses, designing surveys and better targeting of questions.

Chart 1.2　Unemployment Rates, Percentage of Labour Force

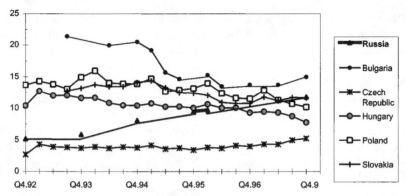

Sources: Authors' estimates based on *Statistichesky bulleten,* no. 3 (53), May 1999,[7] Goskomstat, Moscow; *OEC Short-term Economic Indicators Transition Economies* 3/1995 and 1/1997; and OE CD-CCET labour market data.

Table 1.1 presents developments in the basic demographic structure of unemployment for Russia and international comparisons with several transition countries. While the table clearly indicates a worsening in the Russian unemployment situation over time, it also shows that the other transition countries faced worse conditions (with the exception of the Czech Republic). According to the Russian LFS data, groups experiencing relatively high and increasing unemployment rates included notably youth and those with educational attainment at the primary level or lower. However, in Russia the ratios of the overall unemployment rate to the unemployment rates for these groups were not worse than in the other countries shown in the table. As in the other countries, youth unemployment was about twice the rate of total unemployment. The unemployment rate for the less educated in Russia amounted to about 1.4 times the total unemployment, while in the other countries this ratio was higher (with the exception of Poland).

The overall rate of long-term unemployment in Russia remained relatively modest by transition country standards, but was increasing and accounted for nearly one-third of total unemployment. Of the countries shown in table 1.1, only the Czech Republic had a lower rate (in 1996). Throughout the early years of the transition, the pool of unemployed in Russia experienced relatively high turnover. As Commander and Tolstopiatenko point out, for the years 1992 through 1995, Russia had lower inflow rates into unemployment and higher outflow rates than Bulgaria, Hungary, Poland, and Slovakia.[31] More important, they note that the rate of outflow *to jobs* in Russia was significantly higher than in these other countries; in 1995 the Russian rate was about two to four times greater.[32]

Labour Force Participation

Declining labour force participation helped to mitigate the increase in unemployment in Russia. As shown in table 1.1, the participation rate fell by about 8 percentage points for both men and women between 1992 and 1998. This factor accounted for more than 50 percent of the employment decline during that period, that is, more than one may associate with growth in unemployment. Russian workers left the labour market for many reasons in the 1990s, with discouragement figuring as one major factor. Many former employees found themselves without the skills and competencies required to find a job under the new economic conditions and, ultimately, decided to withdraw. This was sometimes the case, for example, for individuals of retirement age who had pension entitlements.

Employment, Underemployment, and Wages

Despite the overall decline in the employment/population ratio, it remained higher than in most of the other countries shown, except for the Czech Republic. As noted earlier, Russian enterprises adjusted to the new economic conditions through a combination of relatively limited change in employment levels and structure and through substantially increased flexibility in the utilisation and remuneration of labour. This flexibility functioned as a shock absorber, enabling firms to avoid lay-offs, a tendency that is highlighted in table 1.2.

The share of lay-offs in total separations never reached 10 percent. Despite substantial quit rates, significant overstaffing (estimated by some to have been roughly 20 percent in Soviet-era industry[33]) continued to exist in most continuing enterprises. This overstaffing is further illustrated by the substantial underemployment in the form of administrative leaves and short-time working (see table 1.3). Nearly 5.8 million workers were affected by these phenomena when they peaked in 1996, and they still touched some 3.4 million in 1998.[34] Estimates based on RLMS data show that between 1994 and 1996 (when the underemployment was rising) the mean duration of administrative leaves was forty-five days, with women and low-paid workers among the most likely to be affected.[35] In 1997–1998, underemployment measured in shortened working hours tended to decline but was effectively replaced by mounting delays in wage payments. The evidence suggests that employers began to rely more on price adjustments than on quantity adjustments in their labour policies. Indeed, relative to the volume of the output decline, the downward adjustment in hours through administrative leaves was modest.[36]

Over the period from 1992 to 1998, wage adjustments moved in fits and starts. Large drops were followed by periods when wages tended to recover partially. The first drastic fall was associated with the price liberalisation of early 1992. After that, real wages tended to stagnate or even grow slowly until late 1994. A

Table 1.2   Nature of Separations (Medium & Large Enterprises and Organisations; Percentages of Total Separations)

	1992	*1993*	*1994*	*1995*	*1996*	*1997*	*1998*
Lay-offs	8.4	5.8	7.9	6.5	8.4	9.4	8.8
Quits	n.d.	65.1	64.2	68.3	67.0	66.1	67.5
Other	n.d.	29.1	27.9	25.2	24.6	24.5	23.7

Source: Kapeliushnikov, "Russian Labour Market: Adjustment without Restructuring," 150.

Table 1.3   Indicators of Underemployment

	Working Short-Time		*On Unpaid Leave*		
	% of Total Employment	*% of Employment in Large & Medium-Sized Enterprises*	*% of Total Employment*	*% of Employment in Large & Medium-Sized Enterprises*	*Average Duration of Administrative Leaves, Days**
1993	2.3	2.9	0.8	1.0	7
1994	3.0	4.0	2.0	2.8	10
1995	3.1	4.1	1.7	2.3	10
1996	5.2	7.2	1.7	2.4	10
1997	4.0	5.8	0.9	1.3	9
1998	3.2	4.8	1.0	1.5	10

* for those on leave in December.
Source: Kapeliushnikov, "Russian Labour Market: Adjustment without Restructuring," 152.

sharp rise in inflation in October 1994 (and its aftermath) cut the value of wages by over a quarter. In the period after early 1995, wages began to recoup slowly some of their earlier losses. The growth remained weak and levels remained lower than at the beginning of the transition, but no new large losses occurred until the financial crisis of August 1998. At the same time, the growth in the volume of wage arrears offset both declining short-time working and recovering nominal wages. Across Russia, incomes became significantly less equally distributed during this period and poverty increased.

CONCLUSION

This chapter serves as an introduction to the Russian labour market in transition. A key point is that the labour market developments were strongly affected by the initial conditions in the country, the incomplete economic and political reforms, the inadequate institutional redevelopment, and the interaction of these factors with Russia's social dynamics. These factors gave birth to a particular mode of labour adjustment dubbed by some experts "the Russian way."

The Russian transition differs in many respects from those observed in most Central and Eastern European countries. Although radical and positive changes were made in establishing key elements of a market-oriented framework for the Russian labour market, this reform was neither coherent nor sufficient. On the positive side, employment legislation was reformed to provide for greatly expanded freedom of choice for labour market participants and unemployment was officially recognised, instruments for social protection were introduced (including the State Employment Service), wage-setting machinery was deregulated, trade unions were freed from state control, and collective bargaining became the norm. On the negative side, many new laws were adopted that had inherent defects or were weakly enforced, while institutions were often managed inefficiently and policy was sometimes poorly targeted. These factors distorted constraints and incentives for both firms and individuals, led to poor contract and law enforcement, and ultimately made the labour market arena largely a de-institutionalised space.

As a result of these shortcomings, the reallocation of labour resources was fairly slow. Declines in employment and increases in unemployment were disproportionately modest when seen against the large fall in output. The labour market retained significant dynamism with massive job and labour flows but with substantial churning. A unique combination of underemployment and wage arrears became an important manifestation of labour market flexibility.

Were the particular Russian patterns of labour market adjustment ultimately useful in facilitating transition and cushioning social tensions? Or did they needlessly delay the transition and result in workers being worse off than they would have been under a more systematic and market-oriented policy framework that encouraged creation of new jobs in expanding sectors? Did they offer a measure of social protection to workers at a time when labour market and social protection institutions were only poorly developed? Indeed, was labour market and social policy appropriately structured in view of the situation? Was an alternative approach possible? If so, what might have been the interlinkages with other policies? Is an alternative approach still feasible even today? The following chapters will explore these and other questions in more depth and offer a first assessment as to what adjustments might be made.

NOTES

1. Janos Kornai, *The Socialist System: The Political Economy of Communism* (Princeton, N.J.: Princeton University Press, 1992); Janos Kornai, *From Socialism to Capitalism: What Is Meant by the "Change of System"?* (London: Social Market Foundation, Centre for Post-Collectivist Studies, June 1998).

2. See Olivier Blanchard and Michael Kremer, "Disorganization," *The Quarterly Journal of Economics* 112 (November 1998): 1091–1126.

3. Martha De Melo, Cevdet Denizer, Alan Gelb, and Stoyan Tenev, *Circumstance and Choice: The Role of Initial Conditions and Policies in Transition Economies* (Washington, D.C.: World Bank, Policy Research Working Paper no. 1866, December 1997).

4. For more information on the functioning of the labour market in the late socialist period, see books and articles by Silvana Malle, Sheila Marnie, and Susanne Oxenstierna, among others.

5. De Melo, Denizer, Gelb, and Tenev, *Circumstance and Choice: The Role of Initial Conditions and Policies in Transition Economies.*

6. For more detailed accounts of the Russian macroeconomy in the 1990s, see *World Development Report* (Washington, D.C.: World Bank, 1996) and *OECD Economic Surveys: The Russian Federation* (Paris: OECD, 1995 and 1997).

7. *OECD Economic Surveys: The Russian Federation,* 1997, 29.

8. In earlier periods, inflation eroded the real value of outstanding government obligations while pushing up certain taxable revenue streams into higher tax brackets.

9. *Russian Economic Trends* 7, no. 9 (1998).

10. For details of the early stage of privatisation in Russia, see Maxim Boycko, Andrey Shleifer, and Robert Vishny, *Privatizing Russia* (Cambridge, Mass.: MIT Press, 1995). See also *OECD Economic Surveys: The Russian Federation,* 1995, 66ff.

11. E.g., Wendy Carlin, John Van Reenen, and Toby Wolfe, "Enterprise Restructuring in Early Transition: The Case Study Evidence from Central and Eastern Europe," *Economics of Transition* 3, no. 4 (December 1995): 427–458; and Richard Layard and Andrea Richter, "How Much Unemployment Is Needed for Restructuring: The Russian Experience," *Economics of Transition* 3, no. 1 (1995), 39–58; among others.

12. See Barry Ickes and Randy Ryterman, "From Enterprise to Firm: Notes for a Theory of the Enterprise in Transition," in *The Post-Communist Economic Transformation: Essays in Honor of Gregory Grossman,* ed. Robert Campbell (Boulder, Colo.: Westview Press, 1994), 83–104; Tatyana Dolgopyatova and Irina Evseeva, *Strategii vyzhivaniya gosudarstvennych i privatizirovannych predpriyatiy promyshlennosti v perechodny period* (Survival Strategies of State-Owned and Privatized Enterprises under Transition) (Moscow: Higher School of Economics, 1994).

13. Alberto Alesina and Dani Rodrik, "Distributive Politics and Economic Growth," *The Quarterly Journal of Economics* 109, no. 2 (May 1994): 465.

14. Chapter 7 deals extensively with the impact of politics on the labour market.

15. Janos Kornai, "Transformational Recession: The Main Causes," *Journal of Comparative Economics* 19, no. 1 (August 1994): 39–63.

16. Nonemployment is defined here as the population of working age that is either unemployed or not participating in the labour force.

17. This was delayed somewhat in the case of the Czech Republic.

18. Richard Layard and Andrea Richter, "Labour Market Adjustment in Russia," *Russian Economic Trends* 3, no. 2 (1994): 85. Many CIS countries, however, follow the Russian labour market model closely. So, it might be called "the CIS way."

19. Rostislav Kapelyushnikov, "Russian Labour Market: Adjustment without Restructuring," in *Issues on Theory of the Transition,* ed. Vladlen Martynov et al. (Moscow: IMEMO, 1999), 85. This should not be taken too literally, however. As discussed in

chapter 2, it must be acknowledged that there was some restructuring and reallocation of labour resources even if the scale of change fell short of expectations.

20. Calculated for the period from 1989 to the end of the output decline in each country (i.e., 1993 in Hungary and 1991 in Poland).

21. In Russia, the ratio was somewhat higher for medium and large enterprises during 1992–1995, when a 50-percent decline in output in medium and large industrial enterprises in Russia (i.e., those with employment of 200 or more) resulted in a 30 percent employment decline; that is, each one percent decline in output resulted in an employment decline of 0.6 percent.

22. Kapelyushnikov, "Russian Labour Market: Adjustment without Restructuring," 131.

23. This new ministry was the result of the merger of the Ministry of Labour, Ministry of Social Protection, and the State Employment Service.

24. Salaries of employees at the federal level of the SES, the Federal Employment Service, were paid from the federal budget, however.

25. See Tatyana Chetvernina, Pavel Smirnov, and Natalia Dunaeva, "Mesto profsoyuza na predpriyatii (Role of Trade Unions in Enterprises)," *Voprosy ekonomiki,* no. 5 (May 1995): 84.

26. Vladimir Mikhalev and Nils Bjorksten, *Wage Formation during the Period of Economic Restructuring in the Russian Federation* (Paris: OECD, 1995).

27. During the course of 1998, Goskomstat released partially revised data on labour force developments during the transition years. Generally, these data indicate a trend that is comparable to the data originally released, but with somewhat higher levels of overall unemployment (+ ca. 0.2 percentage points in the average year).

28. The definition of working-age population used here is subject to certain exceptions for the countries shown. For example, the data for Hungary and Poland reflect a higher retirement age for women (sixty years) and for Poland, a higher retirement age for men (sixty-five years). For complete details, see the methodological notes to the *OECD-CCET Labour Market Database 1990–1997,* no. 2 (Paris: OECD, 1997).

29. See *Employment Outlook* (OECD: Paris, 1987), 125, for more details on this definition of unemployment.

30. The Czech Republic was a notable exception. There, unemployment showed a modest initial increase, followed by several years of relative stability and then some acceleration when economic conditions worsened in the late 1990s.

31. Simon Commander and Andrey Tolstopiatenko, "Unemployment, Restructuring and the Pace of the Transition," in *Lessons from the Economic Transition: Central and Eastern Europe in the 1990s,* ed. Salvatore Zecchini (Paris: OECD, and Dordrecht, Netherlands: Kluwer Academic Publishers, 1997), 331–350.

32. Grogan and Van den Berg provide additional information on the duration of unemployment during the period 1994 through 1996. Using RLMS data, they found that unemployed people with higher education and unmarried women tended to have relatively short spells of unemployment, whereas married women tended to have relatively long spells. In general, they note that exit rates from unemployment increased over time as the unemployed reduced their reservation wage levels (see Louise Grogan and Gerard Van den Berg, *The Duration of Unemployment in Russia,* Discussion Paper No. TI 99-011/3, Tinbergen Institute, Amsterdam [January 1999]).

33. See *A Study of the Soviet Economy,* vol. 2 (Paris: IMF/WB/OECD/EBRD, 1991).

34. *Russian Economic Trends* 8, no. 1 (1999): 104.

35. Please see the Data Sources Annex for a description of the RLMS data set.

36. Louise Grogan, *Worker Characteristics and Administrative Leave in the Russian Federation* (Amsterdam: Tinbergen Institute, unpublished paper, 1998).

37. For details see the Data Sources Annex.

38. *Labour Statistics for a Market Economy,* ed. Igor Chernyshev (Budapest: CEU Press, 1994).

2

On Movers and Stayers: Labour Market Dynamics

OVERVIEW

The possibilities for labour market adjustment in transition economies are sometimes described using a simplified model consisting of just two sectors: one with "old" jobs in the public sector and another with "new" positions, mostly in *de-novo* private firms. According to this model, as the transition advances, a significant portion of "old" jobs are destroyed and laid-off workers are pushed into unemployment, while new firms generate "new" jobs and pull cheap labour from the pool of laid-off workers.[1] In the old-jobs sector, separations due to lay-offs are expected to increase, while hirings are greatly reduced or stopped. The growing gap between separations and hirings is supposed to bring significant downsizing in old firms. In some transition countries, such as Poland and Hungary, the reality in the early transition period began to approach the conditions described in the model. Consequently, the introduction of economic reforms in Russia created expectations of a substantial reallocation of labour.

Actual labour market developments in Russia turned out to be somewhat different. During the transition period through mid-1998, the separation rates at large and medium-size firms (which tended to be older firms) were in fact relatively high. However, the contribution of lay-offs to the separation rate was minimal. Instead, separations were driven mostly by so-called "voluntary" quits. At the same time, large and medium firms generally continued to hire substantial numbers of new personnel, replacing many of those who quit. Although the hiring rate was generally less than the separation rate, net employment loss still did not keep pace with output declines. Labour hoarding existed in many older firms, alongside the modest growth in employment in expanding firms. The older firms did not take full advantage of the opportunity that the separation rates might have provided to decrease hirings and adjust employment more rapidly to falling output. As a result, there was a gradual, but cumulatively substantial, outflow of labour from these older firms.

These developments were influenced by the considerable flexibility in the Russian labour market as evidenced by the substantial wage adjustment (discussed in chapter 5). Flexibility influenced labour turnover in two directions. On the demand side, by reducing the cost of retaining workers or hiring new ones, it enabled employers to maintain employment at levels higher than would otherwise have been possible. On the supply side, low wages and deteriorating employment conditions probably boosted labour turnover. Although most separations were recorded as voluntary, the worsening of the terms of employment in many cases left workers with little choice but to quit. The reliance on voluntary quits for employment adjustment is significant in that it enabled employers to avoid severance pay obligations (up to three months' wages). At the same time, it inhibited their use of more direct adjustment approaches. Although the pace of lay-offs appeared to increase somewhat during the period studied here, according to one estimate they still accounted for less than 20 percent of separations in medium and large industrial firms in 1994.[2]

During the early years of economic reform, most individuals appeared to avoid a spell of recorded unemployment in their labour market transitions; indeed, a majority of transitions were probably job-to-job. Still, for those who fell into unemployment, the relatively high rates of labour turnover probably improved their chances of finding work; vacancy rates were higher than otherwise would be the case, particularly for low-skilled positions. In this regard, labour mobility may have contributed to slowing the rate of increase in long-term unemployment. At the same time, the relatively modest inflows into unemployment persisted and the stock of unemployed grew to substantial proportions during the period considered here.

The discrepancy between analysts' expectations and these labour market developments has posed a puzzle for observers. Why did hiring rates and voluntary quit rates remain rather substantial? Why did labour turnover continue at relatively high levels and with this particular configuration? At the time, economic literature recognised this issue but did not offer a complete and convincing explanation.[3] A further puzzle is the seeming contradiction between two common views of the Russian labour market. The first view highlights the labour hoarding in state-owned or recently privatised enterprises, focusing on the many workers who were particularly immobile and the paternalism and "social responsibility" of employers who aimed to "keep workers' collectives together." This view highlights the links between the current situation and practices inherited from Soviet industry and industrial institutions. At the same time, a second view emphasises the fairly high level of labour turnover among the numerous "movers" and substantial cumulative reallocation of labour. Each of these views is supported by arguments and empirical evidence, often illustrated by official statistics, case studies, and business surveys.[4] But which one is valid?

The goal of this chapter is to shed light on these and related questions by describing key elements of the dynamics of the Russian labour market during the first five years of transition and highlighting some aspects relevant to policy-making. The labour market dynamics are considered at three different levels. At the aggregate level, we examine gross flows between the three labour market statuses—employment, unemployment, and nonparticipation (i.e., a status of being out of the labour force).[5] At the enterprise level, labour turnover is assessed based on hirings and separations and in comparison with job turnover (see box 2.1). At the individual level, dynamics are assessed in relation to worker characteristics. The analysis incorporates data from a range of official and unofficial sources in an attempt to gain a fairly comprehensive view of labour market dynamics in the course of the ongoing economic restructuring.[6]

SOURCES OF DATA ON LABOUR MARKET DYNAMICS

No single complete and comprehensive source of information is available on labour dynamics in Russia.[7] In order to obtain a relatively comprehensive picture, one must employ a combination of enterprise and household data sets. It requires use of aggregate data, as well as—where available—microdata from individual enterprises and households. While detailed information on these data sets is provided in the Statistical Annex, it is appropriate here to highlight their main characteristics.

Enterprise data on labour turnover are drawn mainly from the administrative reporting of firms, with some supplementary information drawn from surveys.[8] In addition to aggregate statistics, a special administrative data set is used here to provide an in-depth look at large and medium-size firms in four study regions in 1996.[9] The data set covers state-owned, municipal, and newly privatised enterprises; public associations; and a sample of *de-novo* private firms, and includes firms in industry, construction, and wholesale and retail trade.[10] These aggregate and regional administrative data have a few serious drawbacks for monitoring labour turnover. First, most of the smaller relatively dynamic enterprises (up to 90 percent of which are privately run) are not included in key statistical indicators such as separations and hires.[11] Second, the data do not distinguish between continuing enterprises, start-ups, and closures. Third, the data lack information on the composition of flows by the characteristics of the individuals concerned. Fourth, in the case of the regional sample, only four regions are covered and for just one time period. Thus, an analysis of the composition of labour turnover by major social or demographic properties requires additional data sources.

A number of other enterprise sources are used to complement the basic administrative sources. These include the Russian Economic Barometer (REB) survey conducted by a team from IMEMO of the Russian Academy of Sciences and the All-Russian Labour Monitoring Survey of the Ministry of Labour. These surveys provide information on labour turnover and job tenure. In order to gain insights into the labour market transitions and job tenures of

Box 2.1   Basic Definitions and Concepts

Labour turnover is calculated as the sum of hirings and separations during a specified interval (H + S), usually a one-year period. It provides a measure of gross labour reallocation, covering movement of individuals into or out of jobs, regardless of whether the jobs themselves are newly created, ongoing (and subsequently filled by others), or whether the jobs themselves disappear (*Employment Outlook* [Paris: OECD, July 1996]). Dividing the sum of those separated and hired by the average annual employment gives the corresponding rate of labour turnover. The difference between hirings and separations (H-S) yields the net change in employment.

Separations may be voluntary (e.g., quits) or involuntary (e.g., lay-offs). Hirings may be aimed at filling a vacated job or a new opening. For an individual, a separation may be associated with the transition across any of the three labour market statuses: moving into new employment (i.e., "a job-to-job transition" to a new permanent or temporary job), entering the pool of unemployed, or moving out of the labour force. Likewise, a hire may involve the transition of an individual from outside the labour force, from unemployment, or from employment in another job.

Labour turnover may also be split into movements due to net employment change and "additional labour turnover." The latter includes attrition (e.g., some workers separate due to retirement or disability and must be replaced just to maintain a desired level of employment), mismatch between labour supply and demand (e.g., due to the particular distribution of skills across the labour force, in some cases two or more transitions may be required to achieve a one-person change in employment level), job-to-job transitions (which by definition involve two transitions: a separation and a hire), and friction (e.g., problems in scheduling that may result in a temporary hire to fill a gap in staffing pending a permanent hire). Thus, labour turnover includes movements of personnel beyond those that are absolutely essential to arrive at a given net employment change. This excess movement is sometimes called "churning."

Job turnover is defined as the sum of job creation and job destruction. In practice, job creation is measured as the sum of all employment gains from opening establishments and expanding establishments, while job destruction is the sum of all employment losses from closing or contracting existing establishments. Although official aggregate data on job turnover and its components are not produced in Russia, information can be gleaned from nonofficial surveys and from the administrative reporting of individual enterprises.

Box 2.1   *Continued*

Labour turnover equals job turnover plus the movements into and out of ongoing jobs. While labour turnover provides information on the cumulative labour market transitions of individuals throughout an interval, job turnover provides information on the net reallocation of employment (that is, occupied jobs) across enterprises between two points in time.

---

individuals, the following analysis is broadened using household survey data. Theanalysis here draws on the Russian Labour Force Survey and the Russian Longitudinal Monitoring Survey (RLMS).

TRENDS IN LABOUR TURNOVER

Labour Turnover during the Soviet Period

Socialist enterprises had few constraints on their demand for labour. This was especially true with respect to blue collar workers and professionals in production industries. Quitting one's job was regarded in a strongly negative light by employers, and employees whose job history was marked by frequent job-to-job movements were considered poor and unreliable. Institutional and legal arrangements in the country were deliberately designed to limit uncontrolled labour mobility (e.g., through the use of residence permits called "*propiska*," rewards for long job tenures, distribution of social benefits through enterprises, and moral condemnation of active job-shopping, among other methods). Still, due to widespread inefficiency, there was a permanent and widespread drive from enterprises to hire more labour. The result was a fairly high level of labour turnover. By changing jobs, employees could often obtain wage premiums and better access to scarce social goods distributed through enterprises. Neither administrative nor economic policy measures were able to prevent voluntary job-to-job mobility.

No comprehensive data on labour turnover exist for the Soviet period. Labour mobility occurred in an environment with a rather high degree of employment security and easy job placement. Indeed, until the late 1980s employment in the USSR grew continuously and open unemployment had not existed at all. It is known that during the 1970s voluntary quitting, which accounted for the bulk of all separations, amounted to about 20 percent of employment in manufacturing and about 30 percent in construction. Then during the 1980s, the rate of separations began to slow: in manufacturing to roughly 12 percent of employment and in construction to about 17 percent.[12]

Labour Turnover in the Transition Period

The first half of the 1990s marked a change in the trend. Total employment began to contract in 1990, although this was a gradual process. By 1996, employment had declined by about 12 percent and employment in general became much more fragile. In industry, the contraction of employment was more significant and amounted to 25 percent of all jobs at large and medium-sized enterprises. This loss of employment took place against the background of much a deeper decline in the GDP.[13]

The change in the labour market, with growing unemployment and the likelihood of fewer available jobs, might lead one to expect a substantial slowdown in labour turnover or, at least, a contraction of hirings and a decrease in voluntary quitting. Involuntary separations (e.g., through lay-offs) might have been expected to increase. While a slight deceleration in labour turnover occurred in the second half of the 1990s, it was less than one might have expected (the dip in the indicators in 1996 notwithstanding, table 2.1). Overall, during the period from 1992 to 1998, annual labour turnover ranged between 43 and 50 percent. The official statistics indicate that the annual separation rate fluctuated between 24 and 27 percent of average employment and the annual hiring rate between 19 and 23 percent.

Sabirianova assessed the impact of the economic transition on the magnitude and destination of flows as compared with the pre-transition pattern.[14] She concluded that: (i) the labour market in Russia became more dynamic during the transition years; (ii) mobility within employment increased; (iii) changes in the likelihood of interstatus mobility (except mobility of unemployed into inactive) tended to increase unemployment; (iv) this increase was contained only by large flows into nonparticipation; and (v) the unemployed remained the most dynamic group in the labour market. The evidence of labour mobility may appear surprising, as it comes in the face of such factors as: (i) a severe recession and consequent employment cuts that might have been expected to decrease turnover, lowering voluntary quitting and new hires; (ii) a traditional labour ethic, whereby Russian labour was considered by some as committed to traditional patterns of job attachment; and (iii) the continued existence of institutional rigidities constraining labour mobility (such as housing constraints and use of residence permits in some areas). A more detailed examination of the composition of labour turnover in the following sections helps to shed light on this unexpected mobility.

How Do the Russian Labour Turnover Levels Compare Internationally?

Labour turnover in Russia was comparatively high for a transition economy in the early stages of economic restructuring (table 2.2). In Poland, where small and medium-sized enterprises were developing rather dynamically and restructuring was under way in older enterprises, labour turnover in 1993 was 42 percent for the total economy and 46 percent in industry. The corresponding rates in Russia that year were several points higher (46.2 for the total economy and 48.9 percent in industry). In countries such as Romania and Bulgaria, where the speed of transition was more comparable to that of Russia, the turnover rates were 24 and 32

Table 2.1   Labour Turnover in Russia: Large and Medium Size Firms, 1992–1998 (National-Level Data)

	1992	1993	1994	1995	1996	1997	1998
Hirings	22.9	21.1	20.8	22.6	18.9	19.9	21.0
Separations	26.9	25.1	27.4	25.7	23.9	24.5	24.9
Turnover (H+S)	49.8	46.2	48.2	48.3	42.8	44.4	45.9
Net employment change (H-S)	–4.0	–4.0	–6.6	–3.1	–5.0	–4.6	–3.9

Source: Goskomstat

Table 2.2   Labour Turnover in Selected European Countries, in the Early Transition Period (percentages)

	Hirings	Separations	Turnover (H+S)
Bulgaria (1993)			
Total	10.8	20.8	31.6
Industry	10.1	21.7	31.8
Hungary (1988)			
Total	10.7	11.3	22.0
Industry	21.6	19.4	41.0
Poland (1992)			
Total	17.9	22.4	40.3
State sector	18.4	11.9	30.3
Industry, total	21.6	17.1	38.7
State sector in industry	18.6	10.8	29.4
Poland (1993)			
Total	20.6	21.0	41.6
Industry	25.0	20.7	45.7
Romania (1992)			
State sector employees	5.4	18.4	23.8
Industry	5.2	17.7	23.9
Russia (1992)			
Total	22.9	26.9	49.8
Russia (unweighted average 1992–1996)			
Total	21.3	25.8	47.1
Industry	19.7	28.8	48.5

Sources: Vladimir Gimpelson and Douglas Lippoldt, "Labour Turnover in the Russian Economy," in *Labour Market Dynamics in the Russian Federation*, ed. Douglas Lippoldt (Paris: OECD, 1997), 43; Goskomstat.

percent, respectively. The rate of labour turnover in Russia remained lower than the OECD average but within the range for OECD countries.[15]

LABOUR MARKET FLOWS: WHERE FROM AND WHERE TO?

Labour mobility can vary in its impact on an economy, depending on the structure and magnitude of its component flows (as highlighted in box 2.2 with respect to labour turnover in particular). The most general picture of labour comes from looking at gross flows between the three labour force statuses.

Boeri and others have reviewed the basic evidence on labour reallocation in Central and Eastern Europe (CEE) during the transition years.[16] They highlight a situation where, despite various indicators suggesting that structural change in the region advanced at quite a fast pace, the unemployment pool remained stagnant with low turnover and growing long-term unemployment. Table 2.3 gives an overview of labour market dynamics in the transition countries based on these studies.

The outflow from employment has two destinations: unemployment and exit from the labour force (nonparticipation). Across the CEE countries, the total annual outflow from jobs varied from 5.6 percent of the employment stock in Slovakia to an annualised rate of about 20 percent in Bulgaria. In most of the countries shown, more individuals left the labour force than became unemployed. The lowest outflow from employment to unemployment was in the Czech Republic at just 1 percent of the stock, a development reflected in its low unemployment rate. Outflow from unemployment varied from 39 percent of the unemployment stock for Slovakia to 63 percent for the Czech Republic. Most of the outflow went to jobs while outflow into nonparticipation was relatively limited everywhere. About half of all unemployed remained in this status at least a year and thereby entered the ranks of the long-term unemployed. The highest rate of total outflow from unemployment in the region was in the Czech Republic. These developments stand in contrast to some OECD countries, particularly the United States, where the total outflow from unemployment amounted to almost 95 percent of the stock between 1992 and 1993 and where long-term joblessness is relatively low.

In Russia, the pattern of flows contrasted in key aspects with those of the other transition countries cited earlier. In particular, the overall outflow from unemployment was greater and its composition different. This was evident already in the early transition years, and even more so by the mid-1990s. According to the RLMS data (table 2.3), nearly three-quarters of the unemployed surveyed in 1995 had moved out of that status by the following year. Some 40 percent moved into employment and 33 percent moved out of the labour force. Compared to the early 1990s, however, the rate of annual outflow to jobs fell by over 11 percentage points, while the share moving into nonparticipation doubled. During the period

Box 2.2   Labour Turnover: Advantages and Disadvantages

As pointed out in the OECD *Jobs Study*, there are advantages and disadvantages to both high and low labour turnover. On the one hand, high labour turnover can potentially facilitate adjustment if firms that need to decrease or restructure their staffing can utilise attrition and lay-offs to adjust, and if workers can profit from hiring and job opportunities to secure better job matches. On the other hand, as the OECD study points out, "frequent job changes involve a loss of job-specific skills and transaction costs for workers and employers." If those insiders who have been trained are likely to quit and outsiders can easily fill vacant positions, there are clear disincentives for employers to bear major training costs. This generates "a free-rider" dilemma that may affect on-the-job training practices and lead to a decline in training and skills. Also, larger flows may bring more fragility, less security, and more uncertainty to workers.

At the same time, there are certain advantages to lower labour turnover. Potentially, these include enhanced worker motivation and commitment to corporate goals, lower resistance to change (in light of a perception of employment security), and increased incentive for employers to invest in training their workers. However, long-term employment arrangements may create problems of flexibility and adjustment, especially in the face of market fluctuations. This raises a risk of labour market segmentation, where core workers enjoy long-term employment security while other workers carry the major burden of adjustment.[18]

At any given level of labour turnover, an assessment of the structure of flows is important for a proper understanding of the direction and pace of change in the labour market. For example, a decomposition of flows can help to highlight a situation where long-term unemployment is building up due to problems with the outflow to employment. This was the case in Poland during the early 1900s, where high overall flows were dominated by job-to-job transitions, that bypassed the unemployed, leaving them trapped in a stagnant, but rising, pool of unemployment.

1995–1996, Russia's outflow from jobs to unemployment was about average, but there was also a significant share moving from employment out of the labour force (chart 2.1). These rather intensive shifts into nonactivity (from both employment and unemployment) helped to contain open unemployment, but the growth in flows to nonparticipation also were indicative of growing numbers of discouraged workers.[17]

Returning to the last line of table 2.3, one can get a sense of the scale of the overall flows in relation to the labour force. Summing the movements between

Table 2.3 Labour Market Flows in the Selected Transition Countries (percentages of the stock)

	Employment to unemployment	Employment to out-of-LF	Unemployment to employment	Unemployment to out-of-LF	Out-of-LF to employment	Out-of-LF to unemployment	Employment to employment
Bulgaria[a] (June 1994– Mar 1995)	5.9	9.2	32.3	24.4	5.5	4.4	—
Czech Rep.[b] (1995–96)	1.0	5.6	47.1	15.6	6.7	0.4	—
Poland[b] (1994–95)	3.5	5.5	38.0	15.6	6.0	3.2	—
Slovakia[b] (1995–96)	2.9	2.7	34.8	4.2	2.0	1.6	—
Slovenia[b] (1994–95)	2.4	5.8	38.7	19.4	6.3	2.1	—
Russia[c] (1992–93)	3.3	5.9	51.2	16.0	9.0	1.7	—
Russia[d] (1995–96)	3.4	7.2	39.9	32.8	10.9	6.4	15.5
Russia (1995–96) Flows as a % of LF[d] (total flow = 37.4%)	3.2	6.8	2.9	2.4	4.9	2.9	14.3

LF = labour force

Sources: (a) Tito Boeri, Michael Burda, and Janos Kollo, *Mediating the Transition: Labour Markets in Central and Eastern Europe* (London–New York: CEPR-IEWS, 1998);

(b) Tito Boeri and Randolph Bruno, "A Short Note on the Characteristics of Labour Turnover in Central and Eastern Europe," in *Labour Market Dynamics in the Russian Federation*, ed. Douglas Lippoldt (Paris: OECD, 1997), 156–157;

(c) Mark Foley, *Labour Market Flows in Russia: Evidence from the Russian Longitudinal Monitoring Survey* (unpublished paper, 1995);

(d) Authors' estimate based on RLMS 1995–1996.

Chart 2.1   Russian Labour Market Flows, 1995–1996

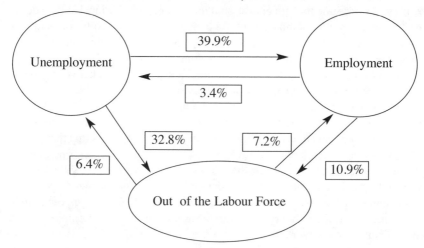

Notes: N = 6167. Each flow is shown as a percentage of the stock of the originating group.
Source: RLMS 1995 and 1996.

the three labour force statuses, it can be seen that 23 percent of the labour force changed status within one year. Adding those who moved job-to-job, one finds over 37 percent of the labour force moved during this period (and that does not take into account those who in addition experienced short-term transitions during the course of the year but returned to their original status by the time of the next survey).

KEY FEATURES OF LABOUR FLOWS IN RUSSIA

Worker Characteristics and Labour Turnover

Labour turnover also reflects a reallocation of employment across major population groups, as well as a reallocation of workers among enterprises. An examination of the evidence on variation in labour turnover helps to shed additional light on enterprise staffing decisions and adjustment behaviour of occupational, age, gender, and educational groups, for example.

Based on a few case studies, we have found some evidence of differences in labour turnover rates between certain groups of blue collar workers and other occupations, and that these differences contributed to the reallocation of labour.[19] In industry, during the early transition years, it appeared that most hiring was focused on getting either very skilled workers with particular professions or, on the contrary, low-skilled employees for poorly paid jobs. Among the latter groups were many young people coming directly from educational institutions. Hiring decisions in such cases may have been encouraged by the low cost of this labour, by previous agreements with educational institutions, and by local authorities trying to prevent youth unemployment. As to separations, blue collar/manual workers quit twice as often as white collar employees. While, as noted earlier, the total separation rates were driven largely by voluntary outflows, it also appeared that variation in the propensity to quit constituted a key difference between groups in terms of their adjustment capacity and behaviour.

Comprehensive and precise data are not available on labour turnover by major occupational groups. Nevertheless, for those parts of the economy covered by the available Goskomstat data on hirings and separations, it appears that there are significant differences in labour turnover between blue collar workers and other employees.[20] The data available for the period from 1994 through 1995, for example, imply that hiring rates for blue collar workers averaged some 3.2 percentage points higher, while their separation rates averaged 3.9 percentage points higher.

The net effect of the divergent patterns was a recorded rate of employment decline for blue collar workers (in medium and large establishments in industry) that was half again as large as the rate for white collar employees during this period. Thus, the share of white-collar employment in the total industrial employment tended to grow during 1994 and 1995. Given that output declines outpaced overall employment declines, and assuming that other factors such as technology remained constant, the implication is that labour hoarding among white collar workers may have increased. Since in the past Russian industry had relatively high shares of white-collar employment, it is questionable whether such an increase would indicate a more efficient allocation of labour resources.

Chart 2.2 draws on data from the All-Russian Labour Monitoring survey to provide additional information on the occupational composition of labour turnover in industry in 1995.[21] These data indicated rates of employment decline and turnover for manual workers that were roughly twice the corresponding rates for managers. Slow turnover and a lower rate of replacement for white collar employees implied that they faced a much narrower range of labour market opportunities in industry; there was simply a smaller proportion of positions vacated by quits and in need of filling. The low mobility of the white collar employees in large and medium enterprises in industry probably reflected a number of factors related to the labour market, such as a longer potential duration of unemployment as well as social and psychological tendencies among a portion of this population (e.g., a lower propensity to switch jobs and capacity for adjustment to change). The view of unskilled workers as having the least stable job matches is reinforced by the data in the chart. While this group of workers contracted more rapidly than others, it also had the highest replacement rate (some 65 percent of separations were offset by a hire).[22] While a high demand for skilled manual labour may have been explained partly by rigid technology and by industry and technology-specific considerations requiring employees to have certain skills, the implicit rationale for such intensive hiring of low-skilled workers posed a puzzle to ana-

Chart 2.2   Labour Turnover by Occupational Group, 1995 (Percentage of Average Employment)

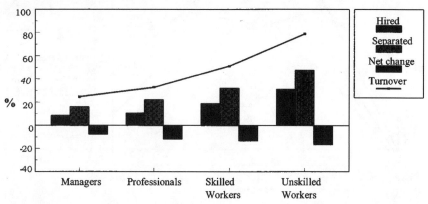

Notes: 1995, N = 326 firms.
Source: Authors' estimates based on *Vserossiyskiy Monitoring Sotcialno-Trudovoy Sfery* (All-Russian Labour Monitoring Survey) (Moscow: Ministry of Labour of the Russian Federation, 1996).

lysts. As Commander with co-authors noted at the time, "In short, restructuring decisions, including those on skills, appear not to be the dominant motivation behind hiring."[23]

The 1995 All-Russian Labour Monitoring enterprise survey data suggest that age was an important factor associated with mobility among employees in industry. Industrial firms tended to hire younger individuals, with the highest share of hiring—over one-third of all hires recorded by the survey—going to those under thirty years old (chart 2.3). At the same time, the under-thirty age groups made up less than one-fifth of the total industrial employment recorded by the survey. This contrasted with the situation for older workers. The age group over fifty years old was underrepresented in the hiring, providing only about 10 percent of all hires while its share in employment was equal to nearly 20 percent. The age distribution of separations was also skewed to younger age groups, albeit to a lesser extent. Those under thirty years old were the only ones showing shares of separations greater than their shares of employment.

The RLMS household survey data for 1995 and 1996 confirmed the existence of a differentiation by age. Younger groups were shown to be much more mobile. For example, for those in the group aged sixteen–twenty-four years, the probability to move from employment into unemployment was 5.3 percent versus only 1.2 percent for the 55+ group. Correspondingly, unemployed from the younger group had a 44 percent probability to be rehired and a 27 percent probability of moving into inactivity. This contrasted with probabilities of 17 and 69 percent, respectively, for the older group. Thus, younger people were more likely to become unemployed but also much more likely to move back into employment.

Chart 2.3   The Age Distribution of Hires and Separations in Industry

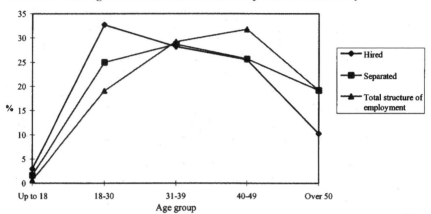

Notes: 1995, N = 326 firms.
Source: Authors' estimates based on *Vserossiyskiy monitoring sotcialno-trudovoy sfery* (All-Russian Labour Monitoring Survey) (Moscow: Ministry of Labour of the Russian Federation, 1996).

The RLMS data also provide information on the flows by gender and education. The outflow from employment for men and women was similar in scale; however, men were more likely to go into unemployment, while women were more likely to leave the labour market. The same pattern is observed if we look at mobility from unemployment: men had higher chances to be rehired while women were more likely to go into inactivity. This illustrates some *gender asymmetry* in labour mobility.

As to educational level, individuals having only secondary education had a low rate of outflow to unemployment but the highest to inactivity. Higher educational attainment showed itself to be an important asset in helping individuals to maintain employment status. Among those with university education, for example, only 5 percent left employment in the interval between the 1995 and 1996 surveys.

Labour Flows and Enterprises

One of the important dimensions of structural change in transition countries is the reallocation of labour from public to private jobs. This process occurs as a result of the mobility of individuals as well as the privatisation of former state companies. One can get a better view of developments by dividing all employed into three groups: those who work in public, private, or self-employment. Sabirianova found a much higher level of job security and stability in the public sector than existed in the other sectors.[24] Seventy-six percent of those working in public sector positions in late 1995 remained in the public sector one year later. The comparable figures for the private sector and the self-employed were much lower, at 48 and 34 percent, respectively. The latter group was exposed to maximal risk and had the lowest probability to keep their status.

The unemployed who found work were most likely to find it in the public sector. However, comparing 1995–1996 with 1992–1993 data, one can see that the private sector absorption capacity appears to have increased. According to Mark Foley, only 5 percent of the unemployed moved to private jobs in 1992–1993. This compares with 14 percent in 1995–1996. It is likely that most of this increase is due to the large-scale privatisation measures in 1992–1994 rather than to more intensive job creation in *de-novo* private sector firms. New firms still were reluctant to hire unemployed and often relied on contingent labourers, many of whom had employment ties to other state or privatised establishments.

Table 2.4 presents the data on the reallocation of labour during the early transition period (1992–1995), presenting the net expansion or contraction in employment by sector (all sizes of firm).[25] It highlights the large volume of annual employment changes by sector, which are less apparent when one looks at multiyear change in a given sector or the net changes in the total economy (i.e., some of the annual changes are offset by changes in subsequent years). In each year, the sum of the change in employment in expanding and contracting sectors was more than twice as great as the net change in employment for the economy as a whole. In total over the period 1992 to 1995, estimated employment declined by 5 million while the change in employment through expansion and contraction of individual sectors amounted to 10.6 million. Here it should be noted, however, that such a measure should be used with caution, as the precise outcomes depend on the classification of the sectors that is used. Nevertheless, the moderate changes in the number of positions due to contracting or expanding employment contrast with the rather high mobility of individuals.

Separations

Separations in the first years of the transition were mostly voluntary and the level of quitting was fairly stable, with only a modest decline in 1996 and 1997.[26] The toughening of financial conditions (e.g., the cut-off of most subsidies to firms) appeared to have only limited influence in increasing the use of lay-offs. According to enterprise reporting, over 68 percent of all those who left their jobs in 1995 did so "by their own choice." Voluntary separations comprised a major fraction of labour flows in any given sector, varying from 40 percent of all separations in the gas industry to almost 90 percent in the social sector (i.e., health care, education, and culture) in 1995. In industry such quits accounted for 56 percent of all separations in that year.

Employer-initiated lay-offs played a fairly minor role in the downsizing of firms during the period from 1992 to 1995, fluctuating between 1.5 and 2.1 percent of

Table 2.4 Reallocation of Labour by Sector, Total Economy, 1992–1995 (All Figures in Thousands)

	1992 Employment	Change 1992–1993		Change 1993–1994		Change 1994–1995		Total Change 1992–1995	
		Expanding sectors	Contracting sectors	Expanding sectors	Contracting sectors	Expanding sectors	Contracting sectors	Expanding sectors	Contracting sectors
Industry	21,324		–519		–2 229		–1,376		–4,124
Agriculture/forestry	10,336	11		181			–28	164	
Construction	7,887		–747		–352		–288		–1,387
Transportation/ communication	5,632		–224		–54		–54		–332
Trade/catering	5,679	695		110		16		821	
Public utilities	2,988	16		38		280		312	
Health care	4,227			151		106		273	
Education/culture	7,521		–282	144		217		79	
Finance	494	87		164		155		406	
Research and development	2,307		–70		–404		–133		–607
Public administration	1,519	130		310			–259	181	
Other	2,157		–310		–127		–320		–757
Column totals	72,071	939	–2,158	1 098	–937	774	–1,082	2,236	–3,083
As a percentage of 1992 Employment	1.3%	–3.0%	1.5%	–1.3%	1.1%	–1.5%	3.1%	–4.3%	

Sources: The underlying data cover the whole economy (i.e., including an adjustment for estimates of employment in smaller firms) and are drawn from *Rossiyskyi statisticheskiy ezhegodnik* (Moscow: Goskomstat, 1996); authors' calculations.

annual average employment or between 6 and 8 percent of all separations. Lay-offs were relatively more frequent in industries facing severe economic pressure, such as data processing (where the rate of lay-offs was 6–7 percent of average annual employment) or geology (where the rate was over 8 percent in 1994). However, even there they accounted for less than a quarter of all separations.

The predominance of voluntary separations over lay-offs is typical in many countries, including most OECD countries. As is pointed out in the OECD *Jobs Study*, "quits usually decline in a recession because attractive job opportunities become rarer, and because quits are the larger component, total job separations also decline in recessions despite the increase in lay-offs."[27] In these countries, labour turnover fluctuates procyclically, increasing in up-turns. The available evidence from transition countries also suggests that, at least in some of them, dismissals have made a major contribution to employment loss. According to Janos Kollo, in Hungary the net attrition (defined as nonreplacement of those who quit) played a complementary role, while dismissals were a major tool in downsizing of firms.[28] The case of Russia seems to illustrate a different pattern. First, the gap between rates of quitting and of lay-offs is markedly larger than in the OECD Member countries. Second, the transformational recession in Russia is more severe than cyclical downturns generally are, but it has not resulted in a substantial decline in quitting and an increase in lay-offs. At the same time, however, the distinction between recorded lay-offs and quits in Russia is less clear than in most other countries.

Two major factors shape employment contraction in state or privatised firms in the transition countries: (i) pulling factors (like outflow to the emerging private sector) affecting the most competitive workers, and (ii) pushing factors where enterprises concentrate on shedding the least productive workers. The latter influence has tended to lead to downsizing (negative net change), while the former may lead to hirings as firms are induced to search for replacements. In Russia, the resultant new hires tended to be unstable, in part because under the transition conditions, managers and workers probably faced a greater lack of information than previously, which made screening more difficult.[29] Newcomers may have come under pressure from pulling as well as from pushing factors that in some cases caused them to re-separate. This re-separation phenomenon had the potential to lead eventually to a sorting process, with the least competitive being pushed out into unemployment or inactivity or the more competitive being matched to positions providing better opportunities. Still, the continued strong pace of hirings delayed the arrival at such an outcome.

HIRING RATES: WHY DID THEY REMAIN SO HIGH?

As noted previously, during the first years of transition, the substantial decreases in jobs at large and medium-sized firms did not eliminate labour hoarding.

Changes in aggregate employment continued to lag changes in gross domestic product. This statistical assessment was confirmed by comments from enterprise managers in industry; about 60 percent of managers surveyed in 1995 and 1996 admitted to the existence of labour hoarding at their enterprises.[30]

Discussions on labour hoarding might lead to a focus on various barriers against lay-offs, such as employment security legislation. However, the observed separation rates were high enough to permit employment to adjust to declining production. In order to shed excess labour, firms could have simply slowed the rate of hiring, even without an increase in separations. Such an approach would seem to be less costly than lay-offs and could have greatly cut excess labour in a one- or two-year period. Nevertheless, this did not happen during the period 1992–1997, when hirings demonstrated surprising stability. Moreover, hiring rates were relatively high in some industries suffering from recession (e.g., food industry, construction, and transportation), as well in those that were relatively better off (e.g., finance, communications, or oil extraction).

The persistence of hiring was probably the result of a variety of factors, including:

- A small portion of the hires can be explained by job creation, although the overall job creation rate remained relatively low. Also, in some cases, firms that experienced net employment loss due to restructuring continued to generate some new positions as part of the process.
- The particular labour requirements of technologies in use in Russia force enterprises drove a certain amount of hiring. However, as discussed in the section below on hiring of replacements, there is some evidence that this effect was fairly modest.
- Another segment of new hires consisted of recent graduates from educational institutions. Especially during the early transition years, some enterprises with long-standing ties with local technical or vocational schools continued to face obligations to hire graduates—even where overstaffing already existed. At the same time, many of these entrants had no intention to stay long, but rather used such jobs as platforms for further job search. Often these recruits subsequently quit voluntarily, further contributing to the churning component of labour turnover.
- Direct and indirect pressure from government also promoted excess hirings. Some local centres of the State Employment Service had special quotas for job placement of young labour market entrants and sometimes subsidised this employment.[31] In addition, local authorities with special political interests in preventing youth unemployment sometimes used administrative or informal leverage to prod employers to hire young people. (Admittedly, it is hard to estimate the actual extent of these patterns.)
- Hiring rates were inflated by the high proportion of very short-term matches. Based on data from the REB, Kapeliushnikov and Aukutsionek argue that the

real effective rate of filling vacancies was one-half of that indicated by the hiring rate.[32] These data indicate that half of those hired by the surveyed firms had quit within the first year of service. Therefore, firms actually may have needed to hire two people in order to get one successful match. Also, the RLMS data confirm the relatively high propensity of newcomers for further mobility.

- Some financial and political benefits accrued to enterprises that maintained employment levels, while the cost of retaining workers remained relatively low.[33] Also, prior to the abolition of the excess wage tax in 1996, companies derived some advantage from maintaining a large employment roster at any given level of gross wage expenditure. This helped to reduce the average wage level and consequently the excess wage tax liability.[34] Moreover, a high level of employment provided managers with political influence or bargaining power vis-à-vis local (and sometimes federal) authorities in order to gain financial support. Once hired, a worker whose services were momentarily not required could be placed on short time or administrative leave to minimise the cost to the enterprise (while avoiding the cost of a formal lay-off). However, on balance, it is not clear whether these benefits had a greater impact as disincentives to lay-offs or as incentives for substantial numbers of new hirings.

While this list may not be complete, it does capture some of the main contributing factors in the persistence of hiring. And it highlights the situation of many employers, who may have faced relatively limited barriers to shedding labour but who also had a variety of incentives to hire and relatively low direct costs from hoarding labour.

THE REGIONAL DIMENSION OF LABOUR TURNOVER

Labour turnover varied significantly across the Russian regions. In 1995, for example, separation rates ranged from about 10 percent in Dagestan to 41 percent in Sakhalin; hiring rates ranged from 8 percent in Dagestan to 37 percent in Kanty-Mansy Autonomous Okrug.[35] Separations and hirings by regions had a strong positive correlation and similar distributions. The group of regions with the lowest rates (of both hiring and separation) mainly included those lagging behind in the transition to the market. Among them were both older, traditional Russian regions (Voronezh, Penza, Kursk) and regions with high concentrations of non-Russian ethnic groups (Dagestan, Ingushetia, Chuvashia, Mordovia, among others), which were mostly rural and mainly agricultural. Those with more intensive worker flows tended to have economies based on resource extraction (Tyumen, Karelia, Komi, and Khanty-Mansy, among others) or have access to the sea (Sakhalin, Kaliningrad, Kamchatka, and Chukotka).

It is noteworthy that the regional patterns of labour turnover resembled the distribution of other economic features by region, such as mode of economic development (e.g., degree of reform), type of economic structure, level of per capita income, and living standards, among others. The logic appeared to be simple: the higher the level of economic activity and the better the adjustment, the more new jobs were likely to be created and the greater the number and extent of vacancy chains that might be generated. All this affects both job-to-job mobility and outflows from unemployment.

The relationship between the regional hirings and separations for large and medium-size enterprises and regional unemployment rates was not immediately evident from the data. No statistically significant correlation could be found with either registered or survey unemployment.[36] One of the possible interpretations is that most of the net outflow did not enter unemployment but was rather split between direct job-to-job movement (e.g., to small enterprises) and those leaving the regional labour force. Those leaving the labour force tended to stay inactive in the same region, possibly engaged in unrecorded activity. In general, the interregional differences in labour turnover were not associated with substantial interregional migration. While labour mobility tended to remain relatively high at local level, it was limited across regions by institutional and housing constraints, among other factors.

Regional Case Study

The aggregate data presented herein give a general picture of regional developments, but they do not provide information on the association between observed labour turnover developments and enterprise characteristics such as sectoral, ownership, and firm size effects and employment conditions such as wages and working time arrangements. Using data from enterprise administrative reporting in 1996 in four regions (Chelyabinsk, Chuvashia, Krasnoyarsk, and Moscow), the analysis now takes a look at the relationship between these factors and labour turnover.

Table 2.5 presents pooled data from the regional sample highlighting the scale of labour turnover (H + S) and its components according to sector, ownership, and firm size.[37] The data indicate that industrial firms had the lowest turnover rates while construction had the highest. Construction, although the most dynamic of these sectors, nevertheless experienced the biggest net employment loss, amounting to 15 percent of annual average employment. Trade, in turn, had the lowest net loss, the lowest rate of lay-offs, and the biggest rate of hiring into newly created positions. Across ownership types, the lowest rates of turnover were found in state and municipal enterprises; the highest rates were found in enterprises owned by public associations and those with mixed ownership. Hirings were strongest in mixed and privately owned firms, while they were weakest in state and municipal enterprises. Separations were

Table 2.5 Labour Turnover Characteristics by Ownership Types, Firm Size, and Sectors, 1996 (Ratios to Annual Average Employment; Pooled Sample and National Data)

	Hirings	Separations	H + S	H – S	New jobs	Quits	Lay-offs	Number of observations
A. Pooled sample								
Ownership								
State	.195	.281	.476	–.086	.008	.199	.015	1,261
Municipal	.199	.273	.472	–.074	.008	.222	.010	582
Public	.260	.534	.794	–.274	.006	.300	.026	73
associations								
Mixed	.332	.436	.768	–.104	.011	.374	.006	1,727
Private	.276	.389	.665	–.113	.008	.255	.008	2,686
Firm Size								
< 20	.303	.437	.740	–.134	.022	.321	.043	585
21–50	.291	.380	.671	–.089	.009	.335	.023	1,725
51–100	.312	.418	.730	–.106	.011	.337	.027	1,187
101–200	.277	.391	.668	–.114	.009	.291	.030	1,140
201–500	.249	.335	.584	–.086	.006	.229	.024	968
501–2,000	.205	.308	.513	–.103	.005	.186	.028	567
2,001–5,000	.163	.275	.438	–.112	.004	.155	.029	102
> 5,000	.166	.243	.409	–.077	.003	.122	.014	61

Sector							
Industry	.225	.339	0.564	-0.114	.008	.229	.035	1,986
Construction	.307	.457	0.764	-0.15	.007	.310	.026	1,452
Trade	.296	.366	0.662	-0.07	.012	.325	.023	2,897
Total sample	.28	.38	.66	-.10	.01	.29	.03	6,335
B. National data								
Russia (all sectors)	.189	.239	0.428	-0.05	n.a.	.160	.020	n.a.
Industry	.169	.270	0.439	-0.101	n.a.	n.a.	.032	n.a.
Construction	.290	.425	0.715	-0.135	n.a.	n.a.	.031	n.a.
Trade	.256	.345	0.601	-0.089	n.a.	n.a.	.036	n.a.

n.a. = not available

Sources: Goskomstat data from administrative reporting of large and medium size enterprises, selected regions (Moscow City, Chelyabinsk Oblast, Chuvash Republic, Krasnoyarsk Krai) and reported figures for Russia as a whole; authors' calculations.

strongest in firms owned by public associations and those with mixed owner-ship. In terms of the net employment impact, the greatest proportional loss was in firms owned by public associations.[38]

The data in the sample indicate that firm size was negatively associated with labour turnover, and hiring and separation rates. The trends would probably be more pronounced if the sample were extended to include the more dynamic smaller firms. As it is, the difference across firms by size, as shown in table 2.5, is considerable, with a labour turnover rate among the smallest firms that was nearly twice as high as that of the largest firms. This effect may be partially at-tributed to sectoral and ownership effects as well, however, since smaller-size firms are disproportionately represented in construction or trade and in the private or mixed ownership categories.

Replacements and Job Turnover

Labour turnover may be divided into two broad sets of forces: one associated with worker reallocation across ongoing jobs and one associated with job reallo-cation among firms.[39]

The relationship between hirings and separations at the time of the 1996 re-gional study can be illustrated (for the pooled sample) with a simple regression, as follows: $H = .077 + .526S$ ($R^2 = .38$), where H stands for hiring rate and S stands for separation rate. The coefficient computed for the pooled sample sug-gests that if the separation rate increases by one percentage point, the hiring rate tends to go up by about half a percentage point. This means that every two sepa-rations are likely to lead to one new hire. However, elasticities of hirings to sep-arations vary in their level and significance across regions, sectors, and owner-ship types. The replacement rate is highest in Krasnoyarsk Krai and lowest in Chelyabinsk Oblast. With respect to sectoral variation, industry has a replacement rate that is much lower than those of construction or trade, with the relationship between inflows and outflows in the former case being almost insignificant. This suggests that both hirings and separations in industry may be governed by other, independent factors. The replacement rates also varied across enterprises accord-ing to their ownership. Firms with private and mixed ownership tended to replace three separations with two new hires, while those separating from firms owned by public associations were unlikely to be replaced.

The significant variation in elasticities across regions, sectors, and ownership types casts doubt on the explanation offered by Simon Commander, John McHale, and Ruslan Yemtsov, who wrote that "In effect, the employment deci-sion is determined by technology, which delivers a core membership of the firm."[40] If technology were the key factor, one might have expected to see the highest replacement rates in industry and in state firms (e.g., defence-oriented firms) where technology was more widely applied. Instead, the highest re-placement rates were observed in smaller private firms operating in trade or construction, sectors that were less dependent on special skills complementary to technology. Furthermore, one might have expected a preponderance of skilled workers among all newly hired. However, the demand for skilled workers appears to have been fairly limited, while the bulk of those recently hired consisted of unskilled workers.

In the study regions the job creation rate was very low, amounting to less than 2 percent of average annual employment in 1996.[41] Job destruction was more than five times greater, amounting to 11 percent. Job turnover amounted to less than 20 percent of labour turnover and was dominated by job destruction.[42] That is, for the pooled sample of regional data, some four out of five employment transitions were linked effectively to movement of individuals into or out of ongoing jobs, while one in five transitions was due to a net change in the number of jobs at a particular enterprise. As in Russia overall, because of the generally short duration of matches, often more than one hire was needed to fill a given job slot.

The data also highlight the distribution of the flows according to firms' employment developments (table 2.6). In the study regions, one separation was associated with 1.2 hirings in expanding firms but less than 0.4 hirings in contracting ones. Expanding firms made up only about 23 percent of the total sample, accounting for 21 percent of employment, but accounted for about one-third of all hirings. Firms without significant net employment change (about 14 percent of all firms) were smaller in size and had lower overall labour turnover. They accounted for only 2.5 percent of total employment and generated only 1.0–1.5 percent of hirings and separations. Firms with declining employment were in the majority, amounting to two-thirds of the sample and accounting for 76.5 percent of total employment. However, they continued to hire at a substantial rate (22 percent in 1996); in fact, they accounted for about two-thirds of all new hires.

Hirings, Separations, and Use of Working Time

The regional data set can be used to develop two variables reflecting underemployment in the form of underutilisation of potential work time: compulsory unpaid or partially paid leave and short-time work. These variables are computed as: (i) the number of person-days lost due to administrative leaves per employee (*losttime1*) and (ii) the number of person-hours lost due to short-time work per employee (*losttime2*).

Table 2.7 reports on the bivariate correlations between these indicators of the use of working time, on the one hand, and labour turnover rates, on the other. The signs and significance of the coefficients hint at different types of effects associated with administrative leave and short-time work. Administrative leave was associated more strongly with changes in employment than with short-time working. Increases in person-days of leave appeared to stimulate separations, especially lay-offs (yielding the highest coefficient), and correspondingly to decrease new hires. As to the reductions in working hours, their effects were much

Table 2.6 Components of Labour Turnover in Firms Grouped by Net Change in Employment, 1996 (Pooled Sample)

	Hiring rates (H)	Separation rates (S)	Quit rates	Lay-off rates	Share of firms in sample	Share of hirings in sample	Share of separations in sample	Share of total employment in sample
	(Percentage of employment)					(Percentage of firms in sample)		
All firms	27.6	37.8	29.2	2.7	100.0	100.0	100.0	100.0
Expanding firms (H > S)	51.7	31.6	26.7	1.0	22.8	31.9	15.5	21.0
No net change (H=S)	13.5	13.5	9.9	0.1	14.2	1.5	1.0	2.5
Contracting firms (H < S)	22.0	45.5	34.3	4.0	63.0	66.5	83.5	76.5

Sources: Goskomstat data from administrative reporting of large and medium-size enterprises. selected regions (Moscow City, Chelyabinsk Oblast, Chuvash Republic, Krasnoyarsk Krai); authors' calculations.

Table 2.7 Bivariate Correlations: Enterprise Performance and Components of Labour Turnover, 1996 (Pooled Data for Selected Regions)

Indicators	Hirings	Separations	Quits	Lay-offs
Employment				
Net change/empl.	.2985***	−.5713***	−.4056***	−.4949***
Lognetemployment	.3708***	.1344***	.0981***	.0541**
Log(netemp/emp)	.6337***	.2425***	.2668***	.0794***
Employment	−.0294**	−.0291**	−.0503***	−.0063
Logemployment	−.0701***	−.0728***	−.1267***	−.0138
Financial and output				
Logoutput per employee[a]	.0348*	−.0482**	−.0683***	−.0602***
Output per employee[a]	−.0143	−.0163	−.0161	−.0021
Logprofit per employee[a]	.0002	−.0394	−.0524*	−.0089
Logprofit, total[a]	−.0179	−.0802***	−.1036***	−.0148
Loss-maker (1/0)[a,c]	.0271	.0908***	.0891***	.0495**
Arrears[a,b]	.0144	.0025	.0016	.0116
Net credit position[a,b]	−.0296	−.0228	−.0188	−.0116
Receivables, total	.0306	.0262	.0208	.0329
Receivables, overdue	−.0070	.0050	.0005	.0086
Payables, total	.0298	.0232	.0191	.0336
Payables, overdue	−.0139	−.0011	−.0013	−.0081
Underemployment				
Administrative leave (Losttime1)	−.0457***	.0836***	.0641***	.1038***
Short-time working (Losttime2)	−.0365***	−.0170	−.0242*	.0173
Compensation and labour costs				
Logwages	−.0038	−.0809***	−.1163***	−.0520***
Monthly average wage	−.0111	−.0819***	−.1192***	−.0369***
Social benefits per employee	−.0234*	−.0378***	−.0510***	.0058
ULC (wage fund/output per employee)[a]	.0225	.0158	.0093	.0317

*−p<.1; **−p<.05; ***−p<.01;
(a) Construction and industry;
(b) Net credit arrears 1: net amount overdue/sales; net credit position 2: net (receivables-payables)/sales;
(c) If a loss-maker: 1, otherwise: 0.
Sources: Goskomstat data from administrative reporting of large and medium-size enterprises, selected regions (Moscow City, Chelyabinsk Oblast, Chuvash Republic, Krasnoyarsk Krai); authors' calculations.

weaker and not so straightforward. They affected hirings negatively but also quits, although both coefficients are not very high. Surprisingly, the correlations between short-time working and separations and lay-offs were not significant.

Why do the modes of working time reduction differ so much in their effects on turnover? One plausible explanation concerns the sequencing or degree of measures introduced by management if the financial situation of the enterprise deteriorates. Often, the first step taken by management was to introduce short-time working hours *(losttime2)*; this may not have been considered by workers as a signal for exiting.[43] If reductions in working hours (e.g., from forty to thirty-five hours per week) proved to be insufficient to adjust labour to declines in output, and if the situation continued to worsen, managers might have then begun shifting workers to unpaid leaves *(losttime1)*. This measure was perceived as more serious and was often associated with growing lay-offs; workers considered it as a form of pressure on them to quit. Managers stimulated voluntary separations, in part, by placing low-priority workers on administrative leaves, which drove up overall separation rates. A further adjustment measure, the use of wage arrears, was also widely practised, but unfortunately, the regional data set does not contain information on it.

Hirings, Separations, and Wages

What was the relationship between wage levels and labour turnover? A priori, one might hypothesise either a positive or a negative correlation. On the one hand, an enterprise that paid relatively high wages may have experienced lower labour turnover, for example, as the higher price reduced demand for labour and made both hirings and separations more expensive (the latter due to factors such as severance pay obligations). On the other hand, if higher wages reflected higher marginal labour productivity and profitability at the enterprise, they might correlate with higher rates of new hirings and labour turnover due to job creation or changes in skills mix. Alternatively, in the latter case, wage increases might have also been associated with deep restructuring and acceleration in downsizing, with a similar positive correlation with labour turnover. While the regional data set does not provide conclusive information on the relationship, it does provide some insights.

Table 2.7 reports bivariate correlations between components of labour turnover (as a share of employment) and indicators of compensation and labour costs. Most of the coefficients of correlation were significant and negative but not high. That is, higher wages and benefits were associated with lower labour turnover, but the relationship appeared to be weak. Moreover, the correlation between wages and hiring was small and not statistically significant. This may indicate that higher wages were not incompatible with new hiring, a point that is developed further in the next subsection. Across the pooled sample population, quit rates (the main component in total separations) decreased in relation to higher wage levels. However, lay-off rates also declined in relation to higher wages. The story with social benefit costs was somewhat similar. They were negatively associated with separations and quits. However, they did not show a significant correlation with lay-offs. Also, they seemed to be associated negatively with the hiring rate.[44]

Hirings, Separations, and Financial Performance

One might expect the financial performance of firms to affect demand for labour and, therefore, to be reflected in hiring and separation rates. A priori, firms in financial distress might be thought to have low rates of hiring and, possibly, to be seeking to reduce overall employment, perhaps through the use of lay-offs. Was this simple logic valid in Russia during the first transition years? If yes, then most hirings and separations should be concentrated within types of firms that were significantly different in their financial outcomes. If not, how can this deviation be explained?

The regional data set includes financial data only for firms in industry and construction, so this section will only consider these two sectors (N = 2302). The available data permit calculation of several indicators of financial performance, including: (i) reported annual profit (or loss) per employee (millions Rbl) and a dummy reflecting whether the firm is a loss-maker; (ii) reported sales (output) per employee (millions Rbl); (iii) accumulated receivables (debts from purchases of products and services), both total and overdue, presented as ratios to annual sales; (iv) accumulated payables (enterprise debts to suppliers and creditors), both total and overdue, presented as ratios to annual sales; and (v) arrears and net credit position (receivables minus payables), presented as ratios to annual sales.

Before the analysis is presented, it is important to consider the particular caveats concerning any financial data from firms in Russia. A significant share of transactions were handled on a barter basis, which may have been incorrectly valued or only partially included in the enterprise books.[45] Also, significant informal sector activity was not reflected in the enterprise accounting.[46] Moreover, it may be that more profitable enterprises had greater incentives to hide a portion of their activity (e.g., to avoid taxes) than enterprises that were relatively worse off. Thus, the financial data may be subject to a number of biases and should not be considered precise.

The enterprises considered here can be divided into two broad groups: loss-making and profit-making. According to the data, the two categories accounted for 32 percent and 68 percent, respectively, of the sampled firms. The components of labour turnover for the two groups are shown in chart 2.4. The differences in *hirings* between loss-making and profit-making firms were not statistically significant, providing a hint that the effect of the financial situation on the intensity of recruitment was not clear-cut. As noted earlier, loss-making firms still

Chart 2.4   Components of Labour Turnover, by Type of Enterprise, 1996

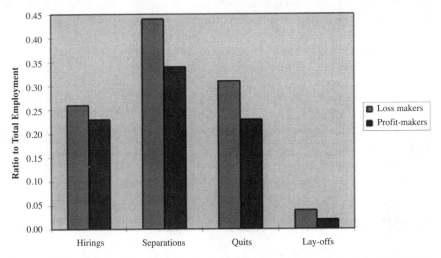

Sources: Goskomstat data from administrative reporting of large and medium-size enterprises, selected regions (Moscow City, Chelyabinsk Oblast, Chuvash Republic, Krasnoyarsk Krai); authors'
calculations.

hired to replace a portion of those separating. Profit-making firms hired replacements and, driven by the potential to raise profits, they sometimes expanded their
personnel rosters.

Separations, however, were differentiated across firms, depending on their
overall financial status as measured by losses or profits. The separation rates were
higher for loss-making firms, including overall separations, quits, and lay-offs—
though in the latter case both rates were rather low. Most separations were in the
form of "voluntary" quits, which are more frequently observed in loss-making
firms. Such firms had a tendency to offer lower wages, pay wages with delay, and
shift workers to unpaid leaves or reduced working time. This worsening of the
terms of employment pushed many in loss-making firms to quit. Ultimately, loss-
makers downsized more rapidly but still maintained substantial hiring rates,
which together with the elevated separation rates drove up the total labour
turnover in this group.

These preliminary conclusions are supported by bivariate correlations between
labour turnover and financial indicators as reported in table 2.7.

A more profound assessment of the relationship of enterprise economic performance to labour turnover can be made using multivariate regression. Two sets
of regressions were run, with each set focused on one component of labour
turnover (hirings or separations) regressed on one of three economic performance
variables [logwages, logproductivity or logprofitability] while controlling for
firm size, sector, region, and ownership. The results indicate little relationship

between the economic performance variables and hiring (table 2.8, columns 1–3). Only productivity had a modest significant positive relationship to hirings. On the other hand, among the control variables, firm size and industry (as well as Moscow location) tended to be significant and negatively associated with hirings. A significant positive relationship appeared with respect to hirings and mixed or private ownership in all three regressions shown in the table. With respect to overall separations, a significant and negative relationship to the financial performance indicators tended to arise (table 2.9). There tended also to be a significant and negative relationship between separations and firm size and industry. A significant positive relationship appeared with respect to separations and mixed or private ownership.

It should be noted that the explanatory power of the regressions was limited with respect to separations, as shown by the low adjusted R^2 scores. Perhaps this

Table 2.8   Multivariate Regressions of Hirings on Enterprise Performance Variables, Controlling for Firm Size, Sector, Region and Ownership, 1996

	1	2	3
Constant	.29*** (5.23)	.375*** (8.19)	.280*** (5.20)
Logwages	.022 (1.23)	—	—
Logproductivity (output per employee)	—	.029* (1.86)	—
Logprofitability	—	—	−.002 (−.13)
Firm Size			
Logemployment	−.07*** (−5.93)	−.06*** (−3.77)	−.024 (−1.22)
Sector			
Industry (1/0)	−.03** (−2.31)	−.07*** (-3.58)	−.081*** (-3.54)
Region			
Krasnoyarsk (1/0)	—	—	—
Chelyabinsk (1/0)	.001 (.07)	−.002 (−.08)	.037 (1.06)
Chuvash Republic (1/0)	−.032 (−1.43)	−.016 (−.55)	.016 (.42)
Moscow (1/0)	−.03** (−2.1)	−.048** (-2.06)	.008 (.26)
Ownership			
State (1/0)	—	—	—
Mixed (1/0)	.12*** (6.88)	.052** (2.3)	.065** (2.44)
Municipal (1/0)	−.019 (-.87)	.027 (.69)	.060 (1.14)
Private (1/0)	.13*** (8.42)	.069** (2.56)	.084*** (2.67)
Public association (1/0)	.78 (1.49)	.003 (.04)	−.022 (-29)
Adjusted R^2	.03	.02	.01

*p<.0.1; **p<.0.05; ***p<0.01   T-statistics shown in brackets.
Sources: Goskomstat data from administrative reporting of large and medium-size enterprises, selected regions (Moscow City, Chelyabinsk Oblast, Chuvash Republic, Krasnoyarsk Krai); authors' calculations.

Table 2.9   Multivariate Regressions of Separations on Enterprise Performance Variables, Controlling for Firm Size, Sector, Region, and Ownership, 1996

	1	*2*	*3*
Constant	.774*** (12.09)	.650*** (13.36)	.515*** (8.23)
Logwages	−.112*** (−5.38)	—	—
Logproductivity (output per employee)	—	−.526*** (−3.20)	—
Logprofitability	—	—	−.028* (−1.86)
Firm Size			
Logemployment	−.075*** (-5.90)	−.082*** (-4.77)	−.084*** (−3.72)
Sector			
Industry (1/0)	−.174 (-1.07)	−.120*** (−5.68)	−.125*** (−4.70)
Region			
Krasnoyarsk (1/0)	—	—	—
Chelyabinsk (1/0)	.017 (.801)	−.004 (−.151)	.024 (.60)
Chuvash Republi (1/0)	−.108*** (−4.21)	−.077** (−2.5)	−.049 (−1.11)c
Moscow (1/0)	−.025 (−1.44)	.030 (1.22)	.0720** (2.01)
Ownership			
State (1/0)	—	—	—
Mixed (1/0)	.142*** (7.35)	.100*** (3.98)	.119*** (3.83)
Municipal (1/0)	−.032 (−1.22)	.003 (.08)	.041 (.67)
Private (1/0)	.132*** (7.43)	.109*** (3.82)	.131*** (3.56)
Public association (1/0)	.230*** (3.75)	.010 (.15)	−.021 (−.24)
Adjusted R^2	.03	.04	.04

*p <0.1; **p <0.05; ***p <0.01; T-statistics shown in brackets.
Sources: Goskomstat data from administrative reporting of large and medium-size enterprises, selected regions (Moscow City, Chelyabinsk Oblast, Chuvash Republic, Krasnoyarsk Krai); authors' calculations.

leads to one of the main points that can be gleaned from this set of multivariate regressions. While the enterprise performance variables tended to have some significant association with separations, this was relatively modest in scope. Much of the variation appears to be explained by other factors. Also, in each equation at least one of the control variables has a greater weight than the enterprise performance variables (with the exception of the negative relationship between log productivity and separations). It may be that financial factors influence hiring and separation decisions indirectly, depending in part on the type of ownership and management that an enterprise has. These decisions may be driven largely by managers and their perceptions of a range of factors, including financial factors, but also possibly depending on other factors such as the political or social environment. The latter points are probably linked, for example, to the low incidence of lay-offs.

LABOUR TURNOVER AND JOB TENURE

Another way to follow changes in worker mobility is to look at job tenure. Job tenure is one of the most transparent indicators of labour mobility in terms of definition. Using job tenure data based on household sampling allows the analyst to overcome certain limitations of the enterprise reporting data, most notably the incomplete coverage of employment in small enterprises. At the same time, information on job tenure can be drawn from enterprise reporting, which may offer more precise information on tenure. For the purposes of this chapter, the key variables derived from job tenure include the share of short-tenured workers (with tenure less than one year) and the average tenure. These variables have a close relationship with labour turnover. The share of short-tenured employment usually has strong positive correlation with labour turnover and hiring rates, while the separation rate and average job tenure are negatively correlated.

The job tenure indicators drawn from various available sources are shown in table 2.10. The first two columns are based on enterprise data and refer to industry in the former USSR. The 1977 and 1987 data for the USSR show an increase in average tenure and a corresponding decrease in the share of short-tenured employees. Column 3 presents tenure data for Russian industry obtained through the REB enterprise survey for 1994. Although not strictly comparable, the REB data provide an indication of continued trends for both the average and short-term tenures.

The increase in labour turnover during the transition might have been expected to cause a reduction in worker tenure, whereas in fact the opposite trend was observed in industry.[47] A possible explanation for this might be found in labour segmentation. Part of the industrial labour force may have experienced a strong increase in labour turnover, while the remainder experienced little external mobility. In other words, an evolving polarisation probably developed between "stayers" and "movers." This scenario is consistent with findings from certain case studies and with the observation made by Kapeliushnikov and Aukutsionek that REB respondent firms in 1994 actually needed to hire two employees to fill one vacancy.[48]

The figures shown in columns 4–7 of table 2.10 are based on household data drawn from the RLMS and cover all sectors. Since these data were drawn from a household survey, they refer to all employees irrespective of type of employer and are not comparable with the enterprise data cited previously. In part, the shorter tenures indicated by the RLMS reflect the more complete coverage of the household survey data (including workers in small firms and new service sector

Table 2.10 Job Tenure Indicators

	Industry			All employees[c]			
	1977[a] (1)	1987[a] (2)	1994[b] (3)	1994 (4)	1995 (5)	1996 (6)	1998 (7)
Average job tenure, years	8.2	9.5	11.2	9.2	8.9	8.8	8.5
Share of workers with < 1 year tenure, %	15.1	12.5	8.0	17.4	18.3	17.5	17.0

Notes: Columns 1–3 refer only to employees in industry. Columns 4–7 provide tenure data for all employees, irrespective of the industry or type of firm.
Sources: (a) USSR industry, based on enterprise reporting, *Trud v SSSR* (Labour in the USSR) (Moscow: Goskomstat SSSR, 1988), 257–258;
(b) Large and medium-sized industrial firms, REB data from Kapeliushnikov and Aukutsionek, "The Labour Market in 1994," *The Russian Economic Barometer*, no. 2 (1995);
(c) Fourth quarter, all employees, household survey (RLMS); authors' estimates.

firms where short-tenured employment is likely to be more prevalent). These figures highlight once again the significant level of labour mobility in Russia.[49] In comparison, labour mobility as indicated by the share of short-tenured employment appeared to be notably lower in certain other transition countries. For example, in 1994, the shares of employees with less than one year job tenure were 14.7 percent in Poland and 15.3 percent in Slovenia.[50]

Tenure Distribution and Its Determinants

Variables that are likely to affect the tenure distribution can be divided into two groups. First are the characteristics of the employees (e.g., gender, age, wages, occupation, education, values, and attitudes) and, second, the characteristics of the employers (e.g., size and age of firm, ownership, sector, and wage arrears). Although tenure information is in limited supply, the RLMS data offer some information linking certain characteristics with variations in job tenure in 1995.

The data show a correlation between short-tenured employment (i.e., tenure of one year or less) and younger age, better pay, and male gender (all differences are statistically significant). It is notable that a statistically significant and negative, but modest, correlation arose between job tenure and wage level. This means that there was some tendency for higher wages to correspond to lower tenure. One explanation for this may be that external mobility (especially when related to new private sector jobs) tended to yield more wage gains than long-term matches in older enterprises. The RLMS 1995 data indicate a negative and statistically significant correlation between job tenure and willingness to quit. Those willing to quit had an average tenure of 6.2 years, while those not willing to do so were with their current employer for an average of 9.2 years. Among short-tenured employees, 43 percent were willing to move to another job, a view shared by only 32 percent of those with tenure over four years. Thus, the propensity to quit for the sake of better employment was significantly stronger among short-tenured employees, that is, the "movers."

Higher education seemed to have a positive effect on job tenure, but most of the differences were not statistically significant. Those respondents with university diplomas had an average tenure close to the survey average. The tenure for employees with post-university education was much longer, amounting to fourteen years. This contrasts with the relatively short tenures for those with vocational backgrounds. Thus, in the case of those with vocational school plus higher education, the respondents had an average tenure of 6.8 years, while those with only vocational training had an average of 7.6 years. This is consistent with the data on labour turnover described previously, showing blue collar hiring and separation rates exceeding those for white collar employees. The tenure data give another angle for viewing the same trend.

As might be expected, given that the transition was only a few years old, employees at privately run firms had the shortest average length of service (4.2 years). Those at foreign-owned or jointly owned firms had an average tenure of 6.2 years, while those at state-owned enterprises had an average employee service length of 8.5 years. Employees at privatised firms had an average tenure of about 11 years. In this group only 14 percent of those surveyed had tenure less than one year, while at private firms such employees made up 54 percent of the total. The RLMS data also indicated that short-tenured employees tended to work for smaller and younger firms.

The deterioration in conditions of employment at some firms may also have influenced employee propensities to quit and, consequently, tenure and labour turnover. Often such deterioration involved wage arrears, wages paid in kind rather than in cash, and/or unpaid leaves. Calculations based on the RLMS data clearly show that those employees who faced such conditions tended to have longer tenure. It may be that such irregularities worked as a device pushing potentially mobile employees out of their jobs, while leaving behind those who had strong commitment to the job or a lack of resources for getting a better one.

CONCLUSION

In comparison with certain other transition countries, the evidence presented here paints a picture of the Russian labour market as being relatively dynamic with fairly substantial hiring and separation rates. Moreover, the experience of Russian enterprises and workers was not uniform and, in disaggregating the flows, the chapter highlights a portion of the underlying differentiation.

The relatively large worker flows contrast, however, with the very modest rates of job creation. In general, job turnover—that is, net change in recorded employment at the enterprise level—accounted for a modest share of labour turnover. This provides an indication that a fair amount of churning took place in the labour market, whereby the actual worker flows were well in excess of those required to accomplish the enterprise level employment changes that occurred. This is not to say that the effect of these net employment changes was modest over time. The sustained nature of the outflows from employment in large and medium enterprises resulted in fairly substantial employment contraction in this group of firms by the end of the period considered here. Much of the job turnover appeared to be linked to reallocation of labour from these enterprises to smaller firms. This movement was also associated with a substantial reallocation of labour across industries, although in some sectors net change in one year was partially offset by opposite movements in following years.

The evidence presented in the chapter indicates that the Russian labour market during the first transition years should not be viewed as being composed of either "movers" or "stayers." From the analysis of the flows, it appears that both views have some validity and are not mutually exclusive. Continued labour hoarding in state-owned or recently privatised enterprises existed at the same time as fairly high labour turnover. Despite continued reductions in employment, these enterprises continued to hire large a number of workers. Much of the movement was associated with job-to-job flows, while there were also significant flows out of the labour market or into unemployment. Thus, the characterisations of "movers" and "stayers" are each relevant for a specific segment of the labour force. Indeed, the notable variation in labour turnover across industries, regions, groups of firms (e.g., by ownership), and employee groups (e.g., occupational and age groups) highlights the interaction of movers and stayers to form a complicated mix.

Many of the best skilled, most competitive, and most adaptable workers departed the state-owned and mixed ownership enterprises for better jobs in private sector enterprises or in self-employment. The separation of these workers, as well as others pushed to act by deteriorating conditions of employment, largely occurred through voluntary quitting. At the same time, a sizable group of generally less competitive workers either preferred, or were constrained by circumstances, to stay. Even in the face of deteriorating conditions of employment, they continued their attachment to their existing employers, often supplementing their income through alternative sources if possible. The result of this segmentation is visible in job tenure data that show peaks in short-term employment and long-term employment (controlling for age). Surprisingly perhaps, this segmentation can also be seen in the relatively high propensity of blue collar workers to change jobs and white collar workers' relatively low propensity to do so.

The available data do not permit a resolution of the puzzle of the persistence of hirings, but they do help to characterise it and provide some tentative indications (table 2.11). According to this limited sample, the hiring rates are greater in smaller firms, in less profitable firms, in construction and trade, and in firms with mixed ownership. They tend to be higher in more productive firms and those that

Table 2.11   Enterprise Characteristics Associated with Selected Components of Labour Turnover

I. Based on groups with greatest ratios to total employment

Indicator	*Hiring rates are greatest in . . .*	*Separation rates are greatest in . . .*	*Quit rates are greatest in . . .*
Firm size	smaller firms	smaller firms	smaller firms
Loss/profit-making firms	loss-makers	loss-makers	loss-makers
Regions	Chelyabinsk	Chelyabinsk	Chelyabinsk
Sectors	construction and trade	construction	trade and construction
Ownership	mixed	public association	mixed

II. Tendencies (based on correlation and regression analyses)

Variable	*Hiring rates tend to be greater in firms that are . . .*	*Separation rates tend to be greater in firms that are . . .*	*Quit rates tend to be greater in firms that are . . .*
Size	smaller	smaller	smaller
Profitability	less profitable?	less profitable	less profitable?
Productivity	more productive	less productive	less productive?
Labour utilisation	lower underemployment (administrative leave)?	higher underemployment (administrative leave)?	higher underemployment (administrative leave)?
Wage structure	higher paying?	lower paying	lower paying

Note: Entries without a "?" were confirmed through both the correlation and regression analysis, the others by only one form of analysis.
Source: authors' calculations.

pay higher wages, as well as in those that have lower underemployment in the form of administrative leaves. Separation rates are greatest in smaller firms, less profitable firms, construction firms, and firms owned by public associations and to a lesser extent those with mixed ownership. They tend to be higher in firms that are less productive, are less profitable, and pay lower wages, as well as in those that have more underemployment. The data indicate that voluntary quits also tend to be more common in firms with such characteristics. The results indicate a tendency for such factors as firm size and sector, location, ownership, employment conditions, and economic performance each to be related to the extent and composition of labour turnover.

The Russian labour market did not conform to initial expectations of a rapid and far-reaching reallocation of labour between "old" and "new" jobs with many workers transiting unemployment. Still, net flows into "new" jobs cumulatively became fairly substantial. In the next chapters we will look at older state or mixed-ownership enterprises and newer private enterprises, with a view to describing employment practices and their relation to the labour market behaviour and transitions of individuals.

NOTES

1. E.g., Philip Aghion and Olivier Blanchard, "On the Speed of Transition in Central Europe," in *NBER Macroeconomics Annual 1994,* ed. Stanley Fischer and Julio Rotemberg (Cambridge and London: MIT Press, 1994), 283–320.

2. Rostislav Kapeliushnikov and Sergey Aukutsionek, "The Labour Market in 1994," *The Russian Economic Barometer* 2 (1995): 25–40.

3. E.g., Simon Commander, John McHale, and Ruslan Yemtsov, "Russia," in *Unemployment, Restructuring, and the Labor Market in Eastern Europe and Russia,* ed. Simon Commander and Fabrizio Coricelli (Washington, D.C.: EDI—The World Bank, 1995), 147–192; Vladimir Gimpelson and Douglas Lippoldt, *Labour Restructuring in Russian Enterprises: A Case Study (*Paris: OECD, 1996); Vladimir Gimpelson and Douglas Lippoldt, "Labour Turnover in the Russian Economy," in *Labour Market Dynamics in the Russian Federation,* ed. Douglas Lippoldt (Paris: OECD, 1997); Simon Clarke, "Structural Adjustment without Mass Unemployment?" in *Structural Adjustment without Mass Unemployment? Lessons from Russia,* ed. Simon Clarke (Cheltenham, UK: Edward Elgar Publishing, 1998), 9–86.

4. E.g., Simon Commander, Leonid Liberman, and Ruslan Yemtsov, *Unemployment and Labour Market Dynamics in Russia* (Washington, D.C.: EDI—The World Bank, WPS 1167, August 1993); Richard Layard and Andrea Richter, "Labour Market Adjustment in Russia," *Russian Economic Trends* 3, no. 2 (1994): 85–103; Vladimir Gimpelson and Douglas Lippoldt, *Labour Restructuring in Russian Enterprises: A Case Study* (Paris: OECD, 1996); and Sergey Aukutsionek and Rostislav Kapeliushnikov, "Labor Hoarding in Russian Industry," *The Russian Economic Barometer* 2 (1996), among others.

5. For a similar presentation for East European nations, see Tito Boeri and Randolph Bruno, "A Short Note on the Characteristics of Labour Turnover in Central and Eastern Europe," in *Labour Market Dynamics in the Russian Federation,* ed. Douglas Lippoldt (Paris: OECD, 1997), 151–161, which contains a brief sketch of gross flows in the Czech Republic, Poland, Slovakia, and Slovenia.

6. Unfortunately, the available data did not permit assessment of earnings mobility, which is also an important dimension of labour market dynamics.

7. In fact, few countries have comprehensive and complete statistics covering the issue. See *Employment Outlook* (Paris: OECD, 1996). For the data available in the United States, see also Steven Davis and John Haltiwanger, *Measuring Gross Worker and Job Flows,* NBER, Working Paper No. 5133, Cambridge, Mass., 1995.

8. Detailed administrative reporting on labour turnover is required of "large and medium" size Russian enterprises. These are firms employing: over one hundred employees in industry, construction, or transportation; over fifty in wholesale trade; or over thirty in retail trade. Early in the transition, these firms accounted for about 75 percent of total employment in the country. Small firms are only required to provide basic employment information.

9. These include regions with high (Krasnoyarsk, Chelyabinsk) as well as moderate (the Chuvash Republic) turnover. A short description of the regions and basic arguments for this selection is available in Hartmut Lehmann and Jonathan Wadsworth, "Labour Force Participation and the Household: Evidence from Five Russian Regions," in *Labour Market Dynamics in the Russian Federation,* ed. Douglas Lippoldt (OECD: Paris, 1997), 115–134. The preparation of this enterprise data set was sponsored through TACIS-ACE project number T95-4099-R.

10. See table 2.5 for a breakdown of the sample by enterprise characteristics.

11. The inclusion of any small firms at all is probably due to continued participation in the reporting system by small units remaining from the downsizing or break-up of large and medium-size firms. For more on the dynamism of small firms in transition economies, see *Entrepreneurship and SMEs in Transition Economies: The Visegrad Conference* (Paris: OECD, 1997).

12. *Trud v SSSR* (Moscow: Goskomstat of the USSR, 1988), 258. These rates were within the range of variation for OECD Member countries); see *The OECD Jobs Study Part II* (Paris: OECD, 1995), 65.

13. Gimpelson and Lippoldt in *Labour Restructuring* note that during the period from 1992 to 1995, large and medium-size enterprises in Russia faced a decline in output of about 50 percent, but employment in these firms declined only about 30 percent.

14. Klara Sabirianova, "Microeconomic Analysis of Labor Market Dynamics in Russia," *Voprosy ekonomiki* 1 (1998): 42–58.

15. *Employment Outlook* (July 1996): 166, provides a list of countries, periods covered, and units of observation, which are not strictly comparable.

16. See, for example, Tito Boeri, "Unemployment Outflows and the Scope of Labour Market Policies in Central and Eastern Europe," in *Lessons from Labour Market Policies in the Transition Countries,* ed. Salvatore Zecchini (Paris: OECD, 1996), 445–447; Tito Boeri and Randolph Bruno, "A Short Note on the Characteristics of Labour Turnover in Central and Eastern Europe," in *Labour Market Dynamics in the Russian Federation,* ed. Douglas Lippoldt (Paris: OECD, 1997), 151–161; Tito Boeri, Michael Burda, and Janos Kollo, *Mediating the Transition: Labour Markets in Central and Eastern Europe* (London—New York: CEPR—Institute for East-West Studies, 1998).

17. Mark Foley, *Labour Market Flows in Russia: Evidence from the Russian Longitudinal Monitoring Survey* (unpublished paper, 1995).

18. In addition to economic developments, labour turnover rates can be influenced by such factors as the peculiarities of legislation or rigidities caused by prevailing social norms and patterns. See Assar Lindbeck, *Unemployment and Macroeconomics* (Cambridge, Mass.: The MIT Press, 1993).

19. Gimpelson and Lippoldt, *Labour Restructuring.*

20. Labour turnover data for blue collar workers are available only for industry. Given the ratio of white collar employment to blue collar employment (1:4), one can crudely estimate the labour turnover rates for white collars (here taken to mean managers, professionals, technicians, and clerks).

21. *Vserossiyskiy Monitoring Sotcialno-Trudovoy Sfery* (Moscow: Ministry of Labour of the Russian Federation, 1996). Note that the sample includes 326 industrial firms of various sizes and ownership. The survey structure is subject to certain biases (e.g., due to sampling problems) and should be used with caution.

22. By way of contrast, in Hungary the probability of replacement in the case of skilled workers was significantly higher than for the unskilled [Janos Kollo, *Firing, Hiring and Wage Growth in Hungarian Firms* (unpublished paper, 1995), 18].

23. Simon Commander, Sumana Dhar, and Ruslan Yemtsov, "How Russian Firms Make Their Wage and Employment Decisions," in *Enterprise Restructuring and Economic Policy in Russia*, ed. Simon Commander, Qimiao Fan, and Mark Schaffer (Washington, D.C.: EDI—The World Bank, 1996), 24.

24. Sabirianova, "Microeconomic Analysis."

25. These official Goskomstat estimates for employment in the economy draw on the establishment reporting system and include certain additional adjustments for underrepresented portions of the economy.

26. The classification of such separations as voluntary was controversial, because of the pressures employers sometimes applied to bring them about. Quits were often economically, socially, and politically less costly for firms than lay-offs. See also Guy Standing, *The "Shake-Out" in Russian Factories: The RLFS Fifth Round* (Geneva: ILO, Labour Market Papers, No. 14, 1995).

27. *The OECD Jobs Study Part II*, 65.

28. Kollo, *Firing, Hiring and Wage Growth in Hungarian Firms.*

29. E.g., see Sergey Aukutsionek and Rostislav Kapeliushnikov, "Russian Industrial Enterprises on the Labor Market," *Voprosy ekonomiki* 6 (1995): 48–56.

30. Aukutsionek and Kapeliushnikov, "Labor Hoarding in Russian Industry," *Russian Economic Barometer:* 3–14.

31. In practice, however, very few young people were placed into employment through quotas.

32. Aukutsionek and Kapeliushnikov, "Russian Industrial Enterprises."

33. E.g., see Aukutsionek and Kapeliushnikov, "Labor Hoarding in Russian Industry," for a list of the main reasons REB respondents cited for labour hoarding.

34. I.e., some of those on the roster of an enterprise would be on leave with reduced pay or short time and drawing modest compensation. This brought down the average wage relative to the tax threshold.

35. Kanty-Mansy Autonomous Okrug is a region just north of Tyumen Oblast and generally east of the spine of the Ural Mountains.

36. Registered unemployment by region is derived from the administrative data of the State Employment Service; survey unemployment from the official labour force survey.

37. The pooling of data for industry, trade, and construction provides an indication of developments in commercial activity overall. In 1996, these three sectors accounted for over 75 percent of employment in what might be considered commercial activities (excluding agriculture).

38. The sub-sample for this type of firms is, however, too small ($N = 73$) for statistically significant conclusions.

39. Davis and Haltiwanger, *Measuring Gross Worker and Job Flows.*

40. Commander, McHale, and Yemtsov, "Russia," 161–162.

41. Based on the pooled sample for the four study regions.

42. There is a significant dispersion across sub-samples, however, with the figure varying from .16 in Krasnoyarsk Krai to .32 in the Chuvash Republic, from .20 in industry to .26 in trade, and from .18 in privatised firms to .30 in municipal enterprises.

43. In a series of case studies during the early years of the transition, one study team found that employers tended to guarantee wages and hours to their most valued employees, while offering reduced hours and/or wages to a second tier of employees. In this way they actively tried to separate the least valued employees (Clarke, "Structural Adjustment without Mass Unemployment?" 44).

44. Commander and Schankerman have made a similar point; see Simon Commander and Mark Schankerman, "Enterprise Restructuring and the Efficient Provision of Social Benefits," in *The Changing Social Benefits in Russian Enterprises,* ed. Douglas Lippoldt (Paris: OECD, 1996), 115–130.

45. *Transition Report 1997* (London: EBRD, 1997), 26, cites REB data indicating that barter accounts for some 40 percent of industrial sector sales.

46. *Transition Report 1997,* 74, cites data from Kaufmann and Kaliberda estimating the unofficial economy in Russia as 41.6 percent of GDP in 1995.

47. Assuming that the two sources provide roughly comparable estimates.

48. Gimpelson and Lippoldt, *Labour Restructuring,* and Kapeliushnikov and Aukutsionek, "The Labour Market in 1994."

49. The All-Russian Labour Monitoring survey (an enterprise survey) observed shorter average job tenure (8.2 years) but also a lower proportion of short-tenured workers (13.4 percent) in 1995. However, this difference is likely attributable in part to differences in methodology between this survey and the RLMS (a household survey).

50. These data are based on national labour force surveys and were drawn from the Luxembourg Employment Study Data Base (Centre d'Etudes de Populations, de Pauvreté et de Politiques Socio-Economiques).

3

"Old Jobs": Employment in State-Owned and Privatised Enterprises

OVERVIEW

This chapter examines the impact of the economic transition on "old" jobs, which we define as those in enterprises founded before the reforms began in earnest in 1992. It highlights the enterprise-level responses to the change in economic system by using an in-depth case study of four large industrial enterprises.[1] This approach permits us to complement and expand upon evidence from more representative sources and it provides concrete examples of the types of adjustment mechanisms that enabled older firms to resist or mitigate pressures for employment adjustment, at least temporarily. The chapter shows that while already attempting some restructuring during the first few years of transition, businesses such as the case study firms also adopted survival-oriented tactics that partly account for the gap between the initial expectations of deep market-oriented restructuring and the more gradualist and piecemeal reality.[2] This strategy contributed to the particular pattern of labour market adjustment found in post-socialist Russia. And it remained embedded in many parts of the Russian economy through the end of the period considered in this book.

Advocates of reform had hoped that enterprises would become more responsive to market signals, in part by reallocating resources, seeking higher returns, and striving to attain market efficiency. This shift in behaviour was considered to be one of the key indicators of progress in reform. Privatisation and reform of corporate governance were seen by many analysts and policy-makers as forces that would push existing enterprises toward more market-oriented behaviour.

By September 1994, across the whole economy, some 100,000 enterprises had been privatised and 80 percent of the industrial workforce was employed in privatised firms.[3] Given the scale of privatisation, it had great potential for far-reaching social and labour market impacts. Some of these had already begun to emerge during the first five years of transition. For example, the social contract between management and labour began to be reshaped and unemployment, social stratification, and differentiation grew. But the failure of privatisation to quickly and fully clarify the future shape of corporate governance left the ultimate outcomes of the process uncertain. Structures for corporate governance and shareholder rights remained in flux.

The result was a less than full and decisive shift in enterprise behaviour. Clearly, a change had occurred; enterprises no longer acted as they used to under the planning system. However, most enterprises did not yet act fully as market-oriented agents, either. It appears that many firms, including most privatised firms, adopted the survival-oriented strategy. As Ickes and Ryterman (1994) pointed out, this survival-oriented behaviour differed from the behavioural patterns of firms in market economies. In Russia, it was characterised by managers who preferred to avoid the dislocations and pain of restructuring and radical transformation. Instead they implemented piecemeal reforms, sought short-term gains, or adjusted in a passive fashion to the various shocks experienced by the firm—often without a long-term vision for the future. While not universal, evidence exists that such behaviour was typical for many Russian industrial companies.[4]

Such behaviour, however, was not irrational. It was induced by uncertainty in many fundamental aspects of the environment faced by firms, including the rules of commerce, supply and demand, and financial constraints, among others. As a result of this uncertainty, it is understandable that many enterprise managers maintained convictions that budget constraints would soften (as before), that demand on the market for their products would revive, or that the state would not allow their firms to die. The absence of bankruptcy proceedings reinforced this view. Some managers had genuine hope that their firms would revive in this fashion; others used the situation to strengthen their positions or financial control in the enterprise.

Naturally, this situation had direct consequences for the human resource policies of the enterprises. In general, the situation left managers with broad discretion in their management of personnel. One survey found that the majority of large enterprise managers perceived little outside intervention in their decision making concerning labour issues.[5] Managers differed in their reaction to this situation, in some firms by actively intervening and in others by adjusting in a more passive fashion to financial constraints and changing staffing needs.

If deep restructuring at enterprise level occurred in an economy moving from socialism to a regulated market system, what might one expect to see with respect to labour resources? The changes would probably focus on a more effective utilisation of labour while limiting growth in labour costs. The tentative programme of restructuring would probably include at least three major points:

- Labour shedding, since firms would strive to get rid of excessive labour;
- Occupational shifts, since firms would adjust skill mix to production needs

(thereby changing the structure of personnel and cutting nonproductive employment); and
- More flexible labour practices in order to facilitate adjustment and minimise costs.

These points help to shape the discussion in this chapter. Do we see the expected changes? If not, then what do we observe? In considering these issues, the chapter begins with a description of the case study firms, then examines their employment developments and moves on to discuss the factors driving these changes.

THE STUDY FIRMS AND THEIR GENERAL SITUATION

The firms covered by the case study represented metal working and light industry. Two of them were located in Kaluga, a medium-sized city some 180 kilometres west of Moscow. The other two were located in the relatively large Siberian city of Krasnoyarsk. These cities were chosen in part because they offered a contrast in conditions (e.g., geographic location, economic base, population size). The study firms were privatised under various schemes during the period from 1991 to 1994. While this sample of firms was not representative, it nevertheless provided an indication of the situation faced by similar enterprises, at least in these regions and sectors.

Key data on employment, wages, separations, and hirings were obtained from the study firms' administrative records. These data were supplemented by additional statistics from official and nonofficial sources, and qualitative information on local, regional, and national labour markets and on industry. Qualitative information was collected at the enterprise level through interviews with managers, professionals, workers, and trade union activists, and at the local level through interviews with government officials. At each firm, ten to fifteen employees of different statuses were interviewed.

The study firms (renamed here) shared certain common features. They were: (i) privatised and organised as joint stock companies (JSC), (ii) industrial, (iii) medium or large size in terms of employment (i.e., more than 200 employees),[6] (iv) not dominant in their local economies, and (v) suffering from declines in output. At the same time, each firm was unique, differing in such characteristics as sector, ownership, and size.

The Big Turbine company was one of the largest power turbine manufacturers in the Soviet Union, providing turbines for ships and, particularly, for submarines with atomic power. In 1993, Big Turbine was privatised under the first option of the mass privatisation programme, meaning that the employees were given a block of nonvoting shares and were entitled to buy a further block of voting shares at a discount. As a result of privatisation, a foreign concern acquired 20 percent of the shares and gained a seat on the board of directors, while a further 20 percent of the shares were administered by the State Committee for Defence Industries (a government agency). During the early 1990s, defence-oriented output dropped from 65 percent to 5 percent of the total and the enterprise shifted to produce various kinds of turbines for power stations and other civilian purposes.

Lady's Dream garment factory was privatised in 1992 through the second option, meaning that 51 percent of shares were sold and distributed among insiders. The company developed a dependent relationship with an Austrian firm, which owned over one-third of the charter capital (bought at voucher and cash auctions). As part of its restructuring, the firm shifted production so that about 90 percent of output went to Western markets under the label of the Austrian firm. However, due to its focus on exports, Lady's Dream lost its domestic market share and its profit margins shrank as its dependence on one outlet increased. In the second half of 1995, it was declared insolvent and sought to negotiate with creditors and potential buyers.

Until its privatisation in 1992, Old Shipyard was a part of a steamship company on the Yenisei River. It retained ties to its parent, which held 51 percent of the shares. Up to 1994, the enterprise focused on technical maintenance, repair work, and even some production of consumer goods (metal products for household use) and machine building. In 1994, the enterprise was reorganised and the technical maintenance shop and personnel were transferred to the parent company. Among the remaining activities, repair work dominated but continued to decline due to a fall in cargo shipping on the Yenisei River, and the firm fell on hard times.

The Siberian Shoe company was leased and then bought out by the labour collective to form eventually a closed JSC in 1992, with all shares held by insiders. The newly privatised company followed through on projects launched earlier to construct a new shop-floor and office building, acquire new machinery from the West, and retrain key employees. By 1995, it had succeeded in diversifying somewhat its production and strengthening its regional sales base.

The firms studied were no exception to the general decline in output in Russia, although their rates of decline varied. Chart 3.1 shows their output trends from 1991 to 1995. Two of the case study firms (Big Turbine and Old Shipyard—both metal working firms, in effect) had a trend in output similar to industry in general. The light industrial companies demonstrated divergent trends, with one showing a much smaller decline (Lady's Dream) and one a much bigger decline (Siberian Shoe). Lady's Dream lost less than a quarter of its output. This relative "stability" was due, in part, to the Austrian partner firm described previously. Output at Siberian Shoe in 1995 was estimated to be at only one quarter of the 1992 level, but this drastic drop in production was accompanied by restructuring, which appears to have left the firm in a stronger position.

Chart 3.1   Industrial Output: 1991–1995 (1991 = 100, except Siberian Shoe 1992 = 100:

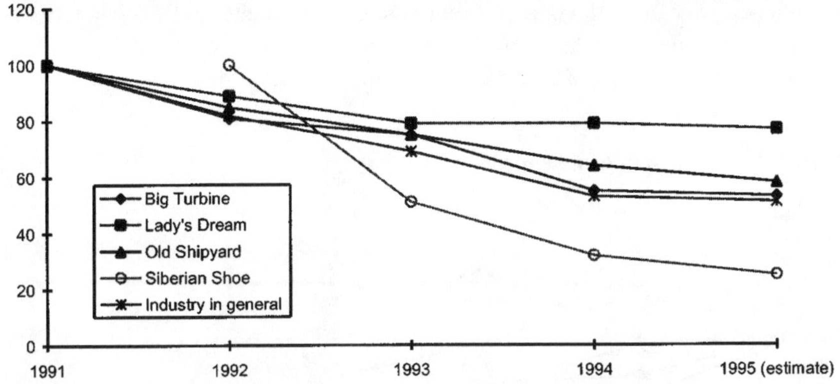

Sources: Company-provided data; Goskomstat.

LABOUR TRANSFORMATION AND ADJUSTMENT IN THE STUDY FIRMS

One might have expected drastically shrinking output to result in a corresponding reduction in employment and that this would occur mostly through lay-offs, freezes in new hirings, and divestiture of nonproductive assets. In fact, the case study enterprises adjusted to the new economic conditions through a combination of change in employment levels and structure, and through increased flexibility in the utilisation and remuneration of labour.

As noted in chapter 1, during the early transition years, the drops in output for the mostly older medium and large industrial enterprises greatly outpaced the declines in employment.[7] Enterprises adjusted largely through use of voluntary quits to achieve employment reductions and through flexibility with respect to hours and wages. In addition, employers increasingly used fixed-term contracts as a tool in flexibly managing labour resources. Shifts in occupational structure also occurred, in part linked to the pattern of voluntary quits and in part by design. The case study firms fit within this general pattern and offered insights into possible explanations for some of these developments. This section of the chapter considers the adjustment that occurred through these various mechanisms.

While the study firms experienced roughly similar employment outcomes, some notable differentiation arose in the trends, particularly between the firms in metal working and the firms in light industries (chart 3.2). Both machine manufacturers reduced their staffing by about 30 percent (table 3.1), with an elasticity of output to employment declines similar to the average for all medium and large firms (i.e., roughly 0.6). The shoe and garment producers tell a somewhat different story; for them, downsizing started with a one- to two-year lag. Siberian Shoe only began to reduce employment in 1993, but by 1994 had been driven to reduce staffing by some 20 percent from the 1992 peak. At Lady's Dream as well, employment levels were maintained through early 1993. Then the firm hit a financial impasse due to unfavourable contractual agreements and exchange rates (causing losses on production for the European market), increasing input costs, and management-related problems, among other factors. Beginning in mid-1993

Chart 3.2   Changes in Employment, 1991 = 100

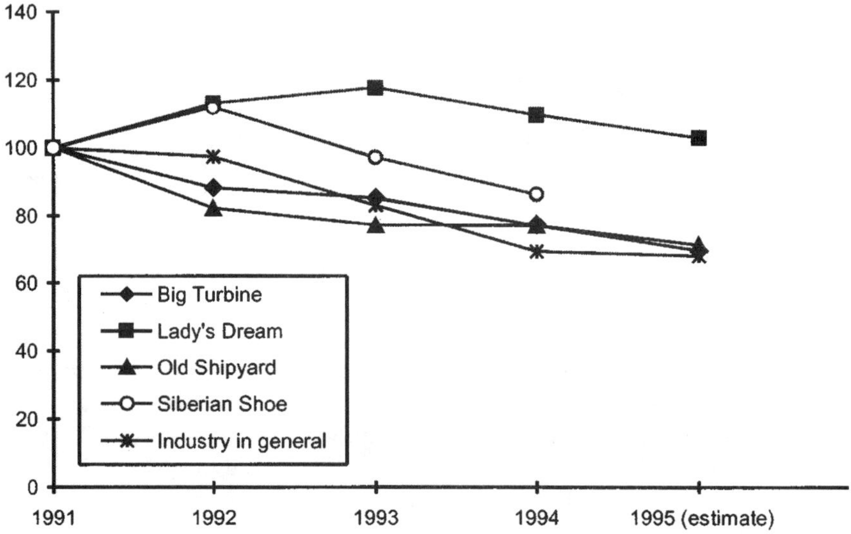

Sources: See table 3.1. 1995 data are based on first half.

Table 3.1   Total Employment

	1991	1992	1993	1994	1995
Big Turbine	11,789	10,407	10,047	9,067	8,197[a]
Lady's Dream	1,740	1,967	2,046	1,906	1,788[b]
Old Shipyard[d]	1,201[c]	988	927	923	855[b]
Siberian Shoe	973[c]	1,089	944	839	n.a.
Industry[d] (millions)	22.4	21.8	18.6	15.5 (Dec)	15.2–15.4 (March)

Notes: In this and all following tables, n.a. means "not available." Also, in all tables and charts for chapter 3, the data for industry refer to medium- and large-size enterprises (i.e., those with employment > 200).
(a) Here and later, the 1995 data for Big Turbine refer to May (unless otherwise indicated);
(b) Here and later, the 1995 data for Old Shipyard and Lady's Dream refer to March (unless otherwise indicated);
(c) 1990;
(d) Large and medium-sized enterprises.
Sources: Company-provided data; Goskomstat.

the firm started to downsize and by the first half of 1995, employment had fallen by 10 percent from the 1993 peak. During the second half of 1995, employment was reduced by roughly 40 percent as an emergency measure. Thus, after initially exhibiting some buoyancy, the light industrial firms also shrank in terms of employment. The changes in total employment represent the combined effects of separations and hirings, as outlined in the next section.

Rate and Structure of Separations

As already discussed in chapter 2, Russian industrial enterprises experienced fairly high separation rates, which were driven mostly by voluntary quits. The intensity of separations in both metal working firms was higher than in the light industrial firms, in part reflecting differences in the labour market opportunities according to the gender and skills of those employed in these two sectors (table 3.2). Interestingly, among the case study firms, involuntary dismissals (i.e., lay-offs and disciplinary firings together) seemed to function as a complement to voluntary quitting. Where the voluntary quitting rate was rather high, there were only minor involuntary reductions.

In general, voluntary quits accounted for the bulk of all separations (table 3.3). Defined as separations initiated by the employee, in reality these quits were often actively induced by employers through prolonged administrative leaves, wage arrears, or other aspects of deteriorating employment conditions (chart 3.3). Lay-offs constituted a relatively minor proportion of total downsizing, although in certain years for certain firms they made significant contributions. For example, Old Shipyard, with significant turnover and downsizing, did not resort to lay-offs until 1995.[8]

Detailed information on the structure of separations by occupational category is available for Big Turbine and Old Shipyard. At these firms, increases in voluntary quits were largely generated by increased outflows of blue collar workers. In 1990, blue collar workers accounted for half of all separations at Old Shipyard, but between 1992 and 1994 they accounted for about 90 percent, with most of their exits occurring via voluntary quitting. Big Turbine experienced similar changes. At both firms, these outflows involved first of all men in various skilled metal working occupations, such as machine tool operators or welders. Most were drawn away by better paid positions, either in other similar large companies or in small businesses. Moves to smaller firms in particular often entailed occupational changes for the individuals concerned.

One explanation for this mobility may be that blue collar workers were better able to adapt to the changes in their work environment than their more educated colleagues. White collar employees often faced even more fundamental changes in their job content following a separation. Far fewer open vacancies existed for professionals and technicians, and those separating had only a slim chance of finding employment in an occupation related to their

Table 3.2 Separation Rates (Percentage of Total Employment)

	1991	1992	1993	1994	1995
Big Turbine	16.5	25.4	24.5	25.8	12.0 (Jan.–May)
Lady's Dream	15.1	11.7	20.1	24.0	10.7 (Q1–Q2)
Old Shipyard	n.a.	39.0	45.0	52.0	16.0 (Jan.–Apr.)
Siberian Shoe	24.0	31.0	35.0	23.0	n.a.
Industry average	n.a.	30.9	33.6	28.8	13.8 (Q1–Q2)

Sources: Company-provided data; Goskomstat.

Table 3.3 Structure of Separations (Percentage of Total for Each Firm Each Year)

Big Turbine

	1990	1991	1992	1993	1994	1995
Voluntary	38.3	35.0	30.6	51.1	54.6	53.8
Disciplinary	3.9	4.1	3.4	5.3	5.4	3.6
Lay-offs	0.0	8.9	0.0	2.6	1.2	21.3
Others	57.8	52.0	66.0	41.0	38.8	21.3

Lady's Dream

	1990	1991	1992	1993	1994	1995
Voluntary	n.a.	45.8	51.7	69.7	48.1	66.8
Disciplinary	n.a.	9.9	21.1	9.7	9.7	11.1
Lay-offs	n.a.	4.2	1.5	0.5	15.6	1.0
Others	n.a.	40.0	25.7	20.1	26.3	21.1

Old Shipyard

	1988	1990	1992	1993	1994	1995
Voluntary	75.8	71.6	59.8	53.5	70.5	77.2
Disciplinary	10.9	20.6	19.4	28.0	15.3	17.6
Lay-offs	0.0	0.0	0.0	0.0	0.0	2.9
Others	13.3	7.8	20.8	18.5	14.2	2.3

Siberian Shoe

	1990	1991	1992	1993	1994	1995
Voluntary	43.9	52.1	50.6	53.3	48.4	n.a.
Disciplinary	11.7	7.8	5.6	5.9	0.7	n.a.
Lay-offs	0.0	0.0	8.5	15.6	22.0	n.a.
Others	44.4	40.1	35.3	25.2	28.9	n.a.

Source: Company-provided data.

Chart 3.3 Voluntary Quitting, % of Total Employment, 1991–1995

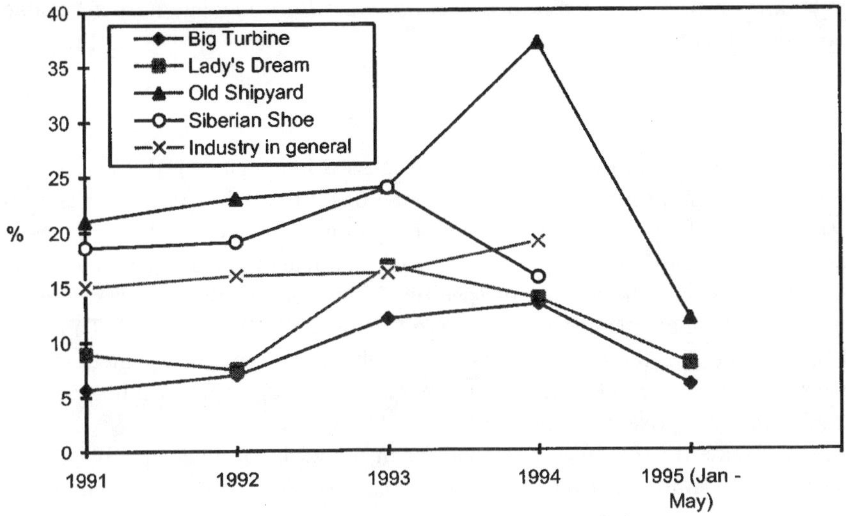

Sources: Company-provided data; Goskomstat.

previous one.[9] Also, the demographic composition of white collar workers was biased toward older women whose capacity to move and adapt to the new labour market conditions has been lower than that of the average blue collar man.

The use of dismissals due to disciplinary reasons exhibited a rather chaotic pattern. Two companies had a rather high rate of disciplinary firing (10 percent and even higher); two others used this policy very moderately. Comparing these data with lay-off rates, one sees that they were negatively interrelated.[10] It may have been that a firm needing rapid cuts in its labour force could have pursued either policy, depending on the particular pressures faced by the manager.

The reliance on quits was in part an avoidance of the politically and socially sensitive action of dismissing employees for economic reasons. Voluntary quits and disciplinary firings gave managers some "cover" during the downsizing. To a lesser extent, this was also linked in some cases to an avoidance of severance pay obligations that come with lay-offs (which amounted to up to ninety days' wages in the event the employee did not find another job during the period). Generally, the gap between quit and lay-off rates meant that the outflow went mostly spontaneously. The domination of voluntary separations left managers less discretion over the shape of the enterprise workforce. In the face of the strong pressure to downsize, managers may have attempted to encourage or discourage quits (e.g., by shifting relative wages), but the influence was indirect. The absence of more direct approaches led to deskilling (in terms of the average employees' capacities) as more competitive workers exited; it also represented a loss of managerial power vis-à-vis the pool of remaining high-skill or firm-specific skill holders, upon whom managers then became more dependent.[11]

Hirings

As was the pattern in most of industry (discussed in chapter 2), the study firms also persisted in hiring workers well into the transition (table 3.4). Despite continued overstaffing, workers in certain occupations remained in demand. These tended to be skilled workers such as welders and machine tool operators. However, workers with these types of specific abilities and skills often preferred to join new private companies even if it involved an occupational change. Thus, underemployment of the existing personnel at the older firms was sometimes accompanied by an ongoing search for new employees with special skills required to keep the enterprise in operation.[12]

At the same time, although demand for unskilled labour was greatly inflated during the pre-reform period, there remained a very real core demand in industry, including at the case study enterprises. This was in part due to certain production processes where technology lagged and/or that did not require special training or skills. Employers looking for candidates to fill such vacancies may have preferred to hire school-leavers or graduates from vocational schools. In a few cases youth employment was subsidised by Regional Employment Funds, which gave firms not only very cheap labour but additional revenue. Those hired under these circumstances could use these low-paid jobs as platforms for further job search; generally, they were unlikely to stay at the enterprise for a long period.

Hiring through noninstitutional channels played a major role in most of the firms and its significance increased consistently (table 3.5). In part, this was due to the decline in overall hiring and more selective search for highly skilled and experienced workers. This type of employee was much less likely to be recruited through State Employment Service or vocational school channels. Here, social networks and friendly ties were major instruments in job matching. In the context of Russian industrial cities where enterprise-provided housing could form a kind of community, having contacts at an establishment gave broad access to information through a web of weak and strong ties.[13] Sometimes residential areas were populated by workers of several enterprises in similar industries, which created an "informational web" with overlapping networks. Interviews with personnel managers also revealed some unconventional approaches to recruitment. For example, sometimes when they learned of financial hardships (e.g., temporary layoffs or mounting wage arrears) in a neighbouring enterprise, they jumped to poach employees with particularly sought-after skills. However, this did not guarantee a long commitment of newcomers to the new enterprise. In cases where such a firm faced similar troubles later on, those hired sometimes returned to their previous employer or other new employment.

Adjustment in the Occupational Structure

Beyond changes in total employment, the enterprises also adjusted the occupational composition of their workforce. Shifts were achieved through the combined effects of labour turnover and internal reallocation of labour. In view of the distortions inherent in the allocation of labour under the socialist system, the scale and shape of this reallocation provides an indication of restructuring.

As of the time of the case study, the two light industrial firms had similar personnel structures (table 3.6). Managers accounted for about 7 percent of all

Table 3.4   Rates of Hiring (Percentages of Total Employment)

	1991	*1992*	*1993*	*1994*	*1995*
Big Turbine	11.6	17.8	19.1	17.2	2.3 (Jan.–May)
Lady's Dream	17.7[a]	19.1	18.0	21.4	6.9 (Q1–Q2)
Old Shipyard	28.0[a]	39.0	44.0	36.0	9.0 (Jan–Apr)
Siberian Shoe	40.0[a]	42.0	29.0	19.0	n.a.
Industry in general	—	22.2	20.1	18.2	10.4 (Q1–Q2)

a) 1990
Source: Company-provided data; Goskomstat.

Table 3.5   Channels of Hiring (Percentage of Total Hires)

	1991	*1992*	*1993*	*1994*	*1995 (Jan.–May)*
Big Turbine					
—vocational institutions	10.3	9.3	4.9	3.8	16.8
—employment centre	9.2	2.5	2.8	2.4	7.0
—free hiring	80.5	88.2	92.3	94.4	76.2
Lady's Dream					
—vocational institutions	35.0	47.4	29.8	32.9	100.0[a]
—employment centre	0.0	0.0	0.0	0.0	0.0
—free hiring	65.0	52.6	70.2	67.1	0.0
Old Shipyard					
—vocational institutions	5.3[c]	1.8	0.2	0.0	0.0
—employment centre[b]	29.0[c]	0.0	0.0	0.6	0.0
—free hiring	65.7[c]	98.2	99.8	99.4	100.0

(a) Q1–Q2
(b) Here, the EC channel includes centrally organised hiring (orgnabor).
(c) 1990.
Source: Company-provided data.

Table 3.6   Structure of Personnel (Percentage of Total Employment)

	1991[a]	1992	1993	1994	1995
Big Turbine					
—managers, professionals, technicians & clericals[b]	31.0	30.7	31.6	33.5	34.5
—workers	57.4	57.3	58.3	60.2	60.0
Total industrial employment	88.4	88.0	89.9	93.7	94.5
Lady's Dream					
—managers	5.9	5.3	5.5	6.7	6.9
—professionals, technicians & clericals	8.7	7.5	7.5	7.6	7.5
—workers	75.0	76.5	77.9	79.0	81.9
Total industial employment	89.6	89.3	90.9	93.3	96.3
Old Shipyard					
—managers	6.0	7.0	7.0	8.0	8.0
—professionals & technicians	10.0	11.0	11.0	11.0	12.0
—workers	51.0	48.0	45.0	41.0	36.0
—clericals	1.0	3.0	6.0	7.0	11.0
Total industrial employment	68.0	69.0	69.0	67.0	67.0
Siberian Shoe					
—managers	6.5	7.0	7.0	6.5	n.a.
—professionals, technicians & clericals	8.1	8.0	8.0	7.3	n.a.
—workers	75.0	79.0	80.0	79.0	n.a.
Total industrial employment	90.0	93.0	95.0	94.0	n.a.

(a) 1990 for the Old Shipyard and Siberian Shoe.
(b) Separate data were not available for managers.
Source: Company-provided data.

employees, while professionals, technicians, and clerical workers together had only a slightly larger share. The share of blue-collar workers had increased somewhat over time and amounted to about 80 percent. (Most blue-collar jobs at these firms were low or medium skilled and occupied by women.) The share of employees in nonindustrial employment (i.e., with jobs not directly related to the manufacturing process) had decreased and amounted to only about 5 percent.[14] Despite all the differences between the two companies, structurally they were developing in the same direction.

A comparison with the structure of personnel at light industrial companies in the United States might provide some benchmarks for assessing the employment structures and adjustment tendencies. Clearly, a precise comparison is hardly feasible due to differences in available data. However, a rough comparison gives some flavour of similarity or divergence. The industry "apparel and other textile products" in the U.S. classification includes enterprises that are similar to the light industrial firms in this study. In these U.S. enterprises, managers accounted for about 3 percent of total employment; professionals, technicians, and clerical workers made up some 10 percent; and production and operating workers accounted for 83 percent.[15] By this measure, the Russian light industry firms were not dramatically out of line, but some notable differences in organization were evident. In comparison, their structure seemed somewhat top heavy with managers, while having less labour devoted to professional, technical, and clerical tasks and to blue collar tasks (generally related to production). Only in the case of the shares for blue collar workers did adjustment in the Russian firms move toward the share in the U.S. industry.

As one might expect, given the differences between heavy and light industry, the employment structure of the two metal working firms differed from the patterns described herein. Managers, professionals, technicians, and clericals comprised about one-third of employment at both firms and these shares were increasing. Their shares were more than twice as high as in the Russian light industrial firms. The difference in shares for blue collar workers is perhaps even more striking. They accounted for about 60 percent of employment at Big Turbine, a share that had slightly increased during the period considered here. At Old Shipyard, on the other hand, the share accounted for by blue collar jobs shrank from 51 percent to 36 percent of the total. Nonindustrial employment accounted for about 5 percent of the total at Big Turbine and was declining, whereas nonindustrial employment at Old Shipyard was quite substantial at 33 percent with little change over time.

A rough comparison with U.S. enterprises might be made using data for "Industrial machinery and equipment" producers. In those firms, managers, professionals, technicians, and clerical workers accounted for about 40 percent of employment. The share of production and operating workers amounted to about 56 percent.[16] In comparison, Big Turbine and Old Shipyard appeared to devote somewhat smaller shares to these white collar occupations. The share of blue collar workers at Big Turbine was actually greater than the average for the U.S. machinery and equipment firms. But at Old Shipyard, their employment share actually dropped to well below the shares at the other Russian firms (and below the comparable U.S. average). While employment shares for the white collar categories at both Russian metal working firms moved toward the U.S. average, the blue collar shares at the two Russian metal working firms moved away from the comparable U.S. average, albeit in opposite directions.

In sum, the study firms had a tendency to shift their allocation of labour resources to be more heavily weighted in production-related activities. The share of nonindustrial employment declined in three of the four enterprises (Old Shipyard being the exception). A portion of this decline was due to the restructuring of the social assets linked to these firms, particularly at Big Turbine. However, the way in which the firms shifted their allocation of labour (i.e., primarily through spontaneous outflows) highlighted an inability to retain workers with key skills and a deterioration in their stock of human capital. Indeed, this problem was particularly acute at Old Shipyard, with its substantial contraction of blue collar employment. Thus, while on the surface, movement appeared to be toward a more rational occupational structure, this may have been to some extent associated with a decline in the manageability of the firms.

Toward "Russian Style" Employment Flexibility

Economic deregulation in 1992 gave enterprise managers the possibility to exploit a wider range of instruments for expanding labour flexibility at any given level of total employment. Among the case study firms, greater flexibility was achieved primarily through changes in compensation (in terms of overall levels, structure, and relative levels within the enterprise), hours flexibility, and use of fixed-term contracts. A discussion of these instruments is introduced here in the context of the case study firms and presented in greater detail in chapter 5.

Wage Flexibility

Increased wage flexibility at the study firms resulted from more flexible procedures for fixing absolute and relative wages as well as flexibility in payment of wages. Wage setting at Soviet enterprises was usually based on a tariff system, which determined both nominal and relative earnings of almost all blue collar workers. Salaries (absolute and relative levels) for managerial or professional positions were also set centrally by special governmental institutions.[17] In 1992, centralised wage setting was ended for non-state employers. The uniform tariff scale continued to be fixed at the national level, but ceased to be an imperative rule for all enterprises, although many firms continued to take it as a guideline or starting point for their internal wage-setting process.[18] The firms in this study provide an indication of the various approaches to wage setting.

Old Shipyard greatly increased wage flexibility in the early transition period by decreasing the fixed tariff portion of wages to comprise just a minor part of total earnings. Moreover, additional premiums were distributed by managers more or less at their discretion and without any explicit bargaining or negotiation procedure. This approach to wage setting covered a majority but not all of the workers. Wages of others were determined through individual bargaining, by special individual contracts, or by agreements (see the following section on fixed-term contracts) and might exceed the average level by many times. As a result, the role of the tariff system decreased in importance, while flexibility increased.

Big Turbine developed a wage-setting mechanism that combined a special eighteen-grade tariff scale (resembling the uniform tariff scale) with the so-called brigade approach to work organisation.[19] Employees were divided into several occupational categories, each with their own wage rate. The hourly rates included in the collective agreement were supposed to be negotiated between the company and trade union.[20] Each brigade at the plant then got its own wage fund, based on the tariff system; the brigades enjoyed some flexibility in the distribution of earnings among members, according to real contribution and regardless of formal tariff. Some applied flexibility only to the premiums; others felt free to adjust the distribution of the entire earnings package. This practice resulted in increased wage differentials as well.

The light industry firms used more standard versions of the tariff system. In one case, however, the tariff-determined portion of earnings was supplemented by a variable premium of up to 50 percent of the tariff base. The premium markup was allocated using formal criteria such as occupation, skills grade, and plan fulfilment. These premiums also enlarged wage differentials.

In general, decentralisation of wage setting was not accompanied by the introduction of effective collective bargaining procedures in industry, including at the study firms. Central wage setting was replaced in practice by wage setting by management. One result was that actual wage increases did not keep up with inflation. Moreover, the new more flexible wage setting permitted managers to adjust relative wages to reflect economic considerations. At the same time, data for the industries and occupations represented by the case study firms did not, however, show drastic rises or falls. For example, metalworkers in machine building in general maintained a relatively constant wage position with respect to average monthly wages in the economy. In the clothing industry during 1992–1993, relative wages for the main production workers (sewing-machine operators and cloth cutters) were relatively constant and then dropped somewhat in 1994.

The average wages in each of the Siberian firms were roughly double those in the firms in Kaluga, reflecting primarily regional influences on wage developments (chart 3.4). This was, in part, due to the northern location of Krasnoyarsk, which made its residents eligible for a special Northern premium (under the tariff system). It was also, in part, due to a structural factor: industry in Krasnoyarsk was dominated by export-oriented mining and metallurgical enterprises exposed to competitive pressures to adjust. Higher wages paid by such firms put upward pressure on wages for the whole regional labour market. However, these factors were still not enough to drive the average wages in the Krasnoyarsk firms much above the national average.

Divergences in record keeping make it impossible to develop a full comparison between the case study firms for the entire period 1991–1995.[21] Nevertheless, available data suggest that relative wages were diverging between major occupational groups, although not drastically. At the companies that provided full data to us, the ratio of managers'/workers' wages was rising. In 1991, this ratio was less than 1.6 at these firms; by 1995, it exceeded 2.0. These developments would appear to be consistent with the increased managerial control over the enterprises. The professionals/workers wage ratio was smaller. At the Shipyard, the ratio varied over time but tended to increase, rising from 1.03 in 1992 to 1.14 in 1994. At Lady's Dream, the ratio grew from 1.19 in 1992 to 1.79 in 1994 but fell in 1995

Chart 3.4   Relative Wages, 1991–1995, Industrial Average = 1.0

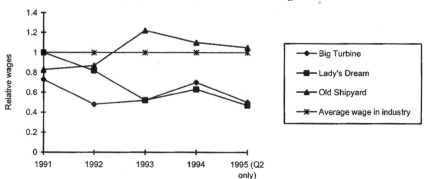

Sources: Company-provided data; Goskomstat.

to 1.29. The relative wage growth for professionals was constrained by the "excess" employment within this group in the labour market in general.

Managers at both metal working companies decreased the wages of nonindustrial employees relative to those of production workers. In both cases, an average production worker by 1995 earned almost two times more than any nonindustrial employee. This policy reflected, in part, a reduction of noncash remuneration provided through social assets held by the firms. While the average worker saw declines in enterprise-provided social services, those working in these service facilities saw their relative pay drop vis-à-vis the average employee in the firms.[22]

Unfortunately, the available data only cover broad groups and do not show intragroup segmentation and differentiation. They conceal the differences within the occupational groups, which the available evidence indicates are becoming more and more significant. This concerns workers as well as managers.[23] For instance, in early 1995 the ratio of average monthly wages for low- and high-skilled production workers at the Shipyard was 1:5, 1 for low skilled (25 percent of employees) and 5 for highly skilled (10 percent of the employees). The latter group of workers earned as much as top managers. A similar situation existed at the other firms.

Increasingly, the movement in relative wages at the case study enterprises appeared to be providing economic incentives and signals to the employees. The system was clearly beginning to reward some employees, while others saw their earnings lag.

Wage Arrears

During the first years of transition, the real value of cash wages could be significantly diminished if they were not paid on time. Although inflation by the end of 1995 had decreased considerably, it remained high by most standards.[24] As a result, the practice by many large and medium-size industrial enterprises to delay wage payments resulted in a considerable loss in real earnings for employees. According to Goskomstat, at the time of the case study in 1995 the total amount of delayed wages in industrial enterprises exceeded the equivalent of the average monthly wage fund. Deliberate delays in paying wages served as a survival strategy for some firms, while for others they served as a source of profit. It made wages more flexible, reducing the pressure for lay-offs and providing an alternative source of credit for the enterprise (sometimes, effectively with a negative interest rate).[25] At the same time, as noted in chapter 2, such arrears probably contributed to labour turnover by generating voluntary quitting, particularly among those who were more skilled and competitive. It also undermined the relationship between work and reward, as well as between the employer and employee. Although failure to pay wages on time might seem illegal, the Russian legislative system lacked any effective enforcement measures against it.

The studied enterprises were no exception in this regard, although their debts to employees were relatively small. Wage arrears caused by financial hardships and poor sales first appeared at these firms in late 1994 or early 1995 and at times expanded to two to three months' wages (up to one month at Siberian Shoe). Delayed payments became one of the most acute issues in terms of trade union pressure and action.[26] Thus, a strike erupted at Lady's Dream in 1995, linked to a call to pay wages on time. The Big Turbine trade union leader informed the study team about a pre-strike situation at one of the large shop-floors, also tied to wage delays. In its attempts to retain key personnel, management at Big Turbine often paid key blue collar workers first, only then paying the white collar staff. This, in turn, led to differentiation by occupational group in terms of wage arrears and affected both nominal and relative real wages.

Hours Flexibility

As noted in chapter 2, reductions in working hours became a very significant feature of Russian enterprise behaviour during the first years of transition. Short hours and unpaid leave policies helped to greatly increase internal labour market flexibility.[27] These policies helped the study firms to minimise employment reductions, by instead cutting working hours for broader groups of workers. At the same time, working time reductions were associated with voluntary quitting.[28] Usually, these reductions were brought on by production stoppages caused by liquidity problems, overstocking, weak demand, or supply problems. Siberian Shoe, for example, introduced a reduced working week and put some of its core workers (mostly women working on the assembly lines) on unpaid vacations on a rotating basis. Thus, for the individual employee, the firm sought to minimise the duration of unpaid leave; at the same time it maintained the overall numbers on unpaid leave. Those who were more competitive searched for other jobs while the less competitive appeared scared by the threat of losing their jobs entirely and accepted the reductions in hours.

Fixed-Term Contracts

As did many Russian firms, all the companies in the case study utilised fixed-term contracts to expand their employment flexibility and to provide greater incentives to certain key employees (box 3.1). At three of the firms only managers had such contracts. They were most extensively used at Old Shipyard where by 1995 all managers, professionals, and workers in twenty-four of the most skilled occupations (e.g., repair workers, welders, and machine operators) were employed via such contracts. By early 1995, contractual employees accounted for up to one-fifth of total employment at Old Shipyard. Contracts were given for one-year terms and could be interrupted by management for disciplinary reasons, alcoholism, violation of regulations, the failure to fulfil plan targets, or due to "other reasons related to respect."[29] Indeed, some of those interviewed in the case study indicated that fixed-term employment was also potentially associated with "increased risk" of arbitrary personnel actions. In the firms studied, however, it appeared that fixed-term contracts in practice tended to be used to reward workers. Contractual employees had wages and benefits substantially above the average level. This approach apparently motivated these employees to work harder and to accept stronger managerial control over their work.

Other Labour Market Adjustment Mechanisms

Training and Retraining Policy within the Studied Enterprises

Although training might be considered a mechanism to facilitate adjustment (e.g., by helping employees to adapt to restructured production processes), its use by the surveyed enterprises during the transition actually decreased and changed in nature. The companies shifted away from the use of external training providers. Increasingly, where training was necessary, the companies were inclined to rely on on-the-job methods. For example, both of the Krasnoyarsk companies used to have contracting relationships with external vocational institutions in their community but shifted to train newcomers entirely on-the-job.

The decline in training activity was primarily explained by the lack of resources to pay to external training institutions and the drop in employment levels. Moreover, training initiatives were reduced in view of the increasing commercial uncertainties; managers had a rather poor vision of future developments and consequently had few clear ideas of whom and how to train. From an employee perspective, incentives to train with a view toward upward mobility within the firm were greatly reduced. In theory, incentives for training and skills transfer could have been provided through special institutional devices like internal labour markets, including job ladders.[31] However, in reality, shrinking employment and the general lack of formal job ladders left many employees with a perception of little opportunity for upward mobility, decreasing their motivation to seek training.

Box 3.1   The Evolution of Fixed-Term Contracts

Pre-reform employment rigidity was strengthened by the fact that almost any placement was unconditional and could hardly be interrupted at a manager's discretion. During the Soviet era, a typical regular employment contract was open-ended and provided a kind of lifelong employment. Fixed-term contracts began to be used more often in the late 1980s, a time of experimentation with deregulation and flexibilisation of employment relationships.

During the first years of transition, fixed-term contracts remained restricted in terms of application. The Russian Labour Code (chapter 17) only allowed such contracts as an exception in particular cases (e.g., for temporary replacement of workers absent under certain conditions or for certain kinds of tasks) and for particular categories of personnel. However, many companies circumvented the regulations and used fixed-term contracts in quite standard cases. The labour laws and rules were perceived as having many loopholes and were basically rather poorly enforced. Those employees whose interests were harmed by the introduction of fixed-term contracts appeared reluctant to resist publicly, due to fear of firing, poor knowledge of the laws, and/or weakness of trade unions, among other reasons.

Enterprises used fixed-term contracts to varying degrees; some offered such contracts only to certain managers while others expanded this practice to include blue-collar workers.[30] These contracts enabled personnel managers to avoid standard labour rules and to strengthen management power over labour. For example, they could be used to avoid severance pay or increase wage differentials. They also introduced a closer association between an employee's responsibilities and his or her conditions of employment, in some cases with special penalties for violating the terms of the contract.

A further problem arose from the increasing dependence on on-the-job training at a time of job cuts. Holders of firm-specific skills had few incentives to transfer their skills, and in some cases they actually sought to oust young newcomers whom they saw as potential threats. The result was particularly high labour turnover for young workers in some areas. To create incentives for skilled employees to participate in training such newcomers, one of the firms launched a special fund to reward those who trained young workers.

Although Big Turbine decreased its training activities, it presented an interesting case. The company had always maintained well-developed training and retraining facilities, investing substantial resources in them. These facilities included a vocational technical school for workers and a technical college for technicians. In addition, the firm had special contracting relationships with other regional educational institutions. Despite the hardships of transition, it managed to maintain its own facilities although the contracting ties weakened. In response to employment contraction and declining demand for internal training, the firm reached an agreement with the regional Employment Centre to use its facilities to teach and train people for other companies. Such a policy was intended to allow the firm to continue to maintain the relatively costly training centre and facilities during what was seen as possibly a temporary downturn in production.

Trade Unions and Collective Bargaining

During the period of transition, the tripartite system in Russia might have served as a mechanism to facilitate restructuring. At first glance, the institutions representing employees' interests in privatised enterprises could give the impression that organised labour had significant power to influence the process. A very high level of unionisation was in place (although lower than in the Soviet past, when almost 100 percent of employees were unionised) and employees were generally shareholders.[32] However, it appears that at many firms—including the case study enterprises—the intrafirm labour institutions offered only weak bargaining power for rank-and-file employees.[33]

Each of the surveyed companies had only one trade union, which was the successor of the traditional one (known as FNPR). The trade union continued to include both workers and managers as members. Within these firms, no observable new alternative union activity occurred, although in one enterprise the local trade union organisation quit the regional branch of FNPR and declared itself independent. In that case, the union's operations remained much unchanged, but it no longer contributed membership fees to the higher union bodies and was less subject to outside intervention. Indeed, it appeared to be dominated by enterprise management and was unlikely to play an independent role.

Three of the four firms had enterprise-level collective agreements. The fourth one maintained an agreement through the first years of transition but failed to prolong it for 1995. In general, the collective agreements represented a kind of statement of intentions compiled in a rather declarative style. No concrete responsibilities or penalties were imposed in case of violation. Thus, the existence of collective agreements hardly constrained the parties.

In June 1995, employees at Lady's Dream went on strike in protest at the buildup of two months' wage arrears. The strike initiated by a group of rank-and-file workers lasted about one week. The momentum was more emotional than rational, and the strikers lacked clear goals or deliberate strategy. The union local backed the strikers but played a rather passive role in trying to mediate between the strikers and managers. After the initial emotional tension dissipated, the strike came to an end without any concrete success for the workers. However, it forced the management to be more attentive and clear in its relations with employees regarding wages.

The trade union at Big Turbine sought to be a more active player. At the time of the case study, about 95 percent of all employees, including the top management, remained in the union local. In practice, it appeared that the union provided managers with additional channels to exert influence. Considering wage-setting procedures a key issue, one local union leader admitted to the study team that management took the lead in labour policy.

In sum, for all the case study enterprises, local trade union activity was rather pro forma and ineffective. The high unionisation did not really give much strength to rank-and-file labour. Rather, the former centralised system of labour administration was largely replaced by managers' discretion. Within the evolving industrial relations framework, the role of trade unions remained modest.

Restructuring of Social Assets

Being both a social institution and an economic enterprise, the socialist factory always provided employees not only with wages, but also with a considerable number of nonwage social benefits, generally delivered through enterprise-linked social infrastructure. These benefits, although declining marginally, continued at relatively high levels during the early years of the transition. Indeed, this notion was confirmed by Commander et al. in an enterprise survey conducted in 1994, which found only marginal declines in the early transition years.[34] Moreover, the firms in their sample did not expect a significant decline in the social provision in the future.

During 1994–1995, however, there was evidence of some change in the situation as enterprises began to shed or restructure the assets associated with social benefits. For example, a survey of ninety-seven enterprises in selected regions conducted in November 1995 by the Institute for Advanced Studies revealed decreasing numbers of enterprise-linked social establishments.[35] Their survey found declines—sometimes substantial—in the number of units beginning even in 1993, but with a sharp drop of 12 percent in 1994.

In general, a positive correlation developed between the amount of social benefits provided by enterprises and enterprise size (in terms of number of employees).[36] Big Turbine, however, was an extreme example. As a key plant for the Soviet military, it was granted substantial additional funding, which allowed the firm to build a large number of housing units and several rather expensive facilities like a swimming pool, "palace of culture," and health care and other recreational establishments. This made the enterprise one of the "richest" in terms of social infrastructure. After the firm's privatisation, this infrastructure became a severe financial burden, but a number of political and social constraints impeded full divestiture of the "assets." As a result, management chose a differentiated policy toward the social assets. The most expensive elements were disposed of, facilities that could do so were made self-sustainable, and those assets that were relatively cheap to maintain or were of direct utility to the firm were retained.[37] By 1995, these measures decreased nonindustrial employment at Big Turbine by two-thirds as compared with pre-transition levels. Meanwhile, the relative wages of those working in these areas dropped from 68 percent to 54 percent of the average level for production workers. In just a few years, these efforts had succeeded in substantially reducing the drag of social assets on the balance sheet (table 3.7).

The case of the Shipyard offers an important contrast, whereby the barriers to divestiture were more explicit. Formally speaking, in 1992 all social assets were transferred into municipal ownership but the financing from the enterprise funds was to continue for ten years. As a special condition permitting privatisation, enterprise-provided financing was fixed in an agreement with the local committee on property. Although the firm management was eager to get rid of this burden, its hands were tied. In terms of costs, the firm had to allocate one-third of the total operating profit to fund social assets. The enterprise tried to squeeze some additional offsetting privileges like tax deductions and exemptions from local taxes. In practice, while forcing the enterprise to maintain social assets, the local authorities closed their eyes to local tax arrears and nonpayment of obligations to local social funds.[38]

Lacking the importance of heavy industrial firms under the former economic system, Lady's Dream and Siberian Shoe had managed to build up only modest social infrastructure. Early in the transition, management at both enterprises acted to divest these assets. This was largely accomplished by the end of 1993, a point confirmed by the declines in the shares of nonindustrial employment.

Thus, all of the case study firms had taken steps to address the problem of unwanted social assets. At Big Turbine and Old Shipyard, these assets still contributed somewhat to the operating costs, but wherever possible managers sought to reduce the drag on enterprise finances. Moreover, social benefits in general had become a rather flexible component of labour costs.[39] Indeed, the case study highlights significant flexibility in terms of social benefits as well as wages.[40] And the study firms appeared to have been particularly successful in reducing employment in social infrastructure.[41]

LABOUR ADJUSTMENT AND PRODUCTION COSTS

The next two sections look at labour adjustment in relation to the production costs at the case study enterprises. Although the available data are only approximate and were not available for all years and firms, it is striking that with some notable exceptions the indicators tended to move in a direction that indicates growing

Table 3.7   Big Turbine: Costs of Social Asset Operation (Percentages)

	1991	*1992*	*1993*	*1994*
Share in profit	21.0	28.0	17.0	13.0
Share in total expenses	4.4	3.6	4.8	2.7
Share in wage bill	13.2	17.1	15.8	10.2
Structure of costs:				
—housing[a]	50.0	53.1	62.7	68.5
—kindergarten	33.0	33.3	23.7	divested
—health care	11.0	4.9	3.8	11.5
—recreational facilities	6.0	8.6	9.8	20.1
Total	100.0	100.0	100.0	100.0

(a) Planned for divestment in 1995.
Source: Company-provided data.

labour costs, both in relation to other production costs and in absolute terms. This was primarily due to the rapid decreases in output relative to labour indicators.

Shares of Wages and Total Labour Costs in Total Production Costs

A degree of convergence transpired in the wage shares as a percentage of production costs, at least in the industries and specific enterprises under consideration here (chart 3.5). The tendency was for wage cost shares to be relatively buoyant over time. Only Big Turbine managed to decrease the share of these costs modestly. Data limitations precluded development of a time series for total labour costs.

Total labour costs included wages and mandatory social charges plus additional elements such as housing, nonmandatory social charges (e.g., private pensions or insurance), training, amenities, and, until early in 1996, the excess-wage tax (EWT). Table 3.8 shows a detailed breakdown of labour costs for Russian firms in the same categories as the case study firms, based on the results of the 1994 Goskomstat labour cost survey. After wages, the most significant costs employers paid were the mandatory social charges. Although some variation cropped up in the effective rates, together these charges generally increased the wage bill by about 40 percent. In 1994, these charges included legally required employer contributions to the Pension Fund (nominally 29 percent in addition to the wage bill), the Social Insurance Fund (5.4 percent), the Medical Insurance Fund (3.6 percent), and the Employment Fund (2 percent). In January 1996, the Employment Fund contribution rate was reduced to 1.5 percent. Employer expenditures on wages and mandatory social charges comprised about one-third of total production costs.

Expenditure on social assets fell mainly in the housing and amenities categories. For engineering and metal working firms the latter two categories together

Chart 3.5   Share of Wage Costs in Total Production Costs (%)

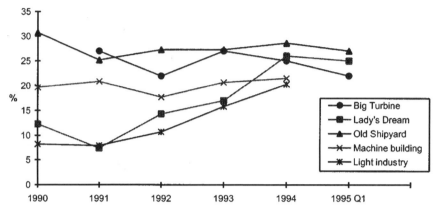

Sources: Company-provided data; Goskomstat.

Table 3.8   Russian Labour Costs in Selected Industries, 1994

| | Engineering and metal-working | | | Light industry | |
	(Total labour costs = 100)	(Wages = 100)		(Total labour costs = 100)	(Wages = 100)
Wages	58.0	100.0	Wages	63.2	100.0
Housing	2.1	3.6	Housing	1.8	2.8
Mand. social fund	24.9	42.9	Mand. social fund	23.2	36.7
Other social exp.	3.7	6.4	Other social exp.	6.2	9.8
Training	0.3	0.5	Training	0.3	0.5
Amenities	2.1	3.6	Amenities	0.3	0.5
Excess-wage tax	7.0	12.1	Excess-wage tax	3.6	5.7
Other	1.9	3.3	Other	1.4	2.2

Sources: "Labour Costs Survey in 1994," *Informazionny statisticheskyi bulleten*, no. 12 (Moscow: Goskomstat, November 1995); authors' calculations.

added some 7 percent to the wage bill. For light industrial firms they cost about 2 percent in addition to the wage bill. Training amounted to an additional 0.5 percent for both types of firms. The EWT amounted to another 12 percent addition to the wage bill for engineering and metal working firms and a 5.7 percent addition for light industrial firms.

Although the EWT was initially introduced as a tool to help curb inflation by keeping down wages, it became a source of considerable revenue for the government.[42] Since the actual amount of EWT to be paid by a firm was dependent on average wages, there was a possible disincentive for enterprises to lay off low-paid employees, even if their services were no longer required. Nevertheless, although the managers from the enterprises studied strongly criticised the EWT, they did not consider it a major factor distorting their labour policies. A similar finding resulted from a REB survey, in which respondents also did not consider the EWT as a factor driving labour hoarding.[43] They tended to prefer various other ways to avoid the EWT, such schemes channelling "excess" compensation through private insurance funds or bank deposits, rather than by padding their employment rosters. The EWT was abolished in early 1996.

In sum, taking the corresponding industry averages for the nonwage labour costs, it might be estimated that in 1994 the share of total labour costs in production costs ranged between 40 and 50 percent (assuming that the firms roughly followed the industry averages).

Unit Labour Costs

Rough estimates of the evolution in unit labour costs (ULC) can be made using the quotient of real annual average wages divided by real annual output per employee. While the ULC for industry by this measure declined about 10 percent between 1992 and 1994, at Big Turbine and Old Shipyard the ULC indicator rose by roughly 50 and 30 percent, respectively. The increase at the metal working enterprises resulted in part from the fact that both firms sought to maintain the average real wage despite the declines in production. Only the garment producer reduced the ULC (about 30 percent). In that case, however, the drop was due to extreme cash flow problems that prevented the full adjustment of wages for inflation as the firm slipped into insolvency. Indeed, the latter case serves as a reminder that no one indicator should be used to evaluate progress in restructuring and that it is important to know the context of developments.

WHAT PUSHED FIRMS TO ADJUST EMPLOYMENT LEVELS AND LABOUR COSTS?

The evidence presented herein points to significant labour adjustments in the early transition years but with a mixed record of both positive and negative results (e.g., increased flexibility but loss of human capital). It appeared that a variety of pressures had pushed management to adopt a blend of passive and active adjustment strategies, even where managers lacked a corresponding long-term vision or policy for labour restructuring.

Financial Stress and Budget Constraints

Enterprise managers were unanimous in regarding liquidity problems as a key factor affecting their labour policies and driving them to introduce changes and adapt.

Financial transfers from government (mostly in the form of subsidies and directed credits) to firms were significant during 1992–1993 but subsequently shrank. Commercial credits were prohibitively expensive. Thus, each firm searched for a unique mix of methods to go beyond the budget constraints that they faced.

One component of such a strategy often was simply to avoid or postpone facing up to obligations through various financial devices. In view of the rapid growth of debt and arrears, it is clear that many firms did not include imposition of strict financial discipline as part of their response to pressures.[44] Although most of firms' supplementary "liquidity" came from arrears in paying wages, taxes, and suppliers, additional resources were available from other sources, such as access to soft loans from special funds controlled by local authorities.[45] The lack of an effective bankruptcy procedure not only deprived enterprises of a potentially positive tool for restructuring, it also shielded them from anxious creditors. In many cases, the local political network of managers played an important role in the successful use of avoidance strategies.

Although not a financial manipulation, it is worth noting that privatised firms also tried to generate revenues by renting out space and equipment they control. For many years Russian enterprises hoarded not only labour but productive resources such as facilities, office space, and land. The general decline in production made this hoarding even more obvious. At the same time, new businesses lacked facilities or space to start operations. Thus, older firms were able to generate revenue from lease of surplus production-related resources, which helped to improve their cash flow.

Privatisation and Corporate Governance Institutions

The Federal Privatisation Program included three options that varied in terms of privileges for insiders but generally resulted in substantial shareholdings being controlled by insiders. The resulting labour-management coalitions could hardly be expected to stimulate radical and forced downsizing under the conditions of the early transition in Russia. Indeed, as noted earlier, much of the labour adjustment came as a result of voluntary separations or management decisions affecting hours or wages. Among the study enterprises, the privatisation process resulted in substantial insider minority holdings in the metal working companies (with up to one-third insider control). Insiders gained majority control of Lady's Dream, and Siberian Shoe was fully owned by insiders. In the latter case, although shareholding was spread among employees, management appeared to maintain particularly tight control.[46]

Across the three firms with outsider shareholding, it appears that outsiders tended to focus on corporate financing and marketing issues rather than labour restructuring. Outsider influence on labour decisions was mostly indirect, coming as a consequence of financial and commercial issues. Moreover, among insiders, trade unions had only a limited influence on labour policies. As a result, managers continued to exert relatively independent decision making authority concerning personnel. As might be expected, in line with the survival-oriented approach, they tended to act cautiously.

Labour Market and Social Policy

Although government labour market and social policy initiatives (discussed in greater detail in chapter 6) could have been used to help facilitate adjustment at the study firms, in practice they had little direct impact—with the exception of the employment-support loans mentioned previously in the case of Siberian Shoe. In some cases, they may have actually had a somewhat distorted adjustment process. Active policy interventions such as training programmes or rehabilitation and employment of disabled persons reached few, if any, employees at the study firms. As for the job-broking services of the State Employment Service— which constituted a major component of active labour market policy—managers in the study firms were aware of the recruitment assistance available but generally hired through other channels.

A similar situation existed with respect to most passive policy measures. Possible exceptions may have included the lay-off requirements, EWT, and, to a lesser extent, unemployment benefits—all three of which may have had a distorting effect. Given the intense financial pressures and inflationary expectations confronting managers, it is probable that certain managers gave some weight to avoiding potential severance pay obligations associated with lay-offs. In the short run, it was less costly to retain workers on unpaid leave or short time or to encourage voluntary quits; however, this impact merely helped to bias the separation process toward voluntary quits rather than blocking it. Despite the statements of managers to the contrary, it is also possible that EWT provisions may have helped to offset pressures to reduce labour hoarding.[47] Unemployment benefits may have had a very modest indirect influence where managers perceived a social obligation to employees. Given the extremely low benefit levels, some managers may have become slightly more reluctant to sack employees.[48]

CONCLUSIONS

A detailed examination of labour market developments in these large industrial firms (summarised in table 3.9) and a presentation of complementary evidence on a more representative population of firms indicate that considerable adjustment took place in these generally older enterprises during the first years of transition. Key features of this adjustment included: (i) changes in employment levels, and (ii) changes in employment structure, with a shift in staffing patterns to focus more on production-related activities, and (iii) use of labour market flexibility to limit the magnitude of the downward adjustment in employment.

Table 3.9 Changes in Labour Market Situation, 1991–1995

	Big Turbine	Lady's Dream	Old Shipyard	Siberian Shoe
Industry	metal working	light industry	metal working	light industry
Decline in output	significant	significant	significant	very significant
Employment reduction	significant	significant (since 1993)	significant	significant (since 1992)
Changes in composition of personal (share devoted to production)	minor positive	minor positive	negative	minor positive
Separations	intensive	intensive	very intensive	intensive
Voluntary quitting	moderate	moderate	very intensive	intensive
Lay-offs	minor	minor	intensive (in 1995)	moderate
Hiring (1993–1995)	intensive, but less than separations	intensive, but less than separations	intensive, but less than separations	intensive, but less than separations
Flexibility in wage setting	moderate	minor	significant	minor
Relative wages	decreasing	decreasing	slightly increasing	n.a.
Effect of trade unionism on wage setting	none	none	none	none
Divestiture of social assets	quite intensive	little to divest, largely accomplished	no divestiture largely accomplished	little to divest,
Share of wages in unit production costs	relatively stable	significantly increasing	relatively stable	n.a.
Unit labour costs	increasing	decreasing	increasing	n.a.
Per management, key factor in personnel management	financial situation of firm	financial situation of firm	financial situation of firm	financial situation of firm

Source: Company-provided data.

Labour market flexibility in these firms was manifested mainly through adjustments in hours and wages, wage arrears, and increased use of fixed-term contracts. From the perspective of the enterprise stakeholders, this flexibility allowed the firms to weather changing conditions (for a while, at least), although perhaps with significant sacrifices (e.g., most workers experienced wage losses). And, substantial opportunity costs to the business may have resulted from the delay of more far-reaching restructuring. From a social perspective, the flexibility helped to cushion the transition for many, allowing them to retain ties to the workplace when they might otherwise have been pushed from employment with little recourse to government-provided social protection. In general, managers tried to avoid controversial or radical steps (e.g., mass lay-offs), preferring a gradualist approach. The result was that in many cases, even after several years of transition, labour costs had still not adjusted in line with changes in output.

It appears that, beyond mechanisms for labour market flexibility, several institutional or systemic factors also made it possible for firms to slow the sometimes painful restructuring process. At the case study firms, managers were resourceful in finding ways to soften budget constraints somewhat by exploiting the opportunities to reduce taxes or secure access to soft credit and outside financial support. Second, the privatisation process left insiders with varying but significant influence over personnel matters in the enterprises. Although with time, managers—and to a certain extent, outside stakeholders—were able to increase their influence, there remained an insider-induced conservatism in personnel management and a tendency to avoid lay-offs. Finally, labour market policy encouraged somewhat the retention of labour, although at the case study enterprises the visible impacts were relatively modest and labour turnover remained fairly high.

At the same time, evidence exists that some enterprises undertook positive initiatives. Among others at the case study firms, they sought new partners (including foreign ones), developed new markets and products, decreased somewhat labour hoarding and inappropriate social infrastructure, and introduced technological and organisational innovations. Nevertheless, interviews with managers at the case study enterprises provided an indication that the adjustment process involved measures that were often ad hoc arrangements in the face of continuing difficulties. Many actions were taken or maintained based on short-term decisions, rather than as part of a deliberate or long-term strategy leading to a resolution of the problem. The result was, in some cases, a contradictory mix of policies and a pattern of hesitant adjustment that persisted into the late 1990s.

NOTES

1. See the Data Sources Annex for a discussion of the advantages and disadvantages of a case study approach in the Russian context. Also, note that much of the case study

evidence presented in this chapter is based on Vladimir Gimpelson and Douglas Lippoldt, *Labour Restructuring in Russian Enterprises: A Case Study* (Paris: OECD, 1996).

2. E.g., Barry Ickes and Randy Ryterman, "From Enterprise to Firm: Notes for a Theory of the Enterprise in Transition," in *The Post-Communist Economic Transformation: Essays in Honor of Gregory Grossman,* ed. Robert Campbell (Boulder, Colo.: Westview Press, 1994), 83–104; Tatyana Dolgopyatova, *Rossiyskye predpriyatiya v perekhodnoy ekonomike: ekonomicheskiye problemy i povedeniye* (Russian Enterprises in Transition Economy: Economic Problems and Behaviour) (Moscow: Delo Ltd., 1995).

3. *OECD Economic Surveys: The Russian Federation 1995* (Paris: OECD, 1995), 77. Also, see *OECD Economic Surveys: The Russian Federation 1997* (Paris: OECD, 1997) for details of the peculiarities of the Russian privatisation process.

4. Ickes and Ryterman, "From Enterprise to Firm" and Dolgopyatova, *Rossiyskye predpriyatiya v perekhodnoy ekonomike.*

5. Only 2 percent of the REB respondents (top managers of 500 industrial enterprises in Russia) considered themselves generally dependent on others when making personnel decisions and just 14 percent felt a severe lack of independence in wage setting (Rostislav Kapeliushnikov and Sergey Aukutsionek, "The Labour Market in 1994," *The Russian Economic Barometer* 2 [1995]: 25–26).

6. In fact, the smallest firm in our sample had a workforce of 839 in 1994.

7. In the first quarter of 1995, Goskomstat estimated the aggregate employment in industry at 19.0 million. This means that industry had only lost in total about 15 percent of its personnel during this period, while the drop in output was several times larger, at about 50 percent. At the same time, however, the aggregate picture includes a significant number of small and new businesses, which influences the total and masks the trends exhibited by medium and large industrial enterprises (most of which are former state enterprises).

8. After the very large earlier losses in human capital at the firm under the earlier ad hoc survival-oriented strategy, the attempt to determine and guide separations beginning in early 1995 came too late to ensure retention of key parts of the original skills base.

9. The spectrum of opportunities for those who separated in Kaluga and Krasnoyarsk was largely the same: a choice between jobs with the same or similar occupation at one of the nearby large enterprises or jobs in the small business sector. Due to very high skill requirements at Big Turbine, any external mobility was likely to be accompanied with a kind of deskilling. Shifts into the small business sector often caused a complete occupational break. In the early transition years, for example, this sector generated more small retail sales positions than skilled industrial positions, for example. Thus those who were occupationally committed tended to seek moves to companies that provided career continuity.

10. This point was also noted in Sergey Aukutsionek and Rostislav Kapeliushnikov, "Russian Industrial Enterprises on the Labor Market" (*Rossiyskiye promyshlenniye predpriyatiya na rynke truda*), *Voprosy ekonomiki* 6 (1995): 48–56.

11. This process is discussed in Galina Monusova and Natalia Guskova, "Internal Mobility and Restructuring of Labor," in *Labour Relations in Transition. Wages, Employment and Industrial Conflict in Russia,* ed. Simon Clarke (Cheltanham, UK: Edward Elgar, 1996), 82–98.

12. For example, among the vacancies at Big Turbine during 1993–1994, blue collar jobs accounted for over 95 percent. In the same years, Lady's Dream and Siberian Shoe also offered some vacancies for highly skilled welders, repair workers, and electricians.

These jobs did not belong to the core occupations at these light industrial companies and were considered there as auxiliary, although they were better paid. Given the generally high demand for such workers, potential job-seekers in these occupations were able to command high wages. This complicated hiring at the light industrial firms, which had to compete hard for candidates.

13. See Mark Granowetter, *Getting a Job: A Study of Contacts and Careers* (Cambridge: Harvard University Press, 1974); Vladimir Gimpelson and Vladimir Magun, "Emploi et mobilité sociale des travailleurs licenciés," *Cahiers internationaux de sociologie* XCVI (January–June 1994): 57–75; Valery Yakubovich, "Institutions, Social Networks, and Market Exchange: Matching Workers and Jobs in Russia" (paper presented at the conference "Economic Sociology at the Edge of 3rd Millennium, Moscow, Russia, January 14–15, 2000).

14. The bulk of this employment consisted of those working in social facilities. However, it also included watchmen and a few other employees not directly related to manufacturing operations.

15. *Occupational Employment in Manufacturing Industries, 1992,* U.S. Department of Labor, Bureau of Labor Statistics, Washington, D.C., Bulletin 2437 (February 1994), 5.

16. *Occupational Employment in Manufacturing Industries.*

17. In theory, the tariff-determined portion of blue collar workers' earnings was to account for three-fourths of the total pay, with the remaining portion consisting of different sorts of premiums and extra payments. Using this combination of emoluments, the wage setters sought to limit wage differentials while providing incentives for better and harder work. The actual wage distribution differed from the model. First, the tariff-based share made up only 35–40 percent of total payments. Second, the supplementary portion was usually allocated in a fixed proportion to the tariff-based one. As a result, the system failed to provide the desired incentives.

18. For a good discussion of Russia's wage policy during transition, see Vladimir Mikhalev and Nils Bjorksten, *Wage Formation during the Period of Economic Restructuring in the Russian Federation* (Paris: OECD, 1995).

19. The brigade system of work organisation was introduced as an innovation starting in the late 1960s. For a discussion of the use of this system in Soviet industry, see Darrell Slider, "The Brigade System in Soviet Industry: An Effort to Restructure the Labour Force," *Soviet Studies* 39, no. 3 (July 1987): 388–405.

20. Comments from employees at the plant left the authors uncertain as to whether there was genuine bargaining over wage rates.

21. Aggregate group wages for 1991–1994 are available for only three of the companies. The fourth firm—Siberian Shoe—provided data on wages by major workers' occupations for 1993 and 1994.

22. Lady's Dream took a different course, actually raising relative wages for these employees. However, two main factors probably accounted for this. First, the nonindustrial group was not numerous and its wage fund was not large in aggregate terms. Second, the average wage paid by the company was very low (almost 40–50 percent lower than the average wage in industry) and there was no margin to push it down further. The lower the average wage, the more difficult it was for the firm to maintain or to increase intergroup differentiation. Also, nonindustrial jobs at the firm required no less skill than any typical worker job at the firm (i.e., the production jobs there did not have high skills requirements).

23. Goskomstat, press release, no. 50 (Moscow, 1994).

24. The annual rate of change in the CPI decelerated from about 16 percent per month during 1992–1994 to about 3 percent per month in the course of 1995 (*OECD Economic Surveys: The Russian Federation 1997*).

25. Richard Layard and Andrea Richter, "Labour Market Adjustment in Russia," *Russian Economic Trends* 3, no. 2 (1994): 85–103.

26. According to Goskomstat reports, most of the strikes that took place in 1994–1995 were responses to wage arrears.

27. Layard and Richter, "Labour Market Adjustment in Russia"; Gimpelson and Lippoldt, *Labour Restructuring*.

28. Vladimir Gimpelson and Douglas Lippoldt, "Labour Turnover in Russia: Evidence from the Administrative Reporting of Enterprises in Four Regions," *Transition Economic Series*, no. 4 (Vienna: Institute for Advanced Studies, 1998).

29. According to managers, during the course of a year about three employees on average were fired for disciplinary reasons, largely due to alcoholism.

30. The use of fixed-term contracts to increase labour market flexibility was common in many OECD countries as well. The share of total employees on fixed-term contracts in the EU varied from 2 percent in Luxembourg to almost one-third in Spain ("Fixed-Term Contracts in the European Union," *Employment in Europe: Policies*, no. 47 [Brussels: European Commission, Autumn 1994]: 30).

31. Peter Doeringer and Michel Piore, *Manpower Analysis and Internal Labor Markets* (Lexington, Mass.: Lexington Books, 1971).

32. According to one survey, the unionisation rate in the Russian economy fell between 1993 and 1995 by about 7 percent. See Tatyana Chetvernina, Pavel Smirnov, and Natalia Dunaeva, "Mesto profsoyuza na predpriyatii (Role of Trade Unions in Enterprises)," *Voprosy ekonomiki*, no. 5 (1995): 84.

33. For more general discussion on the trade unions in Russia and their role in social and economic transformation, see the bibliography for Simon Clarke, Linda Cook, Leonid Gordon, and Eduard Klopov, among others.

34. Simon Commander, Une Lee, and Andrey Tolstopiatenko, "Social Benefits and the Russian Industrial Firm," in *Enterprise Restructuring and Economic Policy in Russia,* ed. Simon Commander, Qimiao Fan, and Mark Schaffer (Washington, D.C.: EDI—The World Bank, 1996), 52–83.

35. Irina Tratch, Martin Rein, and Andreas Woergoetter, "Social Asset Restructuring in Russian Enterprises: Results from a Survey in Selected Russian Regions," in *The Changing Social Benefits in Russian Enterprises*, ed. Douglas Lippoldt (Paris: OECD, 1996), 95–111.

36. E.g., see Commander, Lee, and Tolstopiatenko, "Social Benefits and the Russian Industrial Firm."

37. Housing and kindergartens were the most expensive components. Expenditure in these two categories amounted to 85 percent of all expenditures allocated to social assets. The kindergartens were divested in 1994 and after that housing was divested. Athletic and recreational facilities were converted to function on a commercial basis.

38. Based on a rather rough estimation, it appears that the tax losses brought on by different kinds of avoidance and evasion by the firm may have exceeded the direct costs to local government in the case where it assumed full financial responsibility for the assets; but this remains to be verified.

39. For a more detailed discussion of this issue, see Lippoldt, ed., *The Changing Social Benefits in Russian Enterprises*.

40. A finding that may be contrary to evidence in other studies. See Commander, Lee, and Tolstopiatenko, "Social Benefits and the Russian Industrial Firm."

41. According to findings of a REB survey in 1995, on average 12 percent of all employees at enterprises still worked at social facilities (Aukutsionek and Kapeliushnikov, "Russian Industrial Enterprises on the Labor Market," 55).

42. The EWT was as a tax on the portion of the average wage bill, exceeding a threshold set at six times the official minimum wage; these were called "profits" and taxed at a 35-percent rate. As adjustments in the minimum wage did not keep up with inflation, the volume of wages exposed to this tax increased rapidly.

43. Aukutsionek and Kapeliushnikov, "Russian Industrial Enterprises on the Labor Market," 50.

44. Janos Kornai, *Highway and Byways* (Cambridge: MIT Press, 1995).

45. For example, new investments at Siberian Shoe early in the transition were partly funded by a cheap credit from the local Employment Fund. In 1994 alone, the firm got 200 million roubles "for creating new jobs." During these years, such credits were often allocated at extremely low or no nominal interest. The conditions of allocation subsequently became more rigorous and the interest charges increased (50 percent of the Central Bank refinancing rate). However, these credits remained generous and in some cases they were not repaid at all.

46. There may have been a tendency for managers to gain control in firms wholly controlled by insiders.

47. As noted previously, by retaining low-wage workers, the enterprises could reduce the average wage in the firm and consequently reduce the Excess Wage Tax burden.

48. In December 1994, for example, this benefit amounted to roughly 20,500 roubles; by comparison, the average wage nationally was 354,200 and the official subsistence minimum was on average 145,400.

4

Are "New" Jobs Better Jobs?

OVERVIEW

This assessment of the scale and nature of private sector employment is a critical part of understanding labour market adjustment in Russia. This chapter comprises such an assessment, highlighting the differentiation between the old jobs found in mixed-ownership and state-owned enterprises and those in the private sector.[1] The main goals are: (i) to assess changes in the level and composition of private sector employment in the Russian Federation, (ii) to describe the conditions of employment in that sector, and (iii) to analyse the social and demographic characteristics of those working in the sector.

A few authors have presented detailed discussions on the nature and extent of employment in the private sector as the transition advanced.[2] However, examination of the labour market dimension was hampered by the limited availability of data, and most published studies covering this period relied on either aggregate data or small sample surveys. The analysis in this chapter uses a combination of sources to help close the gaps. It draws primarily on aggregate data based on the Labour Force Survey (LFS) and enterprise administrative reporting combined with the results of a special supplementary questionnaire attached to the March 1996 LFS in five regions (Chelyabinsk Oblast, Chuvash Republic, Krasnoyarsk Krai, Moscow City, and Moscow Oblast).[3] These regional data are unique in that they provide consistent information on a relatively broad set of characteristics, including a relatively clear definition of private sector employment.[4] While the regions covered by the survey are not fully representative of the entire nation, they do represent a broad range of experience and provide an indication of the underlying situation.

In the last years of the Soviet Union, an internal debate arose about the possibilities for unlocking the potential of existing enterprises through privatisation. This was highlighted by the competition in 1990 between the so-called Abalkin and Shatalin reform proposals. As the reform debate evolved, privatisation—together with price liberalisation—came to be seen as playing a key role in reducing distortions in the allocation of resources (including labour) and improving economic incentives. Across the transition countries, scholars such as Kornai (1992) also highlighted the potential of *de-novo* private enterprise development. As noted in the EBRD's Transition Report of 1997, new private sector activity was considered important not only for its direct contribution to growth, but also for its positive impact on other aspects of economic reform, such as creation of opportunities for displaced workers and promotion of competition.[5]

In Central and Eastern Europe, as expected, old firms mostly shed labour and jobs, while job creation came mostly from new economic entities—albeit with some variation.[6] In Russia, as discussed in earlier chapters, employment levels in older enterprises—while trending downward—were nonetheless sticky; many of these firms continued to hire at rates nearly offsetting separations. At the same time, overall job creation rates remained low, despite a relatively good employment performance in certain private firms.[7]

The literature on the situation of Russian enterprises during the first years of transition confirmed the existence of differentiation between enterprises according to their ownership. Firms with mixed ownership (usually the result of partial privatisation) tended to have worse employment performance than others that were more clearly private such as *de-novo* private firms and wholly privatised firms.[8] Some findings pointed to inertia in the behaviour and objectives of many mixed-ownership enterprises, which was partially attributed to the fact that these firms tended to be run by the same "old" managers.[9] In some cases, an infusion of new human capital appeared to be a key factor in improvement of the economic performance of firms. *De-novo* firms (which had it by definition) and those privatised firms where old management had been replaced often performed better than other firms.[10] Still, a substantial unrealised potential remained. A World Bank paper in 1996 summarised the situation saying that " . . . privatisation, as might be expected given its design and the weight given to insiders, has yet to feed through into substantive changes in employment."[11]

THE LEVEL AND COMPOSITION OF PRIVATE SECTOR EMPLOYMENT

Before the nature of employment in the private sector is discussed, it is important to consider that ownership patterns in transition countries were varied and not always transparent to observers. Private ownership in such economies usually arose through either privatisation of former state-run enterprises or the launching of new businesses. However, even where a firm was privatised, assets were sometimes shared with nonprivate entities. Looking at Hungary in 1997, Stark highlighted an example of the complex nature of such mixed ownership: "a limited liability company owned by private persons, by private ventures, and by other limited liability companies owned by joint stock companies, banks, and large public enterprises owned by the state. The new property forms thus find horizontal ties of cross-ownership intertwined with vertical ties of nested holdings."[13] Stark called such networks of firms "recombinets." Thus, when looking at a firm, often one was dealing not with an individual entrepreneurial unit but with a network of firms or, at least, with one segment of a larger network. Such "entrepreneurial" networking allowed enterprises to minimise risks and adjust to uncertainties, conceal profits and evade taxes, deal with bureaucrats, and gain security from racketeers, among other benefits.[14]

Webster and Charap found a similar pattern in Russia in a study of private manufacturing: "In St. Petersburg and Hungary, boundaries between state and private sectors were blurred and integration was relatively high. This pattern may have developed as a result of early reform programs that introduced quasi-private enterprise forms into the state sector—leaseholds and co-operatives in Russia and economic work groups in Hungary. Many enterprises became fully private as new laws were passed, but they continued to maintain strong ties with the state sector. Production equipment was shared, primarily through leasing, and pervasive subcontracting effectively bridged labour forces. Ownership was mixed, most often seen as state enterprises taking equity in private companies. Capital was shared in the form of supplier's credits and other inter-enterprise payments networks."[15]

Strong ties were also common between small private businesses and the state. These firms were sometimes embedded in regional and local business networks dominated or controlled by regional or local authorities. Earle et al. reported in 1996 that "the proportion of total revenue derived from governmental sales on the part of [these firms] is quite high—30.8 percent—perhaps providing evidence of some dependency of the new private sector on the state."[16] They further noted that, "In any case, our results demonstrate the powerful inertia in the relationship between the state and the enterprise sector."

As a result of the blurred demarcation of sectors, most data on the private sector during the early transition were at best approximations of the actual situation. Indeed, the first and most obvious question concerning the issue of private sector employment—"How many people were employed by private firms?"—does not have a simple answer.

Measuring Employment in the Private Sector

In measuring the private sector employment share, one can refer to official Goskomstat data series. However, difficulties of interpretation arise due to such issues as changes in the definition of private firms used in the Russian statistics, lack of clarity in property rights, peculiarities in enterprise reporting practices, reluctance of economic actors to present a full and open accounting, and continuing difficulties with staff training and quality-assurance in statistical offices. In view of the lack of statistical reliability, a cautious approach might be to define a range of estimates, taking into account the biases of the various official measures, ranging from a high-end estimate based on ownership statistics to a low-end estimate based on enterprise size statistics.

Employment, by ownership—Aggregate data on employment by ownership, based on the administrative reporting of enterprises, were published regularly by Goskomstat. The breakdown singled out five ownership categories, including state and municipal, mixed, joint-ventures, public associations, and private.[17] Enterprises with mixed ownership were mostly those privatised in the 1990s within the framework of the mass privatisation campaign but where the state retained a stake in the charter capital. Private firms in this typology included any privatised and newly created entities without a state stake in the charter capital. They were also likely to include old collective farms (or their successors), leased enterprises, and other firms that were clearly not private. This definition, being widely defined, would thus seem to overestimate private sector employment. Table 4.1, based on these data, shows quite impressive private sector growth, with the employment share increasing from 20 percent in 1992 to 43 percent in 1998. This might be considered an upper bound estimate for private sector employment, based on the official data.[18]

Employment in large enterprises—Goskomstat also published aggregate data on total employment and employment in large enterprises, the latter based on spe-

Table 4.1   Employment, by Ownership (Percentages, Unless Otherwise Noted)

	1992	1993	1994	1995	1996	1997	1998
State sector	68.9	53.0	44.7	42.1	42.0	40.1	38.1
Mixed-ownership enterprises (without foreign capital)	10.5	17.6	21.1	22.2	21.0	18.3	16.4
Joint ventures and other firms with mixed ownership and foreign capital	0.3	0.4	0.5	0.6	0.8	1.1	1.6
Public associations	0.8	0.9	0.7	0.7	0.6	0.6	0.7
Private sector	19.5	28.1	33.0	34.4	35.6	39.9	43.2
Total employment (millions)	100 (72.1)	100 (70.9)	100 (68.5)	100 (66.4)	100 (66.0)	100 (64.6)	100 (63.6)

Source: Trud i zanyatost v Rossii 1999 (Labour and Employment in Russia 1999) (Moscow, Goskomstat of the RF, 2000), 55.

cial administrative reporting.[19] These large enterprises were primarily nonprivate. Employment in small and medium enterprises (SMEs) and self-employment can be estimated by considering the residual between total employment and employment in large enterprises.[20] This provides a conservative accounting of SME and self-employment levels, since the data for large enterprises overestimate their effective employment. Large enterprises included a disproportionate share of older establishments, which had substantial numbers of employees on long-term administrative leave, many of whom had little hope of returning to their jobs, as well as other "dead souls" who no longer work at their recorded positions.[21] Unfortunately, no official estimates exist of employment adjusted for this time not worked (i.e., based on full-time equivalents).

Chart 4.1 highlights the growth in the residual between total employment and large enterprise employment. While the economically active population declined somewhat and unemployment grew gradually, employment at the large enterprises declined more substantially. The residual area included SMEs, self-employed individuals, joint-ventures, small public associations, private farmers, and clergy, but the bulk of this vaguely identified employment was likely attributable to the SME sector and informal self-employment.[22] The SMEs included firms with various forms of ownership (including a few mixed-ownership firms that had been large but had "down-sized"), but most were privately owned.

Table 4.2 indicates that the "residual" employment grew from 18 percent of total employment in 1992 to 33 percent in 1998. If the hypothesis of a significant

Chart 4.1 Employment in Russia, 1992–1998 (millions)

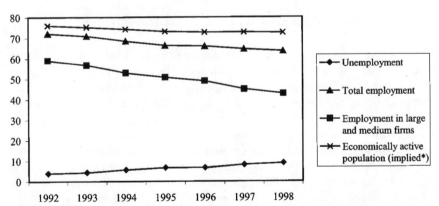

Note: *The implied economically active population (EAP) series is calculated as the sum of the official total employment series (based on administrative statistics) and unemployment series (based on LFS data), as presented in the chart. This approach is used because Goskomstat officials consider the employment series based on administrative data to give the most reliable indication of actual employment levels (they adjust it to correct for undercounting). Thus, there is a gap between the implied EAP and the published LFS EAP series that fluctuated between 1.1 million in 1992 and 5.8 million in 1998 with the implied EAP being substantially higher.
Source: Goskomstat.

Table 4.2   Employment, by Size of Enterprise (Millions)

	1992	*1993*	*1994*	*1995*	*1996*	*1997*	*1998*
Large enterprises	59.0	56.8	53.0	50.8	49.0	45.0	42.8
Other entities (residual amount)	13.1	14.1	15.5	15.6	17.0	19.6	20.8
Total	72.1	70.9	68.5	66.4	66.0	64.6	63.6
"Other" as percentage of "Total"	18.2%	19.9%	22.6%	23.5%	25.8%	30.3%	32.7%

Sources: Goskomstat; authors' calculations.

overestimation of large enterprise employment is correct, then this residual zone may have been even larger. In further disaggregating the residual group of those employed outside of large enterprises and organisations, one might allow for 3 to 6 percentage points of employment in joint ventures and other firms with mixed-ownership, public associations, semi-private farms, and clergy, as well as for errors in the estimates. This approach would yield an estimate for private sector and self-employment in 1998 of 27–30 percent of all employment in the country. This might be considered a lower bound estimate for private sector employment, based on the official data.

THE NATURE OF PRIVATE SECTOR EMPLOYMENT

Private sector employers in Russia were governed by the same labour legislation that regulated state and semiprivate employers. The Labour Code and Employment Law had no special exceptions for private or small businesses. This meant that in most cases employees should have been hired permanently and not on fixed-term contracts, and that any dismissals should have met certain mandatory requirements.[23] The same general rules were applied to most firms with respect to the right to organise and bargain collectively and to the resolution of labour disputes.[24] Nevertheless, the labour legislation was poorly enforced in general and, as evidenced by the growth of the informal sector, it is likely that its application in the private sector was even weaker than in the state sector.

Moreover, for a number of reasons employers and employees may not have been interested in a legally correct employment relationship conforming to the Labour Code.[25] First, employers could seek to minimise labour costs by avoiding mandatory contributions to social security funds.[26] Second, employers may have found it relatively difficult to assess in advance the qualities of job candidates or to check their references (e.g., many candidates cited hard-to-confirm informal sector experience); as a result, many insisted on full flexibility to dismiss those hired.[27] Third, the labour market institutions that were meant to enforce the rules remained underdeveloped, including labour arbitrage mechanisms and courts. Hence, employers sought to keep employment as flexible as possible and concealed it from third parties, while also minimising hiring and firing transaction costs.

These intentions, if realised, might at first seem to have ignored the basic interests of hired labour. However, this was often not the case. Employees entering a new private firm may not have been sure about the prospect of a long-term position there and thus may have preferred to take a secondary subcontracting or part-time job instead of shifting their principal employment to such a firm. In some cases, they were able to do this while maintaining rights to social benefits at their principal place of employment. Moreover, in the face of multidimensional uncertainty, an employee may have preferred to maximise relatively certain short-term gains over possible long-run benefits. Such a person might have assigned higher priority to receipt of a cash wage (with the possibility to evade taxes) than to payment of social security contributions. Consequently, as Commander, McHale, and Yemtsov argued, the expanding private sector may have tended to create unstable jobs, many of which served as secondary employment.[28]

Given such motivations, one can hypothesise that employment relations in the private sector, especially among *de-novo* private sector firms, may have had the following features:

- short-term;
- implicitly semiformal or "noncontractual";
- not transparent to outsiders;
- based on personal networks and trust;
- very flexible and mobile; and
- vulnerable for both employer and employee.

In the next sections, certain aspects of this hypothesis were tested using the regional data from the March 1996 LFS, including information from the supplementary questionnaire on such variables as job tenure, firm size, and income sources. The supplement was completed by the same respondents, aged 15–72 years, as for the main LFS.[29]

Regional Assessment of Employment by Ownership

The five regions covered by the special LFS supplement were chosen to highlight the significant regional variation across Russia.[30] The survey asked each respondent about his or her principal place of employment with the question, "Where did you work during the reference week?" The possible responses included thirteen variants of ownership and employment. These can be grouped into three major categories:

- The *state sector*, including mainly state-owned firms, but also municipal firms, collective farms (*kolkhoz*), and other collective agricultural enterprises. Although the latter were called collectives, they generally remained state-run.
- The *private sector*, which was dominated by private businesses, including production cooperatives, partnerships, family-run private businesses, private farms, and one-owner enterprises, but also included employees working for private individuals and other forms of self-employment. Unfortunately, the questionnaire did not permit a separation of *de-novo* private firms from other private firms.
- The *semiprivate sector*, which was an intermediate grouping containing mostly joint-stock companies, but also leasing enterprises, consumer associations, and other firms with mixed ownership. Many of the joint-stock companies were partly privatised.

Of course, this classification is not very precise and may result in misattribution of employees. For example, it is likely that some employees in the semiprivate sector worked in leasing enterprises or joint-stock companies that were no longer subject to partial state or municipal ownership or control. However, such cases are likely to be a minority.

Table 4.3 suggests that across regions the semiprivate sector varied much more in employment share than did the private sector. Chelyabinsk Oblast had the largest share of the private sector employment, followed by both Moscow Oblast and Moscow City. The rate in Moscow City may at first seem surprisingly modest, but this was the result of the concentration of governmental, educational, and research institutions that were not privately owned. In addition, the city government participated actively in "privatised" enterprises. The lowest percentage of privately employed was in the Chuvash Republic, which was more rural and conservative.

Firm Size

Firm size is usually considered to be a key parameter affecting market behaviour. The Russian economy was dominated by large firms employing hundreds and thousands of employees each. Such behemoths comprised the core of the Soviet economic system, where "diseconomies of scale" did not limit firm size. Development of SMEs was impeded by central planning, which favoured monopolisation and concentration.[31] Only in the late 1980s did the first small private companies begin to emerge. This early experimentation resulted in the establishment of new firms and stimulated disaggregation of some old ones. After that

Table 4.3   Distribution of Employment by Ownership, Firm Size, and Region, March 1996 (Percentages)

Type of ownership	Chelyabinsk Oblast			Chuvash Republic			Krasnoyarsk Krai		
	Total	*E<25*	*E> 500*	*Total*	*E<25*	*E> 500*	*Total*	*E<25*	*E> 500*
State	38.8	19.4	27.8	55.0	25.2	6.9	58.9	17.4	11.7
Private	25.7	30.7	25.1	17.8	38.6	16.7	20.9	36.5	8.8
Semi-private	35.3	3.6	67.7	27.2	13.6	52.1	20.0	5.6	39.5

Type of ownership	Moscow city			Moscow Oblast		
	Total	*E<25*	*E> 500*	*Total*	*E<25*	*E> 500*
State	57.9	9.8	21.1	53.3	12.5	17.9
Private	23.4	43.6	2.8	23.7	35.7	11.9
Semi-private	18.7	15.3	24.4	23.2	7.5	33.7

Sources (for this and all subsequent tables): LFS microdata and authors' calculations.

time, private sector expansion had a tendency to be correlated with growth in SMEs. Notably, the small scale privatisation in the early 1990s boosted the numbers of privately controlled firms, while privatisation of larger firms through the creation of joint stock companies left most with mixed ownership.

As we can see from table 4.3, employment in the private sector was skewed toward small companies. Between 31 and 44 percent of those who identify themselves as being employed in the private sector worked in firms with less than twenty-five employees. The share was highest in Moscow and lowest in Chelyabinsk. In each region, the proportion of private sector employment in large enterprises was less than the proportion in small enterprises. Moscow City represented an extreme case, with less than 3 percent of its private sector employment in large firms. Employment in large firms was concentrated mostly in the semi-private sector.

Labour Turnover

As noted in chapter 2, labour turnover in Russia was relatively high in comparison with some transition economies. Underlying this movement, however, there appeared to be significant segmentation. The rate of labour turnover was relatively high in the private sector, being driven by a number of factors linked to the characteristics of firms and employees.[32] Many new private firms were expanding businesses and generating new jobs that were filled from outside. Survival rates of these jobs appeared to be rather short. This was, in part, due to the relatively low turnover costs linked to poor enforcement of the labour legislation and lack of employment security measures. Also, older privatised firms were adjusting to the new environment and were under increasing pressure to shed redundant labour and reallocate existing personnel in hopes of a better stock and deployment of human capital. It is likely that the private sector tended to attract those with a higher willingness to change jobs and adaptability. All this contributed to the relatively high labour turnover in the sector.[33]

The LFS data appear to confirm that labour turnover in the private sector was higher than in the other two sectors, at least across the survey regions in 1996. The data presented in table 4.4 indicate that the proportion of employees with job tenure less than one year in the private sector was generally two to three times higher than in the other sectors, with the exception of Chuvash Republic. Nevertheless, a portion of the variation was explained by nonownership factors. In table 4.5, the relative effects of variables that were likely to influence labour turnover are considered using logit regression. The dependent variable was "job tenure less than one year," which was used as a proxy for labour turnover (but which did not control for the effects of new job creation and the younger age of private sector firms).[34] On the right hand, the equation included variables for age group, sex, education, occupational group, firm size, sector, and ownership. The regressions were computed for each region separately. In four regions, the coefficients for private sector employment were significant and higher than those of the other ownership types. Among the variables, however, small firm size had the highest impact on the incidence of short job tenure, except in the Chuvash Republic, where the largest coefficients came about with respect to type of activity (trade and services) and age group (31–45 years of age).

Thus, while it appears that a tendency arose for employment in the private sector to be associated with shorter tenures, this tendency was not universal across regions and other factors were also important. For employees working in private firms, low tenures appeared to be most strongly associated not with ownership of the firm, but rather with the size of the firm, its economic activity, or the age of the respondent.

Indicators of Employment Performance: Working Hours and Wage Arrears

Underemployment, a key indicator of employment performance, was often manifested in Russia in terms of short-time working hours or administrative leaves. It was also associated with delays in wage payments. National-level statistics document the difficult employment conditions in large state or semiprivate enterprises, which were viewed as hoarding labour. In effect, these large firms generally adjusted to slack market demand and declining output through underemployment of the existing personnel.[35] One might expect the pattern in the private sector to differ, in part due to the lower average firm age. Many private firms did not experience the drop in demand that hit older firms with the introduction of economic reforms in the early 1990s.

Based on the administrative reporting of large firms, it appears that in the first quarter of 1996 about 3 percent of the labour force experienced short-time working hours and 1.6 percent experienced unpaid or partly paid administrative

Table 4.4   Job Tenure, March 1996 (Percentages)

Type of ownership	Chelyabinsk Oblast < 1 year	Chelyabinsk Oblast > 5 years	Chuvash Republic < 1 year	Chuvash Republic > 5 years	Krasnoyarsk Krai < 1 year	Krasnoyarsk Krai > 5 years	Moscow City < 1 year	Moscow City > 5 years	Moscow Oblast < 1 year	Moscow Oblast > 5 years
State	12.3	57.6	5.3	66.0	12.5	55.7	3.8	77.1	6.5	69.8
Private	23.9	43.2	9.8	56.3	26.5	26.9	14.6	30.9	14.6	44.1
Semi-private	8.8	66.4	8.0	71.2	13.0	55.1	5.3	62.2	7.7	72.9

Table 4.5 Logit Regression: Having Job Tenure Less Than 1 Year, March 1996

	Chelyabinsk Oblast	Chuvash Republic	Krasnoyarsk Krai	Moscow City	Moscow Oblast
Constant	−4.2319	−5.5845	−2.8262	−3.8300**	−3.1602**
Age					
<30 years old	1.6696	.8886	−.7981	.0419	.7604**
31–45	.7383	1.9222	.2355	−.2852	.1110
46–60	.4006	.6060	−.2820	.9847**	−.4819**
>60	—		—	—	—
Gender (male)	.1902	.2565	.3351	.0146	.4427**
Education					
Higher	.5270	−.0705	−.0856	.0606	.0722
High	—	—	—	—	—
Lower	.3354	.1477	.1088	.7467**	.0685
Occupational groups					
Managers	−.5351	−.6163	−.2212	−.5872	−.8834
Professionals	−.3433	−1.1335	.1124	−.2007	−.3636
Workers	.7950	−.2050	.6392	.2810	.3028
Clerks	—	—	—	—	—
Firm size					
up to 25 employees	1.3629**	.7569	.9180**	1.1221**	.8179**
26–100	.7578**	.9986	.2452	.6412*	.1209
101–500	.4394	.6481	−.2168	.1137	.0201
over 500	—	—	—	—	—
Ownership					
state	—	—	—	—	—
private	.4946*	.9041*	.6189**	.7445**	.3177
semi-private	.0290	.2898	.2163	.1873	.0571
Type of economic activity					
industry	−.0904	1.3430*	−.3155	−.3906	−.3953
construction	−.3123	1.2120	−.5732	−.2817	−.5435
transport	-.9094	1.0214	−.8816	.6074	.2033
services	.3771	1.9347**	.0853	−.1784	.1318
trade	.2619	1.8762**	−.3578	.0281	.3066
−2ll	934.6	377.2	1105.8	2012.7	1866.4
N obs	1398	729	1410	5029	3697

*–p< .05 **–p<.01

leave.[36] These rates appear to be higher than roughly comparable indicators for certain other transition countries.[37] Over 1996, 7.5 million employees working for large Russian enterprises (16 percent of their total staff) experienced some spell of administrative leave.

Two indicators based on the regional LFS data can provide more detailed information with respect to the survey's reference week. First, there is the proportion of those working more, less, or the same number of hours as compared to a "normal" week. Second, one can compare the absolute number of hours in the "normal" week with those actually worked. These indicators are subject to the important caveat that they are calculated with respect to one point in time and may be subject to seasonal or other extraordinary factors. This point is highlighted by the fact that in all sectors and regions the respondents reported working fewer than usual hours in the reference week. Moreover, comparisons of variation in working hours by sector are limited by the fact that the state sector includes noncommercial organisations (e.g., hospitals and schools) with little hours flexibility. Therefore, with respect to underemployment, comparisons of working hours are most indicative of the underlying situation in the private and semiprivate sectors. Also, it should be noted that the causes for hours increases or reductions are not indicated by the data.

The shares of those working more, less, or the "normal" number of hours are shown in table 4.6. The data suggest that the private sector had the highest share of persons working more hours than in a normal week (except in Chelyabinsk) and had a lower share of persons working less than normal hours than the semiprivate enterprises. The share of employees affected by reduced working time during the reference week varied across both the regions and types of ownership. According to this indicator, the private sector performed better than the semiprivate sector in all regions but lagged behind the state sector (except in Chelyabinsk, where it performed better than both sectors). Among those working less than normal hours, involuntary reductions account for 50 to 70 percent of all cases.[38] Looking at the absolute figures for working hours, similar trends can be seen. Those employed in the private sector tended to have relatively longer actual and usual work weeks, although there were exceptions in Chelyabinsk and Krasnoyarsk. Each employed LFS respondent was also asked to characterise his or her main job as: (i) permanent or nonpermanent (e.g., fixed-term or occasional) and (ii) full-time or part-time. The data show quite clearly that the private sector used more nonpermanent and part-time employment.

In sum, it can be seen that the private sector performed generally better than other sectors in generating more working hours with fewer reductions. At the same time, private sector employees were more likely to be working under flexible employment arrangements, even though current law places such arrangements under strict limitations. The differences between sectors were, however, not as striking as one might expect and they may have been linked more to the prevailing smaller size of private firms than to ownership form. This point was

Table 4.6 Selected Indicators of Employment Performance, by Region, March 1996

| | Hours Worked Per Week (hours) | | | Worked During the Survey Week . . . (%) | | | Type of Employment Contract (%) | | Have a Second Job (%) |
	Actual hours	Usual hours	Difference	Less than in normal week	More	Same	Permanent	Full-time	
Chelyabinsk Oblast									
State	37.2	37.7	−0.8	6.7	2.7	90.6	98.9	97.2	4.1
Private	38.9	39.4	−0.5	6.6	2.3	91.1	95.5	95.9	1.2
Semi-private	39.1	39.4	−0.8	6.9	0.5	92.6	99.4	97.7	0.9
Chuvash Republic									
State	36.6	38.1	−1.5	1.0	1.7	97.4	99.4	97.9	0.9
Private	36.7	39.6	−2.9	1.5	3.8	94.7	85.4	91.7	2.1
Semi-private	32.3	38.9	−6.6	9.6	1.1	89.3	99.1	94.0	0.5
Krasnoyarsk Krai									
State	36.7	37.7	−1.0	2.0	7.2	90.8	98.8	96.7	2.0
Private	37.5	38.6	−1.1	3.6	11.0	85.4	90.8	90.0	3.9
Semi-private	37.6	39.3	−1.7	5.5	4.0	90.5	98.0	95.4	3.6
Moscow City									
State	37.8	39.0	−1.2	2.2	2.5	95.4	99.0	97.7	2.4
Private	39.6	40.1	−0.5	2.4	5.4	92.2	93.1	95.9	2.4
Semi-private	37.7	39.8	−2.2	4.1	3.5	92.4	98.2	96.6	3.2
Moscow Oblast									
State	37.8	39.5	−1.7	1.8	2.7	95.5	98.8	97.9	1.9
Private	38.4	40.3	−1.9	3.1	4.3	92.5	91.8	95.6	1.1
Semi-private	37.8	39.5	−1.7	3.2	1.7	95.1	98.5	96.2	0.9

highlighted by Russell and Hanneman, who examined the use of part-time labour and subcontractors by small businesses in Russia. They argued in 1997 that "privately owned small businesses in Russia make use of part-time employees and independent contractors at higher rates than enterprises owned by the state," but "they do so not because they are private firms, but because they are small."[39]

Wage arrears were often considered a particular disease of state and former state enterprises. The regional LFS data suggest that although the private sector did perform better in this regard, it was not immune. Significant proportions of employees in all five regions and all types of ownership received their wages with delay or incompletely. As indicated in table 4.7, the private sector had the highest proportion of those getting wages on time and completely and the lowest proportion of those who did not. The largest share of employees affected by delays was in the semiprivate sector. Across the survey regions, the best performance was seen in Moscow City and Moscow Oblast. However, even in such relatively prosperous areas, significant numbers of private sector employees suffered from either delayed or incomplete payments. The other regions had much higher shares of employees facing arrears, including about one-half or more of private sector employees.

The existence of wage arrears in the private sector may have been linked partly to nonpayments in the state and semiprivate sectors. Such a hypothesis would appear reasonable, in that state enterprises and organisations or insolvent semiprivate enterprises may not have funded their obligations toward private enterprises. Wage arrears also affected the disposable income of individual customers of private firms. Moreover, where the government and other nonprivate employers delayed payment of legally contracted wages, and this violation of laws was not punished, it created clear incentives for other employers to follow the practice. Until the economic crisis in the summer of 1998, firms with cash were able to make hefty profits by investing their wage arrears in short-term instruments. Under such circumstances nonpayment of wages was tending to become a norm among employers and risked to shift the whole system to a new equilibrium. Once established, such an arrears trap was difficult to break and might have required politically costly measures to correct (e.g., enforced bankruptcy or punitive fines). Widespread use of wage arrears left employees with few alternatives but to accept the situation, which in effect lowered their reservation wages.

Drawing on the LFS data, logit regression can be used to study the relative importance of factors that may be associated with wage arrears. Table 4.8 presents the results for a regression of the variable for receipt of wages (paid completely and on time) on demographic and enterprise characteristics. It shows that the private ownership effect was rather limited and was significant only in Krasnoyarsk Krai. In all other regions private firms tended not to differ substantially from state ones in paying employees on time and in full. Moreover, the regression highlights firm size and type of economic activity as more important influences. Holding other variables constant, smaller firms in trade were much more likely to have timely wage payments. This was especially clear in Moscow City and Moscow and Chelyabinsk Oblasts. Although these small firms were largely private, one can argue that they performed better not due to ownership but rather due to their size and trade activity.[40] This tendency may be linked to the fact that small firms often existed in the semiformal or informal economy, preferring to operate with cash. In effect, they may have benefited from avoiding social charges on wages, while recruiting and retaining labour by generally paying cash wages in a timely fashion. These benefits may have tended to outweigh the potential gains from use of cheap credit linked to wage arrears.

SOCIAL AND DEMOGRAPHIC PROFILE OF THE PRIVATE SECTOR

If the inflow of new human capital is associated with improvements in economic performance, one might have expected private enterprises to create favourable

Table 4.7   Did You Receive Your Wage on Time and Completely?, March 1996 (Percent of Employed by Enterprise Type in Each Region)

	Enterprise type:			
	State	*Private*	*Semi-private*	*Total*
Chelyabinsk Oblast				
Complete and on time	38.8	42.7	22.7	35.0
Incomplete and with delay	15.3	27.4	34.9	24.7
Either incomplete or with delay	45.9	29.9	42.4	40.3
Chuvash Republic				
Complete and on time	38.2	52.5	34.3	40.8
Incomplete and with delay	13.1	7.2	23.3	14.2
Either incomplete or with delay	48.7	40.3	42.4	45.0
Krasnoyarsk Krai				
Complete and on time	30.7	48.5	28.9	34.9
Incomplete and with delay	20.2	27.6	26.3	22.3
Either incomplete or with delay	49.1	23.9	44.8	42.8
Moscow City				
Complete and on time	74.8	86.9	72.6	77.6
Incomplete and with delay	5.6	2.6	6.9	5.5
Either incomplete or with delay	19.6	10.5	20.5	16.9
Moscow Oblast				
Complete and on time	75.0	75.1	61.7	72.1
Incomplete and with delay	5.5	6.0	9.5	6.7
Either incomplete or with delay	19.5	18.9	28.8	21.2

Table 4.8   Logit Regression: Getting Wage Payment on Time and Completely, March 1996

	Chelyabinsk Oblast	Chuvash Republic	Krasnoyarsk Krai	Moscow City	Moscow Oblast
Constant	−1.4334**	.5976	.0597	2.0465**	2.1667**
Age					
	−.0077	−.0050	−.0020	−.0073*	−.0118**
Gender (male)	−.0674	−.0110	−.0636	−.1356	−.2489**
Education					
Higher	.3041	.3384	.5986**	.0778	−.4261
High		—			—
Lower					
education	−.1307	−.3180	−.0751	−.0125	.0717
Occupational groups					
Managers	.1545	−1.1908	−1.0996**	−.8570**	−.7852*
Professionals	.2318	−.9073	−.9169**	−1.2645**	−.8427**
Workers	.2506	−1.0552	−1.1196**	−.9521**	−1.2666**
Clerks	—	—	—	—	—
Firm size					
Up to 25 employees	.8632**	−.3691	−.1618	1.1716**	.7814**
26–100	.6861**	−.2340	−.4571	.8992**	.8361**
101–500	.1925	−.4787	−.6234**	.3030**	.6591**
over 500	—	—	—	—	—
Ownership					
State	—	—	—	—	—
Private	.1817	−.2314	.7311**	.0053	−.0913
Semi-private	−.3490*	−.4607	−.0926	−.0983	−.3907**
Type of economic activity					
Industry	.4846	.3131	.2997	−.5347**	−.1444
Construction	.3451	.1414	.9009**	.3983**	.2134
Transport	−.4114	1.3731**	−.4395	.4010	−.4433
Services	.7422**	.5795	.6803	−.0009	−.1335
Trade	1.6673**	1.7738**	1.7750**	1.0362**	1.2469**
−2ll	1572.3	889.3	1634.7	4935.7	3994.3
N obs	1402	719	1410	5007	3662

*−p < .05

conditions for recruitment while seeking to structure the employment relationship to maximise profits and productivity. While private firms may offer employees certain advantages, they may also demand more intensive work and offer much less security. Hence, the demography of the sector could be skewed toward younger, more skilled, and generally more adaptive employees.

Household surveys conducted by the Russian Centre for Public Opinion Research (VCIOM) provide some evidence on these suppositions.[41] During the early years of the transition, these surveys were one of very few sources of information on such labour market aspects as the demography of those working for private sector, their motivation and wage differences, and their patterns of labour turnover. According to the VCIOM data, as of 1995 the private sector tended to employ:

- 1.2 times more men than women,
- 1.1–1.2 times more youth under 24 years,
- 1.2 times more college graduates, and
- 1.9 times more skilled workers than other sectors.[42]

The VCIOM data also indicate that 1.2 times more workers had only primary and secondary education (i.e., relatively low educational attainment) and that the proportion of professionals was 1.6 times less in the private sector compared with the others. These data hint at a rather segmented composition of the labour force in private firms; employees with relatively high and relatively low skills prevailed, while medium-skills holders were a minority. Such a configuration can be explained by the coexistence in the sector of firms involved with innovation (e.g., in research and development) and firms involved in retail trade or other areas that did not require high or special skills.[43]

Unfortunately, the VCIOM sample was relatively small and underrepresented those working in the private sector. As a result, in some cases the statistical significance was rather limited. Also, the analysis did not control for variation between the sectors in terms of the type of economic activity or firm size. Thus, these conclusions remain rather tentative.

The regional LFS data permit further—more representative—inquiry as to the composition of employment in the private sector, at least for the selected regions. Table 4.9 suggests that private sector employees were slightly younger than those working for semiprivate or state establishments. The private sector did not distinguish itself as being substantially different in terms of gender and education. Although over half of its employment was comprised of men and the share of men was higher than in the state sector, the share of men was also generally lower than in the average semiprivate enterprise. The only exception was in the Chuvash Republic, where the both state and semiprivate sectors had a similar gender composition.

With respect to educational attainment, the variation across regional labour markets was much larger than across ownership types. In Krasnoyarsk and

Table 4.9   Private Sector Employees, Distribution by Characteristics, March 1996 (Percentages)

	Chelyabinsk Oblast	*Chuvash Republic*	*Krasnoyarsk Krai*	*Moscow City*	*Moscow Oblast*
Gender					
Men	57.7	54.9	59.1	58.4	54.5
Age (years)					
Up to 30	25.9	28.2	26.8	32.8	27.9
31–45	51.5	47.2	49.6	44.3	43.4
46–60	20.2	22.5	21.9	21.3	25.8
Over 60	2.2	2.1	1.7	1.7	2.9
Education					
Primary and incomplete high	17.0	16.2	23.5	4.6	13.5
High	69.9	68.3	57.1	57.2	67.5
Higher	13.2	15.5	19.6	38.4	17.3
Occupational group					
Managers	11.4	15.5	10.7	16.3	9.3
Professionals	12.8	12.7	10.7	25.8	14.6
Clerks	1.2	0.7	2.7	4.7	1.1
Workers	74.6	71.1	75.9	53.1	75.0

Chelyabinsk regions, private firms employed significantly more people with low (primary and secondary) education than did state or semiprivate firms. In Moscow City this proportion was, on the contrary, in favour of the private sector, although the intersectoral difference was minimal. Looking at four broadly defined occupational groups (managers, professionals, clerks, and workers), it appears that the private sector tended to hire relatively fewer managers and professionals but more blue-collar workers. However, this tendency was only partially confirmed in the case of the Chuvash Republic.

The significance of these socio-demographic characteristics in predicting the sector of employment can be tested using simple logit regression with controls for enterprise size and type of economic activity (table 4.10). The dependent variable was the log-odds of working in the private sector, while socio-demographic variables, enterprise size, and activity parameters were specified as independent dummy variables (except for age, which was measured in years).[44] The results highlighted the primary importance of enterprise size and activity, while confirming the importance of demographic factors. Among the variables used, employment in retail and wholesale trade had the greatest effect on the log-odds. For example, in Moscow, controlling for other factors, the odds of working in private firms were 5.8 times higher for those employed in trade than for those employed in other activities. In Krasnoyarsk

Krai and Moscow Oblast these effects were even higher, amounting to 9.8 and 7.7 times, respectively. Although the dummy variables for industry in these regions were also significant, their effects were weaker. This evidently reflects the nature of private activities in Russia as being developed mostly in trade.

Table 4.10 Logit Regression: Being Employed in the Private Sector, March 1996

	Chelyabinsk Oblast	Chuvash Republic	Krasnoyarsk Krai	Moscow City	Moscow Oblast
Constant	−1.3857*	.2116	−2.2289**	−3.3646**	−3.4756**
Age	−.0177**	−.0047	−.0285**	−.0296**	−.0182**
Gender (male)	.3334*	.0140	.3016	.5859**	.4298**
Education					
Higher	.3352	.7964*	.1311	.2903**	.5118
High	—		—		—
Lower education	.4429*	−.0812	.7088**	−.1388	−.0261
Occupational groups					
Managers	.4446	−.8001	−.2447	.2807	1.3629**
Professionals	.0110	−.9468	−.1616	−.0270	.8243*
Workers	.3973	−.9860	.2297	.6505**	1.5347**
Clerks	—	—	—	—	—
Firm size					
Up to 25 employees	2.3130**	.6094	2.3563**	2.9932**	1.9338**
26–100	1.4006**	.4037	1.3327**	2.0985**	.8363**
101–500	1.0950**	−.9752*	1.0160**	1.3053**	.5079**
Over 500	—	—	—	—	—
Type of economic activity					
Industry	−.6259**	−1.6176**	.5993*	.5257**	.8635**
Construction	−1.3997**	−.0418	−.8708*	.0754	−.5721**
Transport	−2.2882**	−.9694*	−1.2189*	−.0013	.4140
Services	−2.3181**	−2.9437**	−1.3215**	.0291	−.5929**
Trade	−.3222	−.5009	.8018*	1.2733**	1.4193**
−2ll	1163.6	480.1	1009.6	3906.8	3001.6
N obs	1402	730	1410	5055	3701

*–p < .05 **–p <.01

CONCLUSION

During the first years of economic transition in Russia, the private sector grew to account for a substantial share of overall economic activity, thereby facilitating labour market adjustment by creating new, and in some cases more flexible, employment opportunities.[45] Roughly speaking, it appears that by 1998 privately owned and controlled firms accounted for between 30 and 40 percent of employment. It is possible that this percentage subsequently increased as the shareholding structure in some joint-stock companies was consolidated and new businesses were founded (offsetting a portion of those that closed).

Returning to the hypotheses on the nature of private sector employment, it seems that private sector ownership was, by some measures, associated with stronger employment performance and greater employment fragility. Private sector firms tended to show better results with respect to hours worked and, in some cases, timely payment of wages. However, there were significant exceptions. In some regions, state firms had lower incidence of short-time working hours, for example. Although private firms often tended to pay wages in a more timely fashion than other employers, many also resorted to use of wage arrears. The data also indicate that private firms utilised fixed-term or part-time employment more often than other types of firms. This sector also appeared to experience greater labour turnover. Yet other factors were also linked to this employment fragility. For example, although private sector ownership tended to be associated with shorter job tenures, in some regions small firm size actually seems to explain more of the variation.

The data confirm a tendency for employees in the private sector to be somewhat younger and probably more adaptable people. Generally, the sector tended to have a smaller share of management personnel than the other sectors. However, here again regional variations and, possibly, segmentation were apparent. For example, in some regions highly educated persons were more likely to be employed in the private sector than in other sectors. At the same time, those with lower educational attainment were also strongly represented in some areas.

Thus, the situation in the private sector was perhaps less clear cut than one might have thought a priori.[46] A question arises as to what extent private sector enterprises could differentiate themselves from other enterprises in an institutional environment that remained to some degree hostile to private sector development and where other types of employers were able to frequently utilise practises such as nonpayments and wage arrears that had competitive impacts. Indeed, it is possible that such factors reduced the ability of the private sector to contribute its full potential to labour market adjustment.

NOTES

1. Much of the material in this chapter is drawn from: Vladimir Gimpelson and Douglas Lippoldt, "Private Sector Employment in Russia: Scale, Composition and

Performance (Evidence from the Russian Labour Force Survey)," *Economics of Transition* 7, no. 2 (July 1999): 505–533.

2. Examples of papers touching on these issues include Andrea Richter and Mark Schaffer, "The Performance of De Novo Private Firms in Russian Manufacturing," in *Enterprise Restructuring and Economic Policy in Russia*, ed. Simon Commander, Qimiao Fan, and Mark Schaffer (Washington, D.C.: EDI—The World Bank, 1996), 253–274; Jozef Konings, Hartmut Lehmann, and Mark Schaffer, "Job Creation and Job Destruction in a Transition Economy: Ownership, Firm Size, and Gross Job Flows in Polish Manufacturing, 1988–91," *Labour Economics* 3, no. 3 (September 1996): 299–317; Valentijn Bilsen and Jozef Konings, "Job Creation, Job Destruction, and Growth of Newly Established, Privatized, and State-Owned Enterprises in Transition Economies: Survey Evidence from Bulgaria, Hungary, and Romania," *Journal of Comparative Economics* 26, no. 3 (September 1998): 429–445; and various studies by VCIOM. A recent article by Simon Clarke and Veronika Kabalina reinforces our findings: "The New Private Sector in the Russian Labour Market," *Europe-Asia Studies* 52, no. 1 (January 2000): 7–32.

3. "Oblast" and "Krai" are designations for Russian administrative regions. The criteria for selection of the study regions and their characteristics are discussed briefly in the Data Sources Annex.

4. The utility of certain other potential data sources such as the Russian Longitudinal Monitoring Survey (RLMS) was limited by imprecise definitions of enterprise ownership. Sampling and data issues are discussed in the Data Sources Annex. It should be noted that the special supplementary LFS questionnaire was supported by a TACIS-ACE project, also described in the Annex.

5. *Transition Report 1997* (London: EBRD, 1997), 96.

6. E.g., see Richter and Schaffer, "The Performance of De Novo Private Firms in Russian Manufacturing"; Konings, Lehmann, and Schaffer, "Job Creation and Job Destruction in a Transition Economy"; and Bilsen and Konings, "Job Creation, Job Destruction, and Growth of Newly Established, Privatized, and State-Owned Enterprises in Transition Economies: Survey Evidence from Bulgaria, Hungary, and Romania."

7. This point was documented in a few studies, such as that by Richter and Schaffer ("The Performance of De Novo Private Firms in Russian Manufacturing"), who reported on employment performance using job creation/destruction rates. Drawing on data from a 1994 World Bank survey of enterprise managers, they found that the annual job creation rate in state firms was 1.4 percent and the job destruction rate was 6.2 percent. In the *de-novo* private sector the ratio was radically different: the job creation rate was 25 percent, while the destruction rate was 6.1 percent. In total, the annual net employment change in the *de-novo* private sector was positive, amounting to 19 percent, while the change in state enterprises was a negative 4.8 percent.

A similar pattern seemed to exist in Poland, where jobs were created largely in the new private sector but job destruction predominated in state enterprises, a process that drove the reallocation of labour. See Konings, Lehmann, and Schaffer, "Job Creation and Job Destruction in a Transition Economy."

8. E.g., see Commander, Dhar, and Yemtsov, "How Russian Firms Make Their Wage and Employment Decisions" or Richter and Schaffer, "The Performance of De Novo Private Firms in Russian Manufacturing."

9. One study found that, by 1995, firms founded prior to the introduction of reforms still tended to retain pre-reform objectives (Simon Commander, Sumana Dhar, and Ruslan

Yemtsov, "How Russian Firms Make Their Wage and Employment Decisions," in *Enterprise Restructuring and Economic Policy in Russia,* 48).

10. E.g., Nicholas Barberis, Maxim Boiko, Andrei Shleifer, and Natalia Tsukanova, *How Does Privatisation Work? Evidence from the Russian Shops,* NBER Working Paper no. 5136, May 1995; John Earle, Saul Estrin, and Larisa Leschenko, "Ownership Structures, Patterns of Control, and Enterprise Behavior in Russia," in *Enterprise Restructuring and Economic Policy in Russia,* 205–252; Richter and Schaffer, "The Performance of De Novo Private Firms in Russian Manufacturing."

11. Commander, Dhar, and Yemtsov, "How Russian Firms Make Their Wage and Employment Decisions," 48.

12. E.g., Philip Aghion and Olivier Blanchard, "On the Speed of Transition in Central Europe," in *NBER Macroeconomics Annual 1994,* ed. Stanley Fischer and Julio Rotemberg (Cambridge and London: MIT Press, 1994), 283–320; Simon Commander and Andrey Tolstopiatenko, "Unemployment, Restructuring and the Pace of the Transition," in *Lessons from the Economic Transition: Central and Eastern Europe in the 1990s,* ed. Salvatore Zecchini (Paris: OECD and Dordrecht, Netherlands: Kluwer Academic Publishers, 1997), 331–350.

13. David Stark, "Recombinant Property in East European Capitalism: The Hidden Character of Eastern European Capitalism," in *Restructuring Networks in Post-Socialism. Legacies, Linkages, Localities,* ed. Gernot Grabher and David Stark (Oxford: Oxford University Press, 1997), 46.

14. Small firm networking is typical for many capitalist countries but operated differently in many transition countries. See Charles Perrow, "Small Firm Networks," in *Explorations in Economic Sociology,* ed. Richard Swedberg (New York: Russell Sage, 1993), 377–402.

15. Leila Webster and Joshua Charap, "Private Sector Manufacturing in St. Petersburg," in *Russia: Creating Private Enterprises and Efficient Markets*, ed. Ira Lieberman and John Nellis (Washington, D.C.: The World Bank, 1995), 217.

16. Earle, Estrin, and Leschenko, "Ownership Structures, Patterns of Control, and Enterprise Behavior in Russia," 227, 233.

17. Public associations were generally nonprofit but also included some organisations that might be construed as businesses.

18. This approach yields results for 1994–1995 that are not dramatically different from the findings of Commander and Tolstopiatenko in "Unemployment, Restructuring and the Pace of the Transition," who estimated the "pure" private sector in 1994–1995 as 31 percent of the total employment.

19. These administrative data are from the mandatory reporting via Goskomstat's form 1-T, which was submitted quarterly by all large enterprises. (According to Russian terminology, these were "large and medium size" firms.) This reporting excluded joint ventures.

20. SMEs were generally defined in Russia to include enterprises with employment of less than 100, but this varied by industry. See the Data Sources Annex for more details on SME statistics.

21. E.g., see Guy Standing, *Russian Unemployment and Enterprise Restructuring. Reviving Dead Souls* (London: Macmillan Press, 1996).

22. By adding employment in large enterprises (about 50.8 million people in 1995), to the residual components, including 8.95 million from SMEs and about 4.7 million self-employed individuals plus 0.4 million from joint-ventures, private farmers, and

clergymen, one approaches the 67 million total employment, as estimated by Goskomstat. See: *Rossiya v tsifrach* (Moscow: Goskomstat of the RF, 1996).

23. There were a few exceptions common for any enterprise and listed in chapter 17 of the Labour Code. Also, see the reference to the federal law "On Trade Unions, Their Rights and Guarantees of Activity" in *Trudovoye zakonodatelstvo (Labour Legislation)* (Moscow: Prospekt, 2000), 146–158.

24. Based on the federal law "On Trade Unions, Their Rights and Guaranties of Activity."

25. See, for example, *Entrepreneurship and SMEs in Transition Economies: The Visegrad Conference* (Paris: OECD, 1997) and Vadim Radayev, *Creating New Russian Markets: Transaction Costs, Forms of Control and Business Ethic* (Moscow: CPT, 1998).

26. Note that mandatory social contribution rates amounted to 39 percent of the basic wage bill.

27. Russian labour law did not provide for a formal probationary period.

28. Simon Commander, John McHale, and Ruslan Yemtsov, "Russia," in *Unemployment, Restructuring, and the Labor Market in Eastern Europe and Russia,* ed. Simon Commander and Fabrizio Coricelli (Washington, D.C.: EDI—The World Bank, 1995), 147–192.

29. This analysis of LFS data considers only employed respondents. See the Data Sources Annex for details of the sample structure.

30. For a map and description of the selected regions, see the Data Sources Annex.

31. A phenomenon well described in Janos Kornai, *The Socialist System: The Political Economy of Communism* (Princeton, N.J.: Princeton University Press, 1992), 399–403.

32. Gimpelson and Lippoldt provide evidence that private firms tend to have higher labour turnover and, correspondingly, their employees have shorter tenures. However, the data sources did not permit them to control for firm age and activity ("Labour Turnover in the Russian Economy," in *Labour Market Dynamics in the Russian Federation,* ed. Douglas Lippoldt (Paris: OECD, 1997), 17–55).

33. Respondents who were hired into their current job during the twelve months preceding the survey were asked to describe which type of job search led to their successful placement. As in most industrialised countries, direct applications and personal contacts were the primary methods, accounting for between 70 and 90 percent of all job matches. Personal contacts were more important for getting jobs in private firms than in state or semiprivate ones. See chapter 6 for more discussion on placement channels.

34. The LFS supplement did not record tenure as a continuous variable. Consequently, the share of short-tenured employees in the labour force is used here, in view of its generally strong positive correlation with labour turnover and negative correlation with average tenure.

35. See chapters 3 and 5 of the book.

36. *Russian Economic Trends* 5, no. 2 (1996): 105.

37. A roughly comparable indicator of underemployment is the share of persons in the labour force working part time but who would prefer to work full time. In the same period such involuntary part-time workers accounted for 0.2 percent of the labour force in Bulgaria, 2.4 percent in Romania, and 0.6 percent in the Slovak Republic. See: *Short-Term Economic Indicators: Transition Economies, Supplement 4/1997* (Paris: OECD, 1998).

38. It should be noted, however, that part-time work was quite rare prior to the economic reforms.

39. Raimond Russell and Robert Hanneman, "The Use of Part-Time Employees and Independent Contractors by Small Enterprises in Russia" (paper presented at the annual meeting of the American Sociological Association, Toronto, Canada, August 9–13, 1997), 29. Although they did not control for firm age, most of these small businesses were likely to have been newly created.

40. As reported by Alfandari and Schaffer in 1996, "ownership shows relatively little correlation with any sort of arrears, whether or not we control for other firm characteristics" (Gilles Alfandari and Mark Schaffer, "'Arrears' in the Russian Enterprise Sector," in *Enterprise Restructuring and Economic Policy in Russia,* 117).

41. *Informatsionny bulleten VCIOM,* 1993–1997, various issues.

42. *Informatsionny bulleten VCIOM,* no. 4, (1995): 41.

43. Vladimir Gimpelson, "Zanyatost i oplata truda v novom chastnom sektore" (Employment and Wages in the New Private Sector in Russia), *Mirovaya ekonomika i mezhdunarodnye otnosheniya,* no. 2 (February 1997): 81–93.

44. Dummies are proxy variables that reflect qualitative factors related to each observation (e.g., whether or not the individual is employed in industry).

45. One example of the operation of this flexibility might be seen in the financial sector during the crisis of August–September 1998. The collapse of that sector affected tens of thousands of employees who were laid-off. However, this did not translate directly into open unemployment because a large proportion of these employees held multiple jobs.

46. The assessment of developments in this sector is made more difficult by statistical problems that prevent an accurate accounting. A lack of basic data forces analysts to infer a portion of the information for some indicators or to derive it as a by-product from statistical tools targeting other economic phenomena. Further problems relate to the difficulty of identifying private firms, given the lack of transparency in ownership and control—that is, the problem of untangling the "recombinets" as described by Stark. Clearly, more focused research and data collection will be required to improve labour market monitoring and sort out these issues in the future.

5

Price Signals in the Labour Market:
Wages, Wage Arrears, and Social Benefits

OVERVIEW

Observers of Russian labour market adjustment are usually struck by the very gradual employment adjustment. During the period 1992 to 1997, employment dropped by about 10 percent, while GDP was halved. Even when one takes account of the actual reduction in working hours due to underemployment, this does not radically change this conclusion. However important, employment constitutes only one labour market dimension, that of quantity. Wages are a second dimension that represents price. This chapter introduces the wage dimension into the Russian labour market story in more detail.

If employment did not fully show the expected response to "the Great Contraction" in output, one might expect a corresponding reaction on the wage side. This is, in fact, what happened. However, the wage response took quite peculiar forms and looked different than in most of the Central and East European transition countries. First of all, the Russian model combined a decline in real wages due with a growing mountain of wage arrears. Second, a drastic increase arose in wage inequality. Third, enterprise-linked social benefits accounted for a nontrivial portion of labour costs and also declined less than expected; the sustained provision of these benefits was probably a factor contributing to the bubble of wage arrears.

Wage reform was a part of the initial reform package of 1992 and it had a few major and interconnected goals. First, it was intended to significantly deregulate wage-setting and provide firms and employees with clear market signals. The market was expected to replace government bureaucrats in shaping labour compensation. Second, new wage-setting machinery was expected to set appropriate levels of compensation that reflected the underlying productivity of labour (and not to inflate wages in a "predatory" fashion).[1] Third, the reform was expected to increase the return to human capital, one of the major

125

factors of economic recovery and growth. Fourth, the new clarity in price signals and the closer relation between wages and productivity were expected to provide incentives for a reallocation and improved deployment of labour.

Relatively cheap but skilled labour could provide an important comparative advantage. It could stimulate investments and job creation in a sustained fashion, especially where upward shifts in labour costs and real wages lagged somewhat behind the growth in labour productivity. Did this happen during the Russian transition? Not quite, although, as the reader will see, real wages did drop significantly. A specific feature of the decline in labour costs (including the real wage components) was the fact that these costs fluctuated independently of shifts in productivity, reflecting rather wage-push factors—and only partially taking into account the financial situation of enterprises. In the years following the drastic drop in wages and total labour costs in 1992, unit labour costs (ULC) recovered twice during two- to three-year periods, in each case significantly outstripping growth in labour productivity. This happened for the first time in 1992–1994 and in 1995–1998 for the second. Both times the gap between productivity and wages was resolved through a major financial crisis (in October 1994 and in August 1998). Both crises resulted in significant devaluations of the Russian currency (making Russian goods more competitive) and brought labour costs down by one-third. Total wage claims (wages paid plus the value of back wages) were also heavily discounted.

In Russia, as in most countries, the formal wage-setting machinery was one of the main factors in determining earnings adjustments. But, under the conditions of the Russian economic transition, earnings outcomes also depended upon a peculiar combination of additional factors. These factors included weak contract enforcement mechanisms and varied opportunities for secondary or informal employment, tax evasion, and nonwage compensation (i.e., pay-in-kind and employer-provided social benefits). Consequently, the analysis begins here with a look at the basic institutional foundations of wage policy, including the minimum wage and the wage-setting rules. It then moves on to consider trends in real wages, wage arrears, and inequality, before concluding with an examination of nonwage aspects of labour compensation and the structure of labour costs.

HOW WERE WAGES SET IN THE UNSETTLED ECONOMY?

The evolution of wage policy in Russia during the 1990s is discussed in detail in a number of recent publications.[2] Under the pre-transition wage-setting system, central planners from the State Committee on Labour and Social Issues assigned wages according to a special occupational wage scale (known as the uniform tariff scale, UTS). This system covered all industries and occupations, creating a rigid web of regulation that defined labour compensation irrespective of the actual utility and productivity of labour. Wage compression was one of the ultimate objectives of this system; another was the centralised allocation of labour across sectors, regions, and occupations. Neither was ever fully achieved. This system of wage planning experienced some modifications over time and finally was critically damaged by Gorbachev's ill-thought-out innovations. Nevertheless, it managed to survive until the end of 1991.[3]

On 2 January 1992, wage-setting was significantly deregulated. The old tariff system was largely abolished as a part of the general liberalisation of wages. Direct state control over wages was retained only for institutions and enterprises funded directly from the state budget. Even in these cases, centralised wage-setting rules were no longer comprehensive and were left to determine only a portion of the total wage or salary. As to private companies, they were granted relative freedom to set wages for their employees through plant-level negotiations. Due to the lack of effective trade union influence, these negotiations were more like informal bargaining rather than a well-institutionalised routine. At the same time, the state did attempt to limit the potential pace of overall wage increases through a tax-based incomes policy. This was implemented via an excess wage tax (EWT) levied on employers, but even this indirect control mechanism was abolished in early 1996.[4]

Minimum Wages

During the transition years, the statutory minimum wage played an important role in Russia, serving as an instrument of wage setting as well as a means of controlling wage growth. The statutory monthly minimum wage was fixed by the president or Parliament and was adjusted from time to time, albeit irregularly. One adjustment occurred in 1992, four in 1993, one in 1994, five in 1995, and two in the first half of 1996. Then, no further changes took place through late 1998. (Interestingly enough, the election years 1993, 1995, and 1996 saw more minimum wage adjustments than any other periods of time, a point discussed in more detail in chapter 7.) This minimum wage setting also influenced the government setting of wages and salaries in the budgetary sector.[5]

Given that the minimum wage in Russia was very low, amounting to less than 10 percent of the average wage during much of the period considered here, its direct effect on employment was probably very limited (chart 5.1).[6] Nevertheless, upward adjustment of the minimum wage was not just a cheap public gesture. It increased the total public sector wage bill, since public sector wage rates were linked to the minimum wage rate through the UTS. Also, in addition to being a guideline for wage-setting in the public sector, the minimum wage was used for calculating most social benefits and family allowances.[7] This enlarged the scope for its use in "vote buying" by politicians in pre-electoral periods and made the minimum wage a sensitive political issue. Therefore, breaking the link between minimum wages and social obligations of the state could have become an important policy measure.

Chart 5.1   The Minimum Wage as a Share of the Average Wage, 1992–1998

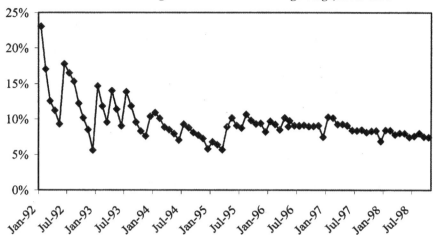

Sources: Russian Economic Trends, monthly series; authors' calculations.

Whereas minimum wage adjustments emerged within an unsettled and poorly institutionalised political process that did not take into account real budget constraints, they risked to strongly affect the whole pool of governmental social obligations, making them fiscally unsustainable. Indeed, they were associated with government arrears and sequestration of major budgetary allocations.

Wage-Setting Rules

During the first years of transition, different wage-setting institutions were operating in the budget-financed, mixed-ownership, and private sectors. In budget-financed institutions (public education, health care, culture, and science, among others) wages continued to be based on the UTS. The UTS scale provided for eighteen grades, in which the first grade was equal to the minimum wage; higher grades were calculated by multiplying the minimum by increasing coefficients. Since the minimum wage was very low and the coefficients were relatively modest, the wage rates based on the UTS tended to be low as well. In many cases, the UTS did not set the final wage rates but rather defined a lower bound at each level and probably affected differentiation. Although wages and salaries based on the UTS were generally dependent on direct state budget funding, where additional sources of revenues were available, the wage rates could be modified upward. For example, such UTS "adjustments" were utilised at the Academy of Science. While its core funding was drawn from the state budget and was declining and received with delays, it was able to raise supplementary funds by renting out office space to outside concerns; rent became a major determinant in the Academy's wage rates. This type of fundraising was widespread among various public insti-

tutions, linking public service and public goods to occasional commercial activities. (Clearly, this did not necessarily lead to improvement in the supply of public goods—or an optimal allocation of such goods.)

Privatised firms were not obliged to use the UTS but often still referred to it in
view of the inertia of their old practices. As suggested by the case studies cited in
chapter 3, the UTS was often used as a guideline and could be applied selectively
to particular groups within enterprises.[8] Although its use may have given some
outsiders an impression that equity considerations were applied by employers in
the treatment of labour, such an impression was likely to be misleading. In fact,
management enjoyed significant discretion over wage rates and wage differentiation. By shifting certain groups of priority employees onto special contracts,
management could pay them much higher wages while other employees saw their
relative wages erode. At the same time, assignment of a particular wage rate did
not guarantee payment at all, given the widespread wage arrears.

Most privatised large and medium-sized firms were heavily unionised and
compensation rates were subject to negotiation. The impact of institutionalised
collective bargaining on wage setting differed across sectors and enterprises;
however, in general it remained very limited.[9] The reasons for this were multiple:
trade unions were rather weak and controlled by management; collective agreements were not enforceable and sometimes set only minimum wage rates (which
tended to be very low); and financial books were nontransparent or inaccessible,
among other reasons. All this resulted in significant inter- and intra-enterprise
wage differentiation. Changes in relative wages reflected not only marginal productivity of workers but also their individual bargaining power, local labour market competitive rates for the most productive workers, and the level of reservation wages (basically, the limit of tolerance) for the least productive workers. The
impact on local labour markets depended largely on the concentration of firms
able to pay efficiency wages or a premium to attract and retain the best quality
labour; these firms were mostly new private businesses or relatively better-
adjusting old firms in export-oriented sectors.

Newly emerged private firms evidently enjoyed the most flexible wage setting,
which tended to be linked mostly to financial performance and efficiency considerations. Surveys provide evidence that these new firms generally were not
unionised and had wage rates set by top managers without the "benefit" of collective negotiations.[10] Typically, these firms engaged in semiformal employment
where, for example, only a small part of compensation was recorded and the bulk
of it was paid on the side. The recorded portion of the wage was likely to be comparable with the average wage in the economy, whereas the actual remuneration
might be 1.5 to 2 times the average.

Extreme wage-setting flexibility led to growing differentiation across firms
and occupations. While the private sector returns to low and medium skills (and
experience) were relatively modest and lay in the same range as in traditional enterprises, high or specific skills could be valued very highly. They could bring a

return as much as ten to twenty times greater than average. What generated this enormous return? No conclusive answer can be given, since the evidence from all measurable factors does not appear explain the total variation.

Brainerd, trying to analyse the factors affecting these returns, considered the residual or unobservable "skills" beyond measurable human capital endowments.[11] They included readiness to take risks, connections, and the luck of being in the right place at the right time, among other elements. "In some senses," she writes, "the Russian economy is like a lottery, with large rents accruing to those well positioned to take advantage of opportunities—but also with substantial losses for those who draw a losing number." Drastic variation in wages across the economy was an indicator that the labour market did not work properly. The transition economy in Russia, with limited competition, poor regulation, and other distortions, offered an environment ripe for all types of rent seeking. Although such rents could potentially erode as arbitrage effects developed along with some increases in competition, this did not happen on a large scale.

Examples of special rents to employees abound.[12] For example, during 1996 and 1997 Moscow newspapers were full of recruitment ads offering various (but mostly white-collar) jobs in private firms with monthly wages ranging from U.S. $200 to $7,000. And this was in an economy where average monthly wages were just over $100. Financial resources for paying such high compensation came from greater efficiency and lower overheads, but also various rents, tax evasion, and redistribution of proceeds from the financial bubble before it burst in the summer of 1998.[13]

Although the "old" and "new" sectors remained quite different, they nevertheless influenced one another. For example, the wage policy of the latter was likely to affect the former. This effect was especially strong when firms from both sectors competed in the same occupational labour market. This drove wages up even in very poorly performing enterprises, forcing them to increase wage differentiation and inflate their wage bills. Since the bankruptcy law was not enforced, even where rising wage bills contributed to insolvency, this did not generally lead to closures or lay-offs but rather to accumulation of wage debts, particularly in the case of state-owned and mixed-ownership companies. In turn, this growth in arrears led to important losses in human capital, as the best workers left for jobs in new private firms; the "old" enterprises thereby closed the window of opportunity for restructuring.

WAGES: REAL AND UNREAL

Wage-setting rules and practices form the core of wage policy, directly affecting nominal and real wage outcomes.[14] Normally, real wages due (to be paid) might be considered a direct indicator of people's well-being. But, in the Russian context, another nonconventional aspect requires a distinction between "real" wages paid and those that are partially "unreal" or "virtual." The discussion here begins with an overview of the major trends and a few key explanations.

Price liberalisation in early 1992 caused a drastic fall in real wages. According to official data, the average real wage in January 1992 amounted to just 34 percent of that of December 1991 (i.e., before price controls were lifted). But, as A. Aslund correctly pointed out, "real wages and incomes in 1991 are a completely artificial concept, as 1991 was characterised by an enormous monetary overhang and massive shortages, while 'real wages' in Soviet statistics were calculated on the basis of official prices, at which few goods were available. Considering the prices Russians actually had to pay in 1991, real wages were much lower than what official statistics still suggest. This was particularly true at the end of the year, as wages were raised sharply in advance of the price liberalisation."[15] If the base point for comparisons is shifted back to 1987, as Aslund reasonably suggests, the fall in real wages in January 1992 was about one-third (instead of two-thirds). If a later date is used for the comparison (somewhat after January 1992), a still significant but more modest decline occurred in calculated real wages.[16]

The trend in real wages due is shown in chart 5.2.[17] During 1993 and 1994, real wages experienced some turbulence, followed by a sudden surge in inflation that hit at the end of 1994, driving the average real wage down by a quarter of its real value within a short period of time. Then, in the period from early 1995 onward, the wage level stabilised and even exhibited a slight upward trend. Meanwhile, the wage level measured in dollars showed a clear upward shift. In 1996 real wages increased significantly while output was still in decline. They rose to a level 13 percent above their 1995 average and yielded their first sustained, but partial, recovery since 1990.[18] In 1997, the real wage rise continued, adding about 4.5 percent on an annual basis. This rise was brought to an abrupt halt with a steep decline occasioned by the August 1998 financial meltdown.

On the whole during the transition period, in relation to the "Great Contraction" in output and the significant tightening of monetary policy, the Russian labour market experienced what might be considered gradual growth in unemployment to double-digit rates. Real wages, on the other hand, experienced several substantial declines, beginning with the launch of far-reaching reforms in early 1992 and then again in late 1994 and the second half of 1998. Although in each case the decline was followed by a partial recovery, real wages remained well below their pre-transition level.

Wage Arrears

In any discussion of wages in Russia, one should bear in mind the serious caveats applied to the official data on this subject. The conventional statistics were based on wages contracted to be paid out to employees and, therefore, may be misleading. In Russia, as noted earlier, a significant gap existed between wages due and

**Chart 5.2   Real Average Wages and Total Real Wage Arrears in Industry,
1993–1998 (December 1995 = 100)**

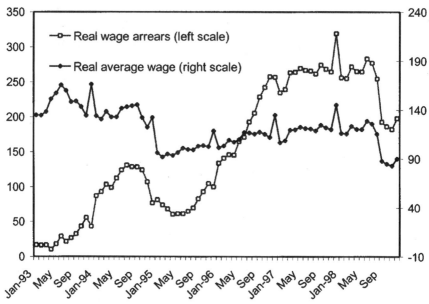

Sources: Goskomstat; *Russian Economic Trends*.

wages paid out.[19] Enterprises often did not pay wages in time or completely, thereby generating wage arrears. Almost from the outset of reforms, the actual take-home pay for a large part of the labour force was lower than the employers' original commitments.

Wage arrears appeared in 1992 as a "technical" consequence of very high inflation. Printing presses were simply unable to catch up with galloping wages and prices. But already in 1993 wage arrears changed in nature, becoming "nontechnical" and rather associated with enterprise adjustment strategies. Nevertheless, nonpayments were still quite limited in size and in the share of the labour force affected. Then, during 1994 and 1995, wage arrears emerged as a salient feature of the looming economic turbulence; the contribution of wage arrears to real wage declines became one of the major manifestations of wage flexibility. By the end of 1996, the stock of unpaid wages accounted for over 20 percent of monthly GDP or one month's total wage bill. It should be noted that this was an average figure for all firms in the main sectors of the economy. In those firms actually running wage arrears, the stock of unpaid wages at the end of 1996 was the equivalent of 275 percent of the monthly wage bill.[20] By mid-1997 unpaid wages accounted for 55.3 trillion roubles, or 128 percent of the monthly wage bill.

Wage arrears were not an independent and isolated phenomenon. They were rather a part of the more general problem of arrears (tax, trade, inter-enterprise, budget arrears) in the Russian economy in the 1990s.[21] All these arrears were to some extent inter-correlated. For example, according to one estimate, one-fifth of the enterprise arrears volume was linked to state budget arrears.[22] The interrelationships between the various actors were rather complex and derived from various factors. For example, a firm facing liquidity problems due to problems collecting receivables (possibly because of nonpayments by the state) in turn may have left the weakest holders of its obligations to be paid last or not at all. Some observers tended to blame the origin of the arrears problem on tight monetary policy and low monetisation linking it to inappropriate macroeconomic measures.[23] However, it is likely that the real reasons for arrears were only partly of a macroeconomic nature but rather were also linked to a mixed basket of microeconomic and fiscal factors.

Gaddy and Ickes explain the growth of arrears by pointing to a lack of restructuring in firms.[24] Still functioning more like Soviet-type industrial dinosaurs, many old firms pretended to add value while in fact they often subtracted or destroyed a portion of the value transferred to them from the energy sector. This provided managers with strong incentives to avoid cash transactions and run arrears. A situation developed whereby much of the economy became "virtual," with major macroeconomic indicators becoming partly "virtual" as well.[25] That is, they were to some extent based on statistical "pretence" and not on the actual value of output. It is hard to say to what extent this accounted for the overall arrears problem, but it seems likely to be a core factor in at least some sectors of the Russian economy during the transition period.

While Gaddy and Ickes's interpretation of events may partially explain the nature of wage arrears, other factors were at work as well. For example, the public wage bill appeared to be a hostage to a troubled political process (this aspect is discussed further in chapter 7). At this point, let it suffice to highlight just two key aspects of the problem: one was the role played by political and institutional factors in initiating inflation of the public sector wage bill; the other was the policymakers' consequent lack of political will to stop arrears from spreading.

The mid-1990s witnessed a particularly strong growth in wage arrears in terms of their volume and the numbers of workers affected. The increase in delays in wage payments is illustrated by household survey data (table 5.1). For example, in March 1993, 62 percent of those interviewed were paid in full and on time, but by November 1996 this proportion had dropped to only 29 percent. Chart 5.2 shows that many of the upward or downward movements in contracted wages were reflected to some extent in the arrears balances, although wage arrears also tended to cumulate and exhibit a generally upward trend.[26] When in late 1994 and early 1995 real wages due dropped by a quarter, for example, wage arrears followed the trend. Overall, the reported real wage figures, if adjusted for accumulated real wage arrears, would have shown a downward trend instead of recovery in the periods between major downward adjustments.

Table 5.1   Wage Arrears in Russia (Percentage of Respondents Paid with Delay)

	Paid in time and completely	Paid with delay under 1 month	Paid with delay over 1 month	Total
March 1993	62	31	7	100
December 1993	48	41	11	100
March 1994	38	43	19	100
June 1994	41	37	22	100
November 1994	40	41	19	100
March 1995	43	40	17	100
July 1995	48	40	12	100
September 1995	44	39	17	100
March 1996	31	45	24	100
May 1996	37	36	27	100
November 1996	29	32	39	100
January 1997	27	33	40	100

Source: VCIOM data.

For a better understanding of how wage arrears were generated, one needs to examine how they were distributed. Although no social group or economic sector seemed to have been entirely protected, the accumulated debts were allocated across firms and employees very unevenly. The distribution reflected the position of different groups in the economy, their resources, and their bargaining power versus other groups of workers, managers and the government. Summing up the evidence available from various studies,[27] it appears that most of the arrears were shifted onto the least competitive and politically vocal part of the labour force. Wage arrears were widespread in sectors experiencing the most difficulty (like machine-building or the social sector), as well as in those that were doing better (for example, oil and gas, construction, or private firms across all sectors). Geography appeared to be a factor: the farther a region was from Moscow, the higher the incidence of accumulated wage debts. Significant intrafirm variation in wage arrears was well documented by Earle and Sabirianova, suggesting possible discrimination within firms against those with less bargaining power.[28] Better-paid employees had more political clout, since they could quit and move to jobs with lower arrears and higher paid-out wages. Lower-paid workers were concentrated in sectors and jobs offering limited exit options. They were less vocal and more likely to acquiesce when facing payment delays. At the same time, because these workers were already among the lower income groups, an accumulation of wage arrears had a much higher probability of reducing them to poverty.

Although Russian managers are sometimes accused of paternalism, this did not appear to be manifested in the allocation of wage arrears: low wage groups did not experience proportionately lower arrears than the high wage groups. Indeed, the situation was the opposite, with wage arrears contributing to further increases in inequality in real wages paid. The association between wage arrears and wage levels can be highlighted by simple calculations based on RLMS household survey data.[29] The RLMS questionnaire included questions on monthly wage paid, amount of wage arrears, and duration of the period when wages were denied (in months). Assuming that wage arrears were evenly distributed throughout the time periods, one can impute the amount of monthly wage arrears and total monthly wage as a sum of the paid and nonpaid elements. On this basis, one can compare the monthly nonpaid wage component with monthly wages paid (Ratio 1) or with monthly wage due to be paid (Ratio 2).

Table 5.2 reports monthly arrears and ratios of unpaid wages to wages paid and wages due, broken down by quintile groups. It shows that in absolute terms, higher monthly wages tended to be associated with higher wage nonpayments (the second quintile was an exception). But higher wages also tended to be associated with smaller proportions of wage arrears relative to wages paid (Ratio 1) and wage due (Ratio 2). The lower the wage level, the higher the proportion of arrears. And the bottom quintile of wage earners, in particular, were hit harder than the other quintiles: employees in the bottom quintile (I) were denied one-third of their wages or salaries, while those in the top quintile (V) failed to receive only 8 percent. This uneven distribution of nonpayments was an additional contributor to wage inequality, which was much greater during the transition than in the pre-transition period (table 5.3).

These examples illustrate the discriminatory effects of wage nonpayments. Lower-paid employees suffered disproportionately from nonpayments, a pattern that seems to reflect a redistribution of the wage fund from less competitive to more competitive workers. The more competitive workers were relative winners.[30] This redistributive pattern fits well with the general picture of large-scale income redistribution in Russia during the transition,[31] which persisted over time. Workers who faced arrears once, for example in 1994, appeared to have had a higher probability of experiencing them again later in 1995 or 1996, based on calculations using the RLMS. This persistence could probably be attributed to low personal bargaining power and/or an individual's commitment to an ailing firm or sector.[32]

Table 5.2 Wage Arrears and Wages Paid and Due, by quintiles, 1996

Quintile	Average wage paid (000 rubles)	Monthly arrears (000 roubles)	Monthly arrears / wage paid (Ratio 1)	Monthly arrears / wage due (Ratio 2)
I	140	203	1.45	.35
II	327	169	.53	.20
III	530	219	.42	.17
IV	852	257	.30	.14
V	2137	263	.12	.08

Sources: RLMS 1996; authors' calculations.

Table 5.3   Wage Inequality in Russia, 1991–1997

	April 1991	April 1994	April 1995	May 1996	October 1997
Decile ratio (ratio of wages in the top decile to wages in the lowest decile)	7.8	23.4	26.4	24.0	25.0
Gini coefficient	.317	.439	.454	.445	.447

Source: Goskomstat.

Wage arrears appeared to be linked to the quasi-stabilisation during the period 1995–1998.[33] For transition countries like Russia, with poorly developed labour market institutions and little recourse for workers, wage arrears helped to close budgetary gaps and formed part of a simple, albeit temporary, stabilisation recipe: "Just do not pay wages or other obligations!" Decreases in money supply imposed serious constraints on enterprises' cash balances and on public spending. In the absence of sufficient fiscal adjustment and stringent bankruptcy measures, soft budget constraints allowed insolvent firms to stay afloat. Instead of pushing enterprises into closure, the situation stimulated them to take on all types of debts, including debts to workers. Chart 5.3 shows the generally inverse relationship between change in the consumer price index and wage arrears (as a percentage of the monthly wage bill). When inflation soared, the level of wage arrears tended to stabilise or even go down. Each attempt to restrain the money supply was followed by a new wage arrears crisis.

While the burden of wage arrears disproportionately weighed on low-paid workers, inflation magnified the negative impacts on this group. Those who were owed back wages tended to be concentrated within particular clusters of economic losers—sectors, regions, and social groups. More competitive workers could seek jobs where they could preserve or improve their wage situation. For many relatively less competitive workers, the choice was between wage arrears and unemployment. And it appeared they often preferred the former option. This left them in a situation where they received some or all of their wages late. They were further penalised when inflation eroded the value of their previously accumulated arrears.

Wage Inequality: How Far Up?

The Soviet economic and political system strongly emphasised social equity and Soviet wage-setting mechanisms were fashioned to promote this.[34] The post-Soviet economy started moving quickly toward the opposite extreme. By 1998, wage inequality in Russia had reached Latin American proportions. The data presented in table 5.3, for example, indicate that between April 1991 and May 1996, the Gini coefficient rose by 40 percent. The decile ratio between the average monthly wage paid to those in the top and bottom declines tripled during the same

Chart 5.3   Wage Arrears and Inflation, 1993–1998

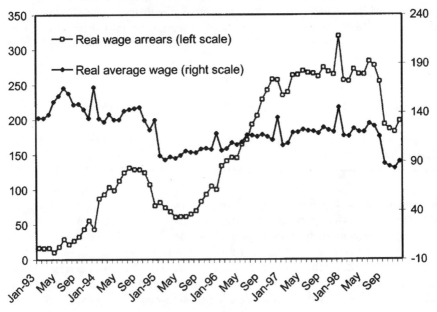

Sources: Goskomstat and *Russian Economic Trends*.

period (to a level greater than it would have been if all wages had been paid on time). Many workers found themselves earning much less than the minimum subsistence level, even if they were employed full time.

A number of factors were at work pushing up wage differentials. One of them was rising market returns to skills and education, while returns to experience declined. As Brainerd concludes, "Less skilled workers have lost substantially in real terms while highly skilled workers have reaped significant gains."[35] Segmentation also materialized between workers in sectors targeting the domestic market and those in export-oriented sectors. As shown in chapters 3 and 4, the case study enterprises and regions experienced increasing wage differentiation between various occupational groups, managers and workers, old and new firms, sectors, and regions. Among these variables, sector was one of the most important. Employees in firms working for cash-rich customers tended to be relative winners, receiving higher cash wages and facing shorter payment delays. During the first years of economic transition, they tended to work in export sectors, trade, finance, or banking. Relative losers were those working in firms oriented toward domestic cash-poor customers or those financed from the state budget. Agriculture, manufacturing, and the social sector (health, education, and science) were among the worst sectors.[36]

The differentiation across sectors can perhaps best be highlighted with an example. In 1991, the average wage in the gas sector (natural gas extraction and transportation) was the highest and amounted to 206 percent of the average in the economy, while the pay in the culture sector was the lowest at just 62 percent of the average. In 1996, the gas sector was still leading, with 424 percent of the average, while pay in the agriculture sector was at the bottom, amounting to less than half of the average.

EMPLOYER-PROVIDED SOCIAL BENEFITS

One reason some workers may have tolerated wage arrears was probably the variety of social benefits they continued received at their place of work—particularly during the first few years of transition. Although the package varied, large employers often provided such benefits as housing, access to sports facilities, child care, and pre-schooling.[37] The provision of these benefits was a continuation of a Soviet approach whereby employers delivered a significant share of compensation in the form of services (box 5.1).

While many enterprises continued to provide some services throughout the transition period, by the late 1990s most also acted to divest or restructure at least a portion of their social infrastructure. Privatisation forced changes in workplace benefits as the new owners were often unable—regardless of their intentions—to absorb the costs and continue to carry such responsibilities for social benefit provision. In general, as a result of the economic reforms, the range of social benefits provided by enterprises declined substantially, although estimates differ as to the exact magnitude of the decline. Child care and recreational offerings, in particular, were cut.[38] In many enterprises, the shares of personnel engaged in such nonproduction activities declined (e.g., see case studies in chapter 3).

By 1995, a household survey found that about one-third of those in employment claimed not to receive such social benefits, and another third placed no economic value on the benefits received.[39] Still, for some, the benefits remained an important supplement. Among the various benefits, for example, employer-provided housing benefits remained particularly important: over 10 percent of Russian employees surveyed in 1995 said they received such benefits.

Table 5.4 highlights the evolution of labour costs between 1994 and 1998. In general, wages (cash and pay-in-kind) generally accounted for less than two-thirds of labour costs. Between 1994 and 1998, nonmandatory social expenditure (such as for child care) and housing declined, while amenities actually rose slightly. This may have been due in part to increasing maintenance and utility costs, as well as to the reluctance of enterprises divest some facilities.[40] Some older Russian enterprises continued to carry a social infrastructure burden that impeded their adjustment processes and their potential to adapt to market economic conditions.

Box 5.1   The Origins of Employer-Provided Social Benefits

Under the Soviet system, social benefits delivered through enterprise-held infrastructure played several important roles. First, they compensated for the relatively low cash wages and helped to maintain a given level of subsistence. Second, their allocation allowed central planners to signal the political and economic priority of certain sectors, enterprises, or occupations. Third, they helped to achieve and preserve (at least formally) paternalistic employer-employee relationships and social cohesion within a given enterprise. Especially in larger enterprises, it was common for housing, health care, child care and pre-schooling, food services, and recreation opportunities to be provided by the employer, usually in collaboration with the trade union and for just a nominal fee, if not free of charge. Enterprises included the costs of the social services they were expected to provide as part of their overhead and transferred them to the state budget or to customers. In any case, firms did not operate in terms of economic profit and loss. In sum, the enterprise-linked social benefits system generated signals that were very important for the planned economy but that were absolutely incompatible with the workings of the emerging market economy.

FLUCTUATION IN RUSSIAN LABOUR COSTS

Unit labour costs (ULC) reflect labour costs per worker and per unit of output. This measure provides a convenient way to track labour costs over time on a roughly comparable basis. Unfortunately, available data for Russia did not cover all of the components of labour costs throughout the 1990s. A rough proxy for ULC tendencies may be imputed by dividing changes in real consumption wages (i.e., average wages deflated using the CPI) by changes in output per worker.

Chart 5.4 shows the evolution of ULC between 1990 and 1998 calculated on this basis. Over the entire period, the chart provides a picture of a generally downward trend in ULC. Labour productivity was in a continual fall throughout much of the period from 1992 to 1998, and the contraction in employment lagged far behind the contraction in output, but real wages also tended to be flat or declining.

At least three important shifts occurred during the period covered by the chart. First, the drop in real wages in early 1992 was followed by a period of wage stability or even slight recovery that led to some upward movement in the ULC index during 1992–1994. Then, the depreciation of the rouble in late 1994 was followed by a sharp rise in inflation in early 1995. This brought the real wage

Table 5.4   Composition of Labour Costs[a,b] (excluding the Excess Wage Tax)

	1994		1998	
	Total labor costs = 100	Wages = 100	Total labor costs = 100	Wages =100
Wages	63.5	100.0	62.5	100.0
Housing	3.0	4.7	2.0	3.2
Mandatory social funds	25.5	40.2	27.9	44.6
Other social expenditure	4.6	7.2	1.9	3.0
Training	0.3	0.5	0.3	0.5
Amenities	1.3	2.0	1.5	2.4
Other	1.9	3.0	3.9	6.2

Notes: (a) Data cover eleven main sectors of the economy.
(b) In order to improve comparability across years, the EWT is excluded. The EWT was abolished in January 1996.
Source: Goskomstat.

down by about one-third and contributed to a comparable decrease in unit labour costs as well. Finally, a slowdown in the fall of productivity and some recovery in real wages due to be paid in 1996 and 1997 produced an upward shift in the ULC. On balance, ULC in 1997 were about one-fifth more expensive than in 1995 but still cheaper than in 1993–1994.

However, the picture presented in chart 5.4 must be viewed with caution as the underlying data were subject to important caveats. First, due to the changes in economic and statistical systems in 1992, the pre- and post-liberalisation data are not strictly comparable. Second, the temporary upward adjustments in the ULC were probably partly just a statistical illusion, due to measured real wage increases that ignored mounting wage arrears. One cannot determine precisely to what extent the swings in ULC were the result of the bubble of nonpaid wages. In any case, the trends shown in the chart clearly reflect the underlying turmoil in wages, highlighting partial recoveries interrupted by steep devaluations. The range of fluctuations seems to reflect a lack of any deliberate strategy and weak institutional ability to keep control over wage claims.

CONCLUSION

This chapter has examined the relationships between prices and quantities in the emerging labour market. The Soviet system of centralised wage planning died in late 1991, together with the command economy. Liberalisation and deregulation in wage setting were considered an important part of the reform package introduced in 1992. "Free" wage setting was expected to generate clear market signals and assist in reallocating labour toward more efficient uses. It was also to contain demand-side inflationary pressures from wages, while rewarding improved utili-

Chart 5.4   Unit Labour Costs (Total Economy) (1995 = 100)

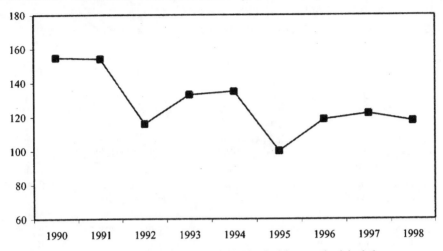

Note: ULC is calculated as the real wage index divided by the labour productivity index.
Source: Review of Economic Policy in Russia in 1997 (Moscow: Bureau of Economic Analysis, 1998), 593.

sation of human capital—a key element needed for economic recovery. However, wage adjustment was far from smooth and transparent.

Although wages were generally deregulated, a number of factors still distorted cost adjustments. Wage-setting institutions, wage competition between old and new firms, insider domination in large enterprises, wage arrears, soft budget constraints, and inherited enterprise-related social obligations were among these factors. As a result, the irregular adjustments in the cost of labour in the Russian economy between 1992 and 1998 were not translated directly into adjustments in employment levels. This relationship was much less transparent and straightforward than that observed in some Central and East European countries. In Russia, wage arrears de facto came to mediate unemployment and wages, with the result that the growth in unemployment was smoothed. At the same time, the burden of the deterioration in wages and the use of wage arrears was unevenly distributed, with the low-paid workers being particularly hard hit by this approach to adjustment.

In this environment, it was difficult for the labour market to move in the direction that policy-makers had initially intended. Wage differentiation grew, but it was not certain to what extent its growth reflected underlying worker productivity differences and to what extent other factors and distortions. The use of wage arrears as a major element in wage flexibility undermined the relationship between workers and employers. While wage flexibility sheltered employers from pressures to restructure and some workers from the hardships of unemployment, it left many facing the hardships of declining wages. In sum, it is probable that the excessive flexibility and other distortions weakened the adjustment process and resulted in nonnegligible social costs.

NOTES

1. As discussed in Tito Boeri, Michael Burda, and Janos Kollo, *Mediating the Transition: Labour Markets in Central and Eastern Europe* (London–New York: CEPR-Institute for East-West Studies, 1998), 60–63.

2. See, for example, Vladimir Mikhalev and Nils Bjorksten, *Wage Formation during the Period of Economic Restructuring in the Russian Federation* (Paris: OECD, 1995); *Paying the Price. The Wage Crisis in Central and Eastern Europe,* ed. Daniel Vaughan-Whitehead (London: Macmillan Press, 1998), and Elizabeth Brainerd, "Winners and Losers in Russia's Transition," *American Economic Review* 88, no. 5 (December 1995): 1094–1116.

3. Rigidity in the central wage planning varied over time. In the 1980s, for example, strong elements of informal bargaining were undermining the whole system.

4. For any establishment, the EWT was calculated as a percentage of the average direct wage, where this wage exceeded a certain threshold. It amounted to 8.5 percent of total labour costs in 1994, for example.

5. Mikhalev and Bjorksten, *Wage Formation During the Period of Economic Restructuring,* 10.

6. By comparison, in Hungary the ratio of minimum wage to average wage was about one-third and in Poland it was even higher. See *Paying the Price,* 33.

7. Even Gorbachev's pension was fixed as a multiple of the minimum wage!

8. Standing came to a similar conclusion. He found that in 1994 a majority of privatised firms were still using the tariff system and that this was especially true for larger firms. Practises such as this reflected the continuing informal and institutional linkages between these firms and public sector systems (Guy Standing, *Russian Unemployment and Enterprise Restructuring: Reviving Dead Souls* [London: Macmillan Press, 1996], 116).

9. See, for example, Franz Hoffer, *Traditional Trade Unions during Transition and Economic Reform In Russia* (Geneva: ILO Working Paper, August 1997).

10. Natalya Dunaeva and Tatyana Chetvernina, "Praktika zaklyucheniya kollektivnykh dogovorov na predpriyatiyakh razlichnykh form sobstvennosti" (Practice of Collective Bargaining at Enterprises with Different Types of Ownership), *Voprosy ekonomiki* 1 (January 1996): 99–100.

11. Brainerd, "Winners and Losers in Russia's Transition," 1110.

12. This does not refer to entrepreneurial income but rather wage competition.

13. The 1998 financial crisis heavily affected private firms, causing drastic wage cuts in many of those that managed to survive.

14. Real wages are defined here as nominal wages deflated by the consumer price index.

15. Anders Aslund, "Social Problems and Policy in Postcommunist Russia," in *Sustaining the Transition: The Social Safety Net in Postcommunist Europe,* ed. Ethan Kapstein and Michael Mandelbaum (New York: Council for Foreign Relations, 1997), 126–127.

16. See also "Na Rusi zhivetsya luchshe, chem schitaetsya," *Izvestia* 4 (December 1997).

17. It should be noted that underreporting of wages was a common practice in Russia. As it cannot be assumed that this practise was constant over time or between groups, all Russian wage statistics should be viewed as approximate with respect to absolute levels, relative levels, and trends.

18. *Russian Economic Trends* 6, no. 1 (1997): 69.

19. Wage arrears were a problem for all the CIS countries. For example, on Uzbekistan see Jeni Klugman, "Wages in Transition: The Case of Uzbekistan," a thesis submitted for a Ph.D. degree at the Australian National University, December 1998.

20. *Russian Economic Trends* 6, no. 1 (1997).

21. For more information on arrears in the Russian economy, see Gilles Alfandari and Mark Schaffer, "'Arrears' in the Russian Enterprise Sector," in *Enterprise Restructuring and Economic Policy in Russia,* ed. Simon Commander, Quimiao Fan, and Mark Schaffer (Washington, D.C.: The World Bank/EDI, 1996), 87–139; Barry Ickes and Randy Ryterman, "From Enterprise to Firm: Notes for a Theory of the Enterprise in Transition," in *The Post-Communist Economic Transformation: Essays in Honor of Gregory Grossman,* ed. Robert Campbell (Boulder, Colo.: Westview Press, 1994), 83–104; Daniel Treisman, "Fighting Inflation in a Transitional Regime: Russia's Anomalous Stabilization," *World Politics* 50, no. 1 (January 1998): 235–265; Nadezhda Ivanova and Charles Wyplosz, "Arrears: The Tide That Is Drowning Russia," *Russian Economic Trends* 8, no. 1 (Winter 1999): 24–35; among others.

22. *Russian Economic Trends* 6, no. 3 (1997).

23. A list of possible reasons is offered, e.g., by Vaughan-Whitehead (*Paying the Price,* 28–29). See also Simon Clarke, "Trade Unions and the Non-Payment of Wages in Russia" (unpublished manuscript, University of Warwick, 1997). One macroeconomic factor of importance was probably the overvalued rouble that existed during much of the transition period. The strong rouble brought significant losses to exporters, placed domestic producers at a competitive disadvantage, and, consequently, decreased budgetary revenues.

24. Clifford Gaddy and Barri Ickes, "Russia's Virtual Economy," *Foreign Affairs* 77, no. 5 (September/October 1998): 53–67.

25. The original usage of the term in this context is attributed to Gaddy and Ickes, "Russia's Virtual Economy."

26. One notable exception to the tendency can be seen for most of the years shown in chart 5.2. Each December employers tended to pay supplements to partially compensate for previously accumulated wage debts (the traditional practice of paying a thirteenth monthly wage or additional year-end bonus was modified to partially compensate for wage arrears). This resulted in temporary increases in real wages and decreases in arrears. Then, each January, both indicators tended to resume their previous trends.

27. Padma Desai and Todd Idson, "The Wage Arrears Crisis in Russia," (unpublished paper, Columbia University, 1997); Hartmut Lehmann, Jonathan Wadsworth, and Alessandro Acquisti, "Grime and Punishment: Job Insecurity and Wage Arrears in the Russian Federation" (Bonn, IZA Discussion Paper no. 65, October 1999); and John Earle and Klara Sabirianova, "Wage Arrears in Russia: An Exploration of Causes and Consequences" (unpublished paper, Stockholm, SITE, 1998).

28. Earle and Sabirianova, "Wage Arrears in Russia: An Exploration of Causes and Consequences."

29. See the Data Sources Annex for an overview of the RLMS.

30. It is also worth noting that managers and entrepreneurs fared best in this regard, as they tended not to suffer from nonpayments of their wages or incomes.

31. See Branko Milanovich, *Income, Inequality, and Poverty during the Transition from Planned to Market Economy* (Washington, D.C.: World Bank, 1998), 44, figure 4.4.

32. These two reasons often coincided.

33. Vladimir Gimpelson, *Politics of Labour Market Adjustment: The Case of Russia* (Budapest, Collegium Budapest, Institute for Advanced Study, Discussion Paper Series, no. 54, November 1998), 15–17.

34. However, ideological goals did not quite fit the reality. In pre-transition Russia, both income and wage inequality were somewhat greater than in most of Central and Eastern Europe and clearly greater than in low-inequality OECD countries like the Nordics. See Milanovic, *Income, Inequality, and Poverty during the Transition from Planned to Market Economy.*

35. Brainerd, "Winners and Losers in Russia's Transition," 1103.

36. It is also worth noting that wage distribution across sectors determined a great deal of geographical differentiation.

37. During the earliest years of the transition, the scale of benefit-related infrastructure was quite substantial. For example, Kapstein cites data from the Russian Economics Ministry showing that as of 1993, enterprises held the majority of the assets related to vacation resorts and sports facilities (80 percent) and kindergartens (61 percent). In the same year, 39 percent of housing assets were enterprise controlled (Ethan Kapstein, *Economic Restructuring and Defence Conversion in a Russian City: The Case of Zhukovsky, Moscow Oblast* [Paris: OECD, 1995]).

38. E.g., see Irina Tratch, Martin Rein, and Andreas Woergoetter, "Social Asset Restructuring in Russian Enterprises: Results from a Survey in Selected Russian Regions," in *The Changing Social Benefits in Russian Enterprises,* ed. Douglas Lippoldt (Paris: OECD, 1996), 95–111.

39. Richard Rose, "Evaluating Workplace Benefits: The Views of Russian Employees," in *The Changing Social Benefits in Russian Enterprises,* 39–60.

40. A presidential decree (no. 168) in 1993 mandated transfer to local governments of prior-existing enterprise-held housing units and certain other social assets. However, this decree was implemented unevenly, constrained in part by the ability of local government to take on management and subsidisation of the facilities. For more details see *The Changing Social Benefits in Russian Enterprises* (Paris: OECD, 1996).

6

Social Protection and Labour Market Adjustment

OVERVIEW

Early in the Russian economic transition, reform-minded policy-makers realised that social protection for labour market participants would play a critical role in winning popular support for economic restructuring, protecting losers in the transition process, and facilitating the reallocation of labour toward more productive pursuits than in the past. Establishment of a new system of social protection was a major undertaking that presented a number of challenges. Not only did it require action on the part of the state to develop a legislative basis, funding sources, and new or restructured institutions, it also involved development of new social norms. Workers and employers had to learn to function under the evolving economic conditions. Unemployed workers had to learn to overcome the stigma associated with their situation and, where necessary, to seek help from the newly created State Employment Service (SES). As the transition period unfolded, the system of social protection did indeed play a significant—but not always positive—role in the Russian model of economic transition and adjustment. This chapter looks more closely at the nature of this role, focusing exclusively on the implications for those participating in the labour market.[1]

Fear of unemployment ran deep in the Russian population. In response, already in 1991 the new Employment Law laid out key protections and guarantees and established the basic principles for the operation of the new SES that would administer unemployment benefits and other labour market programmes. In subsequent years, the designers of the new system gained experience and adjusted the model, often drawing on lessons from other transition and OECD countries and, in some cases, benefiting from a range of foreign technical and material assistance. Model SES local offices were established to test and refine new approaches and then roll them out. While some successes were achieved, this new safety net also proved to be imperfect and in some cases ill-suited to the Russian realities.

Despite the promise embodied in the new policies and institutions, from the out-set questions arose as to the appropriateness and effectiveness of the system in protecting workers and facilitating labour market adjustment. To a certain extent, it is understandable that expectations exceeded the capacity of the new social pro-tection mechanisms. On the one hand, much of the population was experiencing new insecurity; on the other, policy-makers were dealing with a situation for which there had been no precedent. The SES came under attack in the press and in popular perceptions for failure to utilise resources efficiently or effectively, charges that were sometimes unfair and sometimes grounded in truth.

The criticisms of insufficient support for those being laid off focused on only part of the problem. Regardless of its success or failure in offering social protection to dislocated workers, the system offered little effective help to other unemployed and more or less completely failed in its efforts to address the issue of "hidden unem-ployment" (a term that referred mainly to the underemployed). That is, the legal mandate of the SES pushed it to assist first of all the job-losers, then to a lesser ex-tent to provide services or limited financial or material assistance to school-leavers or re-entrants to the labour market. Other job-seekers—such as those in work, but facing deteriorating conditions—could count on only limited placement services.

Little social protection was available to those workers placed on administrative leaves, working short-time, or suffering from wage arrears. Although an act of the Supreme Soviet in 1993 authorised the use of Employment Fund resources to pre-serve jobs at risk (e.g., by providing low-cost loans to support jobs at firms that were "assessed" as being temporarily down on their luck), such support was very limited and, in many cases, probably served mainly to slow restructuring by mak-ing it easier for inefficient firms to avoid lay-offs.[2] In addition, workers on leave without pay or on extended short-time could apply for a minimal benefit (a por-tion of which was reimbursable). These measures did little to ameliorate deterio-rating conditions of employment. Moreover, those workers who quit their jobs in the face of declining real wages were considered to have left their jobs on a "vol-untary basis," an action that deprived them of severance pay.

By the mid-1990s, SES difficulties in delivering services were compounded by shortfalls in Employment Fund revenues, due to a decrease in the legislatively set employer contribution rates and an increase in employer contribution arrears. In many regions, the SES fell behind in the payment of unemployment benefits and was forced to reduce active labour market programmes. Some SES officials com-plained that benefit outlays could have been balanced if only it were possible to limit the size of benefits or exclude certain claimants, such as those with alterna-tive income sources or who had only recently entered the labour market.

The problems in targeting and operating the social safety net were linked, in part, to design flaws in the system of social protection itself. The attempt to establish a full range of labour market programmes more or less exceeded the capacity of the system and institutions to adapt, a problem compounded by the rivalry between the federal and regional authorities for control of resources and policy. Moreover, as one might expect, the system could not be insulated from the overall economic malaise, which ultimately took its toll.

UNEMPLOYMENT

The political debate swirling around the SES was compounded by confusion as to the actual level of unemployment, given the huge gap between LFS unemployment (ILO definition) and registered unemployment (chart 6.1). Hostile politicians pointed to high and worsening survey unemployment and called for more to be done; government sources sometimes cited registered unemployment, which was much lower and which actually began to fall in 1996 as a consequence of administrative changes (linked to Employment Law amendments) and benefit arrears that discouraged registration.

The chart highlights the divergent trends in Russia between the levels of LFS unemployment and registered unemployment, particularly in the period following the Employment Law changes of 1996. It also highlights the large gap between the

Chart 6.1 LFS Unemployment, Registered Unemployment and Persons Eligible Unemployment Benefits ('000s)

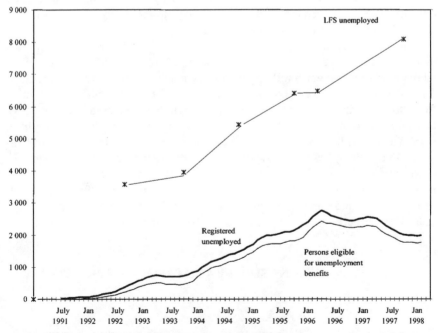

Note: The October 1997 LFS unemployment figure is based on OECD Secretariat estimates.
Sources: OECD-CCET labour market database; *Russian Economic Trends*.

overall number of LFS unemployed and the number of persons registered as being eligible for unemployment benefits. Although the ratio of LFS unemployed to those registered as being eligible for benefits decreased from 16:1 in October 1992 to less than 3:1 in March 1996, it subsequently began to increase, rising to about 4.6:1 in October 1997. Data on unemployment benefit recipiency presented in Commander and Tolstopiatenko (1997) imply that as of 1995, recipiency in some European transition countries amounted to between roughly 25 and 45 percent of LFS unemployment.[3] In Russia, as of October 1997, recipiency appeared to be about 20 percent of LFS unemployment. Although most registered unemployed in Russia were eligible for benefits, most unemployed in Russia were not registered.[4]

Certainly, tracking registered unemployment was useful for administrative purposes and as an indication of the take-up of SES services. But the administrative changes in the mid-1990s that helped to limit the growth in this figure could not mask the worrying increase in the actual number of Russians without work, available for work, and actively looking for work. As shown in chapter 2, job creation rates remained extremely low. Although churning in the labour market helped to provide job opportunities for many unemployed, the number of workers in stable employment was declining. The fact that this happened gradually gave the SES some breathing space and time to develop its capacities. And the SES took advantage of this opportunity to expand its office network, automate many of its systems, and standardise its procedures, among many other enhancements. Nevertheless, such improvements could do little to help the unemployed in the absence of new jobs or sufficient programme resources.

Although many individuals who separated from their jobs were able to avoid a spell of unemployment by moving job-to-job, a significant portion of labour market participants fell into unemployment and some turned to the SES for assistance. Chart 6.2 provides an indication of the gross inflows and outflows to jobs with respect to the pool of unemployed registered with the SES. During the period shown, there were fairly substantial monthly outflows into employment, with some variation. The average monthly rates declined from about 5 percent in 1994 to a low of 4.3 percent in 1996, before recovering to an average of about 5 percent again in the first nine months of 1997. Overall, in the period between the Employment Law changes in May 1996 and the end of 1997, registered unemployment declined from 2.8 million to about 2.0 million, with net outflows occurring in all but five of the intervening months.[5]

THE STATE EMPLOYMENT SERVICE AND LABOUR MARKET POLICY

Structure of the SES

The SES was built upon the previous network of "job placement bureaux" that existed in the USSR under the State Committee for Labour and Social Questions.

Chart 6.2 Registered Unemployment, Inflows, and Outflows to Jobs

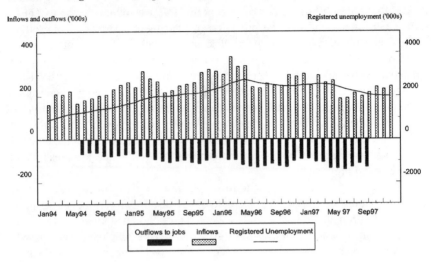

Sources: CCET Labour Market database; Current Statistical Survey

The SES was established as an independent agency in June 1992, with its legal mandate laid out in the Employment Law. This new autonomy led to tensions with the Ministry of Labour, which was cut off from much of its previous resource base and which some ministry staff considered to have lost its rightful authority over labour market programmes. In the early years of the transition, the SES network was greatly expanded and a more client-oriented approach to placement was introduced. The SES and Employment Fund had a three-tiered structure with federal, regional, and local levels. At the national level, the Federal Employment Service (FES) was led by reform-minded administrators who set out to build a nation-wide system with many of the features found in the employment services of wealthier nations. By the mid-1990s, 89 regional and roughly 2,300 local employment centres existed.

From the outset conflict arose over the management of the SES and the Employment Fund resources. The existing job placement bureaux were sometimes linked to local or regional administrations, creating allegiances that carried over into the new SES system, with local or regional groupings opposed to federal intervention. Russian Federation law granted regional civil administrations the right to determine the specific shape of certain government institutions in their territory, a right that regional officials sometimes attempted to exploit with respect to the SES. An act of the Supreme Soviet in 1993 affirmed federal control of the Employment Fund resources, but regional officials still sought to influence its use—sometimes for political ends (e.g., to fund workers helping to bring in the harvest or to support a local company with political connections).[6] The budget control mechanisms of the SES developed slowly.

The SES sought actively to facilitate the functioning of the evolving labour market. In addition to the payment of benefits, this was done—to the extent resources permitted—through the provision of placement assistance, counselling, training, and temporary employment. The proportions in the mix of assistance varied by region or locality, depending on policy priorities. As each job-seeker registered, SES staff would generally first attempt to make a rapid referral to a vacancy. Where no appropriate vacancies were available, the job counsellors would propose options from the menu of available services in an attempt to meet the needs of the job-seeker. Services were provided to employers mainly through referral of candidates, but also via provision of counselling and technical and financial support for small business and start-ups, as well as the job preservation measures cited previously.

SES managers generally sought to emphasise "active" measures, even as budget pressures increased and unemployment benefit arrears began to grow. Sometimes SES managers reluctantly accepted growth in benefit arrears as a way of rebalancing incentives; they sought to avoid giving employed persons who faced wage arrears an incentive to engineer ways to claim benefits. They argued that to pay benefits on time in regions where wages were in arrears would only lead to further labour market distortions.

Even as it expanded, the SES lacked the resources to operate as do public employment services in wealthier countries. In some cases, understaffing and physical conditions in the offices presented serious limitations. Although the staff grew by roughly 50 percent between 1992 and 1994, to reach a level of some 24,000, the SES still struggled with a ratio of staff to working-age population that was low by West European standards (e.g., 0.28 staff members per 1,000 of the working age population, compared to 0.9 in the United Kingdom and 0.6 in Germany). At the same time, it must be acknowledged that the pressure on the SES was reduced to the extent that unemployed Russians failed to register for assistance in the first place.

POLICY IMPLEMENTATION PROCESS

The broad framework and objectives for labour market policy were laid out in the Employment Law and associated decrees, amendments, and additions, although this basis for policy proved to be somewhat flexible. In general, the policy sought to support and promote enterprise, clearing of the labour market, development of skills of the workforce, and social protection and access to employment for job-seekers facing difficulties in finding work. This framework was translated into action through a series of annual or biennial employment programmes that were developed at each level of government. The employment programmes contained an assessment of the current and near term labour market situation in the corresponding administrative unit (i.e., nation, region, or locality), described the policy and programmatic response to be taken, and indicated targets and objectives for planning purposes. They were developed at the initiative of the SES but involved consultation with other key actors in the labour market, such as government officials, trade unions, and employers.

A step toward the standardising and upgrading of SES operations came with the introduction of a "Methodical Handbook," which was first approved by the Federal Employment Service Board in January 1994 and which provided a useful and concrete description of procedures. The Federal Employment Service (FES) also issued regulations to help ensure certain standards in operations. It gave support to regional and local SES structures through review of regional employment programmes, provision of guidance, staff training, and other centralised services.

Staff training, in particular, was the focus of a major SES initiative supported, in part, by foreign technical assistance providers. Many SES staff were completely new to this type of work, having backgrounds in psychology, teaching, or other fields. As with most of the Russian population, the SES staff lacked experience and knowledge of the workings of a market economy. Given the distorted form of market economy that was evolving in Russia, even successful models from abroad could not be transplanted without substantial adaptation, and in many instances particular Russian approaches had to be developed. It was a great challenge to change the "culture" of the staff and to equip them with tools for dealing with the new types of problems they were facing.

FUNDING LABOUR MARKET MEASURES

As noted in chapter 1, labour market programmes depended on an extra-budgetary fund financed largely by employer contributions. The SES had access to some other resources beyond employer contributions, including federal budget contributions that covered the salaries of SES employees at the federal level. Other sources of revenues were relatively minor and were sometimes drawn from local budget resources, voluntary contributions, profits received from commercial activities, or fees paid for some services provided to employers.[7]

The functioning of the Employment Fund was undermined by sizeable arrears due from employers—problems analogous to those affecting the regular state budget.[8] As with all state funding resources, the Employment Fund was caught up in the debate as to what shape fiscal federalism should take on in the Russian context. The amount of federal control and the size of the federal share was challenged by the regions. In addition to these "vertical" challenges to the FES, "horizontal" challenges also cropped up from other federal ministries (e.g., the Ministry of Finance) that sought to appropriate resources for themselves or to consolidate fractured budgets. In the case of the Employment Fund, the debate was poorly informed owing to the lack of transparency in operations and, in the early transition years, the lack of published information on actual expenditures. This situation fuelled initiatives to fold the Employment Fund into the state budget.

The collections of the Employment Fund were split between the regional SES structures and the FES. In the mid-1990s, the regions were authorised to retain 80 percent of the Employment Fund revenues, with the balance to be transferred to the federal level.[9] During the first years of the transition, in most regions the regional and local employment centres managed their own financial resources, which were held in corresponding Employment Fund accounts. The federal agency maintained financial reporting requirements and monitored spending plans through its annual review of each region's Employment Programme.[10] On occasion, the FES succeeded in vetoing inappropriate expenditure plans (e.g., in one case, the proposed use of Employment Fund resources to underwrite harvest activities rather than labour market programmes). Still, FES operational control over regional funds was generally rather weak. In comparison, within regions, the regional SES control of local Employment Fund resources was more effective.

The Novosibirsk region provides an example of a typical region in this regard. In October 1996, the regional office of the SES centralised the Employment Fund resources. Until 1 April 1996, the Novosibirsk branch of the Employment Fund was transferring a 20-percent share of its collections to the federal branch, as required by the federal rules. From that point on, at least through the first half of 1997, no further transfers of funds occurred in either direction between the region and the federal level despite "threats" from the federal side. As a result of the centralisation within the region, delays in payment of unemployment benefits were reduced as local surpluses were used to fund local deficit areas. The stock of arrears declined such that in January 1997 the region was able to pay benefits for November and December 1996; however, a one-month lag remained in benefit payments.

A significant portion of the federal share of Employment Fund revenues was reallocated to employment centres in regions facing shortfalls in revenue. However, to the extent this system of revenue reallocation functioned, it created incentives to avoid surpluses. Running a surplus meant loss of federal subsidies and a risk of having to transfer regional collections to the federal level. Over time, an increasing number of regions fell into deficit and stopped transferring funds to the federal agency. This in turn limited the ability of the SES to reallocate scarce resources to those regions with the greatest needs. As of early 1998, sixty-three of the eighty-nine regions had stopped transferring resources to the Employment Fund at the federal level.

Table 6.1 presents the annual budget for the SES during the 1990s. The share of GDP budgeted for employment services remained less than one-half of 1 percent throughout the decade. This is remarkably low, given the scale of disruption in the labour market. In 1995, for example, the share was comparable to that in the Czech Republic (which had a much lower unemployment rate)[11] and much

Table 6.1   Labour Market Programme Budgets (estimated) Percentage Allocation of Resources

	1993	1994	1995	1996	1997	1998	1999 Q1-3
A. ACTIVE LABOUR MARKET PROGRAMMES	87.5	79.0	62.8	48.0	38.0	38.4	37.6
Vocational training	2.4	4.3	6.6	7.3	5.5	7.3	6.9
Subsidised employment	25.5	17.6	19.8	12.0	6.4	8.0	7.4
Creation and preservation of work places	24.9	16.7	17.8	8.7	4.1	5.6	6.0
Public works	0.5	0.9	2.1	3.3	2.3	2.4	1.4
Employment service and administration	27.6	27.4	14.9	17.2	16.9	18.8	14.5
Maintenance of the employment service							
(includes some resources for job-broking)	27.3	27.1	12.8	17.2	16.7	18.7	14.5
Scientific research	0.3	0.3	0.2	0	0.2	0.1	0.0
Automated information systems of the SES	n.a.	n.a.	2.0	n.a.	n.a.	n.a.	n.a.
Other expenditure							
(includes some resources for job-broking)	32.1	29.7	21.4	11.5	9.2	4.3	8.8
B. PASSIVE PROGRAMMES	12.5	21.0	37.2	52.0	62.0	61.6	62.4
Unemployment compensation	10.3	17.8	29.2	47.6	n.a.	58.3	59.6
Early retirement for labour market reasons	2.1	3.2	8.0	4.4	n.a.	3.3	1.8
TOTAL (A + B)	100.0	100.0	100.0	100.0	100.0	100.0	100.0
Total SES budget as a percentage of GDP	0.227	0.397	0.413	0.339	0.350	0.320	0.278
Memorandum items (billions of current rubles)							
Total SES budget	377	2,407	6,400	7,284	8,822	8,584	8,677
Nominal GDP	166,297	605,893	1,550,465	2,145.7	2,521.9	2,684.5	3,119.2

Notes: n.a. = not reported separately. SES budgets and nominal GDP for 1996–1999 are denominated in "new" rubles.
Sources: Russian Economic Trends, and the Ministry of Labour and Social Development, cited from Tatyana Maleva, "Labour Market Policy" (unpublished paper, Moscow, 2000), 7.

less than was allocated in such transition countries as Hungary and Poland (which allocated, respectively, about 1.3 and 2.25 percent of GDP to such programmes).

Although it must be kept in mind that in Russia budget allocation and budget implementation differed (e.g., due to revenue shortfalls), the table shows the intended priority given in the first half of the decade to active labour market measures such as job-broking, training, and subsidised employment. In the second half of the decade, the SES was forced to substantially reduce such active measures due to growth in unemployment benefit claims and declines in overall budget resources.

Criticism of labour market programmes continued to grow throughout the mid-1990s. This was partly due to claims of SES mismanagement, but also to overdeveloped expectations as to what labour market programmes could accomplish. These programmes were expected to help solve unemployment problems even where the larger economy failed to generate new jobs. Finally, in 1998, the Ministry of Labour succeeded in gaining control over the entire social agenda at the national level. The SES and the Ministry of Social Protection were merged with the Ministry of Labour to form the Ministry of Labour and Social Development, with its main office physically located in the former Ministry of Labour building. Plans were made to bring the Employment Fund back under the full control of a federal agency such as the Ministry of Finance, although delays occurred in implementing the latter change.[12]

ACTIVE LABOUR MARKET PROGRAMMES

The SES allocated large shares of its resources to maintaining the job-broking function (whose costs were spread across several expenditure items, including automation) and to subsidised employment. Job matching was viewed by the local employment centres as one of their key functions, and given the importance of reliable vacancy information, the SES spent substantial amounts and utilised foreign assistance in automating this activity and upgrading staff skills and procedures. The results were positive. Already in 1993, the SES claimed to have assisted in placing over 800,000 job-seekers into jobs; in gross terms, this was over 1 percent of the labour force.[13] However, as the transition progressed, expansion of the placement function was limited by failure to list private sector jobs and by a mismatch between the growing numbers of white collar unemployed and the generally manual job offerings.

Local computer databases were built up to facilitate collection, analysis, and dissemination of information on the jobs available. The Employment Law did not include a specific provision on mandatory listing of vacancies, although it allowed the SES to require employers to submit information on future "labour demand." In practice, the local employment centres often made special efforts to obtain current information on new and filled vacancies from employers on a voluntary basis. This was often done through existing networks of contacts in state and privatised enterprises (e.g., based on personal relationships built through old Communist Party ties or other personal affiliations developed under the old system). However, the lack of good working contacts with new enterprises complicated the work of the employment centres. In many areas, an overreliance on prior existing contacts developed with older enterprises, despite dedication of staff resources to developing employer contacts. At the same time, many employers lacked information or sought to avoid obligations to the SES and did not apply for the assistance on offer for selecting, training, and re-training their personnel.

Returning to the study regions considered in earlier chapters, one can take a closer look at the relative market share of the SES in job matching by drawing on the 1996 LFS data sample. Individual respondents from the five regions who had changed their principal place of employment during the twelve months prior to the survey were asked to specify the main channel by which they had found their new job (table 6.2).[14] In nearly all cases, personal contacts were the main channel for finding a job, particularly in the private sector. Nevertheless, the SES share was nonnegligible, especially among state and semiprivate firms. In the Chuvash Republic, the SES appeared to account for a share of placements comparable to (even exceeding) those in many transition countries. The table hints at substantial variation across the Russian regions, which is not surprising given the influence of local and regional administrations on the SES directly and on the environment for business in general.

Subsidised employment constituted the main SES response to hidden or partial unemployment. Early in the transition, when the Employment Fund was still in surplus, SES managers and many observers defended the SES retaining control of this off-budget fund by citing the high likelihood that a large part of hidden unemployment would translate into open unemployment and that a response would require all available resources. In the meantime, many employment centres began to include in their employment programmes preventive measures aimed at combating mass lay-offs and preserving existing jobs. They offered financial assistance to enterprises in exchange for agreements to create new jobs for the unemployed or to avoid lay-offs. This financial assistance was intended to cover just a portion of the job costs and was intended to leverage SES resources. The support was generally offered through one of two mechanisms: (i) direct subsidies and (ii) interest-free or low-interest loans made via contracts (theoretically with fixed repayment dates). However, the investment in such subsidised jobs gave rise to further criticism. Employment centres were ill-equipped to assess enterprise prospects and make sound business decisions and the allocation of subsidies was subject to political and noneconomic influences probably serving to slow down restructuring slightly.[15]

Other employment subsidies went to support small business development and self-employment. In this regard, the SES sought to stimulate entrepreneurial

Table 6.2   Successful Job Searches: Distribution of Those Finding Jobs within the Previous Twelve Months, by Types of Ownership and Method of Job Search, March 1996 (percentages)

	State	Private	Semi
Chelyabinsk Oblast			
Personal contacts	42.6	63.8	41.7
Direct application	39.4	23.2	55.0
SES employment centres	7.4	2.9	1.7
Ads in media	1.1	2.9	n.a.
Private recruitment agencies	1.1	7.2	n.a.
Other	8.5	2.9	1.7
Chuvash Republic			
Personal contacts	55.2	71.4	58.8
Direct application	24.1	n.a.	11.8
SES employment centres	10.3	14.3	23.5
Ads in media	3.4	n.a.	n.a.
Other	6.9	14.3	5.9
Krasnoyarsk Krai			
Personal contacts	40.7	40.0	33.3
Direct application	47.1	35.0	51.0
SES employment centres	5.7	5.0	7.8
Ads in media	0.7	11.7	7.8
Other	5.7	8.3	n.a.
Moscow City			
Personal contacts	44.8	70.9	55.6
Direct application	33.6	14.2	24.1
SES employment centres	9.6	0.7	5.6
Ads in media	4.8	10.1	7.4
Private recruitment agencies	0.8	0.7	1.9
Other	6.4	3.4	5.6
Moscow Oblast			
Personal contacts	43.3	56.5	51.6
Direct application	37.3	25.2	40.3
SES employment centres	4.0	0.9	1.6
Ads in media	4.7	5.4	3.2
Other	10.7	11.7	3.2

Note: n.a. = not available or not recorded separately.
Sources: Goskomstat labour force survey supplement; authors' calculations.

activity, an approach that marked a distinct break with the old system, in which such activities were considered ideologically unacceptable and illegal.[16] However, the SES initiatives were often not sufficient to overcome the resistance of local and regional governments, which mistrusted the entrepreneurial activity that they viewed as difficult to track and control. The local employment centres could offer counselling, financial support, and sometimes provision of materials and space for business operations, but in many cases this was not enough to overcome bureaucratic hurdles in other parts of government (e.g., in tax offices) or to provide protection from organised crime or other harassment.

In the early years of transition, vocational training was a relatively little used option in the country, with less than 5 percent of the unemployed participating in 1993, for example. This number increased in the mid-1990s but still remained fairly modest. According to the Employment Law and other regulations, the SES was to give priority to referral to training of benefit exhaustees, persons who could not be placed in jobs after participating in public works, and people in dire need of social protection. In these cases training was paid for through the Employment Fund, including basic stipends for trainees. Especially during the early years of transition, vocational training suffered from problems such as poor quality or outdated programmes, lack of modern equipment, and a mismatch between the training offered and available jobs. In addition, given the low levels of job creation, questions arose as to which skills to focus on in training provision. Beyond certain obvious skills, such as computer literacy or modern accounting, that were needed on a large scale, it was not clear how best to equip vocational trainees for the future.

The Kaluga region provides an example of the training issues facing SES managers. There, in the early transition years, the SES managers noted that an excessive enrollment occurred in post-secondary institutions, with an overemphasis on traditional professions that were in decreasing demand (e.g., related to industry). They estimated that more than two-thirds of the unemployed people in need of training were young persons, pointing to serious inadequacies in the structure of standard educational and training programmes and methods of instruction. At the same time, re-training of adult workers also remained a problem. Existing public training institutions tended to be used primarily for initial vocational training of young people. Very few opportunities were offered for upgrading skills or training in the new professions of adult workers, while at the same time many adult workers found it difficult to accept the necessity of re-training, especially where this was brought on by economic restructuring. Overall, the problems with course offerings and content lessened with time, in part as technical assistance contributed to improvement of SES-sponsored training and as private providers came into existence. In Kaluga, the SES actively utilised the services of such providers. Still, training continued to play only a secondary role in the mix of services offered by the SES to most of its clients.

Temporary public works jobs were organised through the SES to carry out socially useful tasks while providing the unemployed with easy access to work (i.e., the jobs generally did not require training). Initially, they were also a little used option, being viewed by most clients as having poor conditions and low pay. Still, the size of public works grew in the mid-1990s and the SES began to expend sizeable amounts on this programme, which was viewed as a way of leveraging resources (similar to employment subsidies). In most cases, public works initiatives were largely financed from employer funds, often municipalities, with resources from the regional Employment Funds covering only 25–30 percent of the cost. Activities under this programme included street cleaning, maintenance of public spaces, and work with public schools and hospitals, among others. Despite the expansion in this programme, the offerings for white collar unemployed remained quite limited.

"PASSIVE" LABOUR MARKET PROGRAMMES

Employment centres sought to give priority to early placement of job-seekers. Under the Employment Law, following the registration of a new benefit claimant, the SES had an eleven-day grace period to attempt to place the individual before the benefits became effective. For those who could not be placed, unemployment benefits constituted the main income support measure utilised by the SES. For school-leavers and re-entrants to the labour market who were registered as unemployed, these benefits offered a first line of defence for income maintenance. For dislocated workers the benefits picked up where legally mandated, employer-paid severance pay left off.

The SES administered the unemployment benefit system according to principles laid out in the Employment Law and its various amendments and additions. The key provisions are summarised in box 6.1. At first glance, the unemployment benefits system would seem to have provided a fair degree of income support; benefit conditions might seem to have been relatively generous and the benefit levels adequate. However, many unemployed failed to register or to satisfy the various administrative requirements. In the first year or two of SES operations, a fair number of registered unemployed were not granted benefits; in December 1993, about one-third of this group was not receiving benefits (although this later improved). Once an individual qualified, inflation quickly eroded the value of the benefits, especially in the early transition years and following the periodic economic shocks. Payments were not indexed and for many claimants they quickly fell to equal the low minimum benefit (roughly the minimum wage), which was insufficient for even a poverty level existence. In December 1994, for example, this monthly benefit was roughly 20,500 roubles; by comparison, the average wage nationally was 354,200 and the official subsistence minimum was on average 145,400. Moreover, the value of the average unemployment benefit relative to the average wage declined over time. Commander and Tolstopiatenko (1997) calculate that this fell from about 24 percent in 1992 to about 9 percent in 1995.

The impacts of the low value of benefits were mixed. It can probably be said that unemployment benefits did not exert a pull on labour from enterprises; indeed, they may have induced some socially minded managers to retain and attempt to protect surplus workers. Also, as noted in chapter 2, most workers who quit their jobs appeared to move job-to-job rather than into unemployment; for these workers, unemployment benefits were generally not a necessity but rather some kind of very modest insurance in the event that their new jobs did not work out. Some individuals, particularly those claiming to be re-entering the labour market, may have seen the benefit as a windfall and, despite the administrative hassle, may have filed a claim even though they had no real intention of working. Also, some unemployed who

---

Box 6.1   An Overview of the Main Features of Unemployment Benefits

The Law on Employment of the Population in the Russian Federation (1991–1996, as amended) laid out the basic unemployment benefit provisions:

Work required to be eligible for regular benefits—Originally, only 12 weeks of work during the previous 12 months were required. This was increased to 26 weeks in April 1996.

Duration of regular benefits—Up to 12 months during an 18-month period. (There were special pre-retirement provisions: persons who were eligible for old-age pensions but had not reached pensionable age could receive benefits for up to 24 months during a 36-calendar-month period.)

Amount—The regular unemployment benefit for job-losers was based on the average monthly wage during last two months prior to the job loss (from April 1996, the average of the last three months' wages). The benefit amounted to 75 percent of the average wage for three months, then 60 percent for the next four months, and then 45 percent for the last five months.

Main conditions—The claimant had to be without work or wage (excluding severance pay), capable of work, available for work, seeking work, and registered with an employment centre.

Minimum benefits—First time job-seekers, re-entrants, and persons "without a profession" were eligible for a minimum benefit amounting to the minimum wage. From April 1996 onward, those exhausting regular benefits were also eligible for this benefit.

Dependent allowance—Benefits for unemployed persons with dependents were increased by 10 percent per dependent (after April 1996, this became one-half of a minimum wage for each dependent, not to exceed a total one and a half times the minimum wage).

Financial and other assistance—Unemployed persons who exhausted their unemployment benefits and dependents of the unemployed were also

---

Box 6.1   Continued

eligible to receive a further ad hoc benefit called a "material allowance" under the original Employment Law and subsequently called "financial and other assistance." This included in-kind assistance and subsidies for housing, use of children's preschool establishments, public utilities, public transportation, health care, and public catering facilities. The amount of material allowance was limited to be no greater than the minimum wage. In practice, until April 1996, material assistance was often used to bridge a spell during which the unemployed person would requalify for unemployment benefits (after 6 months).

Source of funding—The State Employment Fund financed unemployment benefits ad mot other activities of the SES primarily through an employer payroll contribution. This levy was initially set at 2.0 percent of payroll, but then was reduced to 1.5 percent in January 1996.

---

were working informally may have taken advantage of benefits as a kind of subsidy. The SES was not well equipped to monitor disqualifying incomes; checking on these was generally left to the local tax office. The main constraint on such claims was the annoyance of having to report to the employment centre twice a month—which for many probably made the small benefit seem not worth it.

For those who were forced to depend on unemployment benefits following a lay-off, the low benefits had dire financial consequences. Moreover, by 1996, funding shortfalls had led to widespread arrears in payment of unemployment benefits. Many unemployed failed to receive their benefits or were offered the chance to accept goods in lieu of benefit, but these items were often of limited value, generally consisting of surplus production provided by employers who claimed to be unable to pay their contributions to the Employment Fund in cash.

Astrakhan provides a case in point. In that region by May 1997, delays in benefit payments had grown to six months or longer. Managers at the regional SES office complained that the previous system left the population with a widespread attitude of dependence on the state; they felt people were not equipped to take responsibility for their lives under the new system. The SES took a tough approach, informing the unemployed at the time of their registration about the arrearages. Only those with no other source of income received cash benefits sooner than the standard delay, which could extend up to a year. (There was also some deflection of particular hardship cases to the local social protection department.) Astrakhan city pioneered a system whereby enterprises could settle "in kind" a portion of their overdue Employment Fund contributions. The unemployed were offered the opportunity to accept goods (valued at above-market prices) in lieu of benefits.

The regional officials were sufficiently optimistic about this approach that they made a proposal to the Ministry of Labour and Social Development for a legislative change that would codify the system.

For those unemployed who exhausted their benefits, the situation varied by region. Although the original Employment Law provided for the possibility of further assistance, particularly assistance with housing and utilities or other basic needs, in practice this "material assistance" was left to the discretion of regional and local offices. In many regions, prior to the onset of dire shortfalls in the Employment Fund, it appears that exhaustees continued to be paid a benefit at the rate of the minimum wage. While long-term unemployment remained low, this was deemed not to pose too much of a burden on the system. Other regions reported that they routinely cut off most benefits at the end of the basic eligibility period or offered one-time cash payments or in-kind assistance. As the system came under greater financial stress in the mid-1990s, regions tended to become tougher with respect to extending benefits, despite changes to the Employment Law in 1996 that appeared to mandate in many cases the payment of at least a minimum benefit.

In the case of redundant workers, severance pay constituted an additional protection. Employers were required to provide dismissed workers with up to three months of severance pay based on their previous average wage (with a proportionately smaller severance pay awarded if the worker found another job during those three months). In the early years of the transition this benefit was paid prior to the potential payment of twelve months of regular unemployment benefits, effectively entitling workers to unemployment benefits for a period of up to fifteen months. Following the passage of the amendments to the Employment Law in 1996, the unemployment benefits could be paid concurrently with severance pay; the combined payments offered a hope of sufficient income during the first few months following a redundancy.[17] Severance payment requirements probably had an influence on management decisions not to engage in lay-offs. Given the intense financial pressures and inflationary expectations confronting managers, they might be expected to make decisions with respect to short planning horizons. In this situation, managers gave substantial weight to avoiding lay-offs and potential severance pay obligations. In the short run, it was probably less costly to retain workers on unpaid leave or short-time or to encourage voluntary quits.

A further tool available to the SES was the option of early retirement for those unemployed who were within two years of the regular retirement age. Under this system, once early retirement was granted, the regular Pension Fund took on the burden of handling payments to the beneficiary. Up to the regular retirement age the Employment Fund reimbursed the Pension Fund for the cost of these benefits. This arrangement led to tensions between the Ministry of Social Protection and the SES, as the Ministry was already struggling to meet unfunded pension obligations and viewed this as an expansion of its clientele and administrative burdens. Nevertheless, the SES succeeded in expanding the programme in the mid-1990s and it was allocated 8 percent of the SES budget in 1996.

CONCLUSION

The establishment of a system of social protection for labour market participants was seen as a priority by policy-makers hoping to facilitate the reallocation of labour and to cushion hardship. On the one hand, to a limited extent they succeeded. The SES, for example, opened a new channel for job matching that came to play an important role in the functioning of the labour market. Some workers retrained or otherwise assisted by the SES were able to move into new jobs. Severance pay requirements helped some workers who were actually laid off to deal with the short-term financial disruption in their lives. Some unemployed facing particular hardship were assisted through state-provided benefit programmes.

On the other hand—and in some ways this was probably more notable—the system of social protection for labour market participants became a complement to the peculiar Russian model of labour market adjustment. Negative public perceptions of the social safety net probably contributed to worker acceptance of deteriorating conditions of employment and to resistance to risk-taking by many labour market participants. Through its limited scheme of employment subsidies, the SES may have actually supported firms that sought to postpone deep restructuring. The SES contributed to the malaise of arrears through its failure to honour its obligation to pay benefits in full and on time and its failure to enforce mandatory Employment Fund contribution requirements (sometimes with the tacit agreement of Employment Fund managers who were shielding enterprises that were already in distress).

Although the framework for a modern employment service was established, the model was never fully implemented. One critical issue was the failure to integrate all elements into the system, with a balance between the centralised and decentralised elements. Another was the failure to establish clear, authoritative, and transparent budget management, a shortcoming that was particularly damaging to the SES public image. Impediments sprang up in numerous other areas, including uneven quality of management, budget shortfalls in the mid-1990s, and political challenges from other agencies and opposition parties. Although the employment centres demonstrated a capacity to innovate and to take initiative, this was not sufficient to surmount the difficulties facing the agency.

The social safety net would have profited from improved coordination and integration between labour market policy and other policies, as well. For example, in some cases, the administration of early retirement benefits could have been improved. In other cases, little cooperation existed between local social assistance departments and local employment centres in meeting the needs of destitute members of the labour force.

In terms of social protection, a critical issue was the unsatisfactory benefit system, with its relatively broad eligibility, arrears, and low benefit levels. The benefit shortcomings probably contributed to the development of poverty among those who might have depended on unemployment benefits. Narrower targeting of benefits might have ensured better support for those who needed it.[18] A reduction in the range of services offered by the SES might have freed resources for meeting its basic obligations.

The core issue for the SES, however, was that labour market and social policy could not be expected to overcome the larger problems in the Russian economy; policy in these areas could not be expected to address in full the issues of lagging job creation and the need for deep restructuring in enterprises (a problem linked to underemployment and arrears). In an environment of broadly advancing economic reform, the SES would have faced better odds of fulfilling its natural role of providing temporary social protection to dislocated workers in transition and facilitating the clearing of the labour market. The failure to address these broader economic issues while developing a credible and sustainable social safety net probably had political repercussions that contributed to a perpetuation of the malaise . . . a point revisited in chapter 7.

NOTES

1. The discussion here excludes other aspects of social protection related to those exiting the labour market (e.g., pensions) or to those not in the economically active population (e.g., much of social assistance, which targeted primarily poor elderly persons and children).

2. See the Annex to Act No. 5131-I of the Supreme Soviet of the Russian Federation dated 8 June 1993, Regulations for the Federal State Employment Service of the Russian Federation (in Russian).

3. Commander and Tolstopiatenko present data on shares of registered unemployed receiving benefits. Taking into account the ratio of LFS unemployment to registered unemployment, recipiency as of 1995 was roughly: 26 percent in Bulgaria, 39 percent in the Czech Republic, 43 percent in Hungary, and 33 percent in Poland. The actual recipiency rates may have deviated from these percentages because calculations using the aggregate numbers fail to take account of the fact that not all registered unemployed may be considered unemployed according to LFS criteria (Simon Commander and Andrey Tolstopiatenko, "Unemployment, Restructuring and the Pace of the Transition," in *Lessons from the Economic Transition: Central and Eastern Europe in the 1990s,* edited by Salvatore Zecchini [Paris and Dordrecht, Netherlands: OECD and Kluwer, 1997], 331–350).

4. Unlike many transition countries, where generally less than half of the registered unemployed were benefit eligible, in Russia once an individual was registered as unemployed, he or she was—in principle—likely to be eligible for unemployment benefits. In the early years of transition about two-thirds of the registered unemployed were eligible, but by the fall of 1997 this had improved to about 90 percent. In part, the high eligibility was linked to the relatively low levels of long-term unemployment (which helped to limit the number of benefit exhaustees to a lower share of the total than in many transition countries).

5. *Current Statistical Survey,* Goskomstat, no.1 (1998).

6. See the Annex to Act No. 5132-I of the Supreme Soviet of the Russian Federation dated 8 June 1993, Regulations for the State Employment Fund of the Russian Federation (in Russian).

7. The OECD conducted a case study of three local SES centres in 1994 (Lyudmila Nemova and Douglas Lippoldt, "Implementation of Labour Market Policy by the Russian Employment Service," in *The Regional Dimension of Unemployment in Transition Countries*

[Paris: OECD, 1995], 467–509). The 1994 employment fund budgets for these centres, for example, anticipated that employer contributions as a share of total revenues would amount to 94.8 percent in Zhukovsky (Moscow Oblast), 96.7 percent in Kaluga (Kaluga Oblast), and 98.4 percent in Dzerzhinsky Rayon (Kaluga Oblast).

8. One source of difficulty in management of the Employment Fund revenues was the split chain of authority. Employer contributions were collected through the local tax inspections, but employers were also required to report each quarter to the local employment centres about payments made. The employment centre staff were responsible for conducting periodic check-ups. Employers were sometimes able to exploit the gap in bureaucracies to avoid making timely contributions.

9. Until 1 July 1994, the regions were authorised to retain 90 percent of the total.

10. The FES monitoring and control tightened somewhat over time. For example, the SES issued a standardised format for reporting on revenues and expenditures of the State Employment Fund—a procedure approved by Goskomstat in September 1993. Until then, the financial reporting varied across the employment centres, which limited transparency.

11. In 1995, the unemployment rate in the Czech Republic—at 3.6 percent of the labour force—was less than half of the Russian rate.

12. This consolidation was part of a larger federal attempt to regain control of fiscal affairs. According to *Russian Economic Trends* (July 1998), a government review in 1998 found some 28,000 off-budget bank accounts held by various budget-financed organisations, presumably including those of the Employment Fund.

13. However, it should be noted that in Russia, as in OECD countries, it is difficult to track closely outflows from the job seeker register. Some individuals may have been placed more than once during the year; others found employment as a result of an SES referral, but the SES may not have been informed. (Placement data are from Federal Employment Service of Russia, *Rynok truda Rossii v 1993 gody [osnovnie pokazateli]*, Statistichesky bulletin no. 1 (1994) [The Russian Labour Market in 1993: Main Indicators], Moscow).

14. Chelyabinsk, Chuvash Republic, Krasnoyarsk, and Moscow city and region.

15. The effect was modest because the scale of subsidies was dwarfed by the size of the underemployment problem. For example, the entire employment subsidy budget of about 423 billion rubles in 1995 amounted to less than one-eighth of the mid-year total wage arrears in industry, construction, and agriculture.

16. Genuine private activity outside agriculture was legalised in 1987 after the adoption of the Law on Individual Labour Activity, allowing individuals to be self-employed. In 1989, it was estimated that the self-employed accounted for about 0.2 percent of total employment in the USSR.

17. In practice, many workers experienced a decline in real wages prior to lay-off. Often they came from troubled enterprises and had been placed on leaves or short-time. As a result, the severance payments were less than they would have been, based on the individual's previous salary adjusted for inflation. Thus, they were often less generous than they might at first appear.

18. For example, this might have been accomplished by abolishing the previous earnings-related approach and establishing a flat-rate benefit scheme linked to subsistence minima, disqualifying those claimants without recent employment, and taking into account regional variations in living costs.

7

The Politics of Labour Market Adjustment

OVERVIEW

The main characteristics of labour market adjustment in Russia can be summed up in just a few lines. Expectations of substantial job losses early in the transition were not met. Unemployment grew slowly, its growth moderated by increases in certain forms of underemployment and steady declines in labour force participation. Wages were eroded by inflation during the major macroeconomic shocks in early 1992, late 1994, and mid-1998, but recovered somewhat during the intervals between the shocks. These periods of partial recovery, however, also saw growth in the volume of unpaid wages. Ultimately, by mid-1998, wage arrears came to affect almost half of the country's employees. The social groups that bore the brunt of the labour market adjustment costs—manifested in declining incomes—were the ones with the least marketable resources and the weakest political voice.

Negative wage flexibility probably contributed to temporary successes with macroeconomic stabilisation by helping to reduce fiscal outlays and contain potential inflationary demand in the early stages of transition.[1] Together with stalled structural reforms, weak regulatory institutions, incomplete fiscal adjustment, and weak fiscal discipline, it helped to soften budget constraints for existing enterprises and reduce incentives for their restructuring. While this environment helped firms to avoid or delay permanent closures, it also inhibited creation of new enterprises.

A variety of political and economic factors were instrumental in producing these outcomes. This chapter explores the interaction between politics and economic policy and the implications this had for labour market developments. In this context, two interdependent questions are raised:

- How did politics and political institutions contribute to the Russian model of labour market adjustment?

165

- How did this mode of labour market adjustment contribute to political developments? In other words, what feedback was there from the adjustment process to Russian politics?

Despite some achievements in reform, the Russian political leadership during the period from 1992 to 1998 was reluctant or politically unable to introduce and enforce consistent measures to support economy-wide, market-oriented structural and institutional change. It is probable that policy-makers would have perceived proposals to modernise public finance or expose enterprises to the full force of market pressures as being politically too costly. If implemented, such ideas would have negatively affected many powerful groups in the society. Enterprise closures and deep industrial restructuring would have placed a broad spectrum of workers at risk of unemployment; while many managers would have lost possibilities for rent-seeking through their enterprises, many local officials have might faced a loss of power, and already deficient social protection systems might have been stressed to the breaking point, among other possible outcomes. Such fears stimulated a strong opposition to radical reform in general and led to compromises favouring the status quo or piecemeal innovation.

Even the most pro-reform governments (of Gaidar, January–December 1992, and Kirienko, April–August 1998)—had they sought to implement a clear and comprehensive reform vision—were politically too weak and short-lived to get the necessary things done. Indeed, their downfalls were linked in part to strong opposition to their reform orientations. The governments headed by Chernomyrdin, on the other hand, tended to opt for policies of piecemeal reform and muddling through. Throughout the transition period, all of the governments were either weak in the face of vested interests or partly associated with them, or were strongly divided over policy. All were constrained by existing political institutions. Often, all of these factors worked simultaneously.

Political institutions themselves supported wage arrears by inflating the total public sector wage bill. Labour market and welfare institutions, and public fear of a potential unemployment catastrophe, provided incentives for many employees to stay in "old" jobs even where conditions of employment deteriorated. Both the Russian government and stronger elements in society adapted to half-measures in the hope of a "soft landing" that would avoid rapid dislocations. Underpayment and underemployment became components of redistributive politics, shifting major social costs onto the politically and economically weakest groups in society.

WHY DID THE GOVERNMENT TEND TO SET UNSUSTAINABLE WAGES?

As argued in previous chapters, wage arrears emerged as a demand-side response to overstaffing. Instead of adjusting labour costs through lay-offs, firms tried to adjust through widespread nonpayment of wages. This raised the question as to how wages were set in the economy and why unsustainable wage claims emerged. If almost half of all firms were not able to meet their obligations, did this imply an upward institutional bias in the wage-setting machinery? Were there factors pushing all types of employers beyond the limits of their economic capabilities?

Alfandari and Schaffer suggest that wage arrears were in some sense an accounting fiction, representing a way to reduce labour compensation. "In principle, managers always have the choice between paying a low wage (promptly) or essentially promising to pay higher wages with money the firm doesn't have (or the managers won't admit to having) — that is, to accumulate wage arrears. We suspect managers promise wages in excess of the cash they have available so as to turn workers' protests toward the government authorities in order to obtain financial assistance."[2] This would mean that wage arrears in enterprises were a kind of moral hazard case. It might be one of the reasons the firms permitted wage claims to rise when the flow of subsidies first showed signs of drying up. However, the government itself was a major debtor and unable to meet its own obligations, including wage obligations. Ivanova and Wyplosz assess the development of arrears using data for the period from 1993 to 1998.[3] They suggest that financially pressed firms may have initially run up arrears to the government and then resorted to inter-enterprise arrears and arrears to employees.

Early in the transition period, high inflation helped the government and enterprises eventually to meet these nominal claims by discounting their real value. Later on, lower inflation contributed to a more rapid rise in the real value of unpaid wages. Over time the trend became to some extent self-generating, with enterprise arrears to government leading to arrears in government payments, and inter-enterprise arrears leading to further nonpayments.

The persistence of wage arrears, as well as the fact that a considerable portion of arrears was generated by the government itself, indicates that institutional factors may have played a key role in these developments. Further on, we will argue that Russia's politics were one important factor, among others, that contributed to the emergence of wage arrears. Three main features of the political landscape are considered here: (i) the political institutions responsible for fiscal policy, (ii) the multiple elections and unsettled basic political orientation and economic environment, and (iii) the cleft between the interests of the federal and regional governments with respect to distributive politics. Together they worked to push up the wage bill to unsustainable levels, resulting in arrears while limiting employment reductions.

Political Institutions

The public sector wage bill was fixed in the budget and, therefore, was a result of the bargaining between the government and the Parliament over the

major parameters of fiscal policy. The fact that the adopted budgets and revenue shortfalls resulted in persistent shortages of cash to pay wages and
salaries to public employees raises a question as to how public finances were
managed. This question focuses not so much on the day-to-day operations as
on the basic institutional rules and constraints affecting public finance.[4] These
may have offered strong incentives to executives and legislators to distort fiscal policy and, ultimately, the public sector wage policy. In turn, the public
sector wage policy was likely to influence nominal and relative wages in the
economy at large. Although mass privatisation during the period from 1992 to
1994 helped to cut off direct state funding for most enterprises, the government remained the main employer. It directly employed over 40 percent of all
employees and in addition affected wages and salaries through state orders to
firms in private and mixed ownership.

The political environment had the potential to help or hinder economic reforms. Theoretically, the organisation of social interests, the balance between parliamentary and presidential authorities, the fragmentation and polarisation in the
party system, and the nature of executive authorities and electoral systems are
among the political features that matter most. Extensive literature provides both
theoretical arguments and empirical evidence as to how these features affect successes and failures in economic reform and structural adjustment.[5] Although this
literature deals mostly with macroeconomic leverage and outcomes, leaving
labour markets outside the discussion, one can trace the impact of these environmental features on labour markets through the processes guiding macroeconomic
management and fiscal policy. For example, the processes shaping the public sector wage bill (one of the major budgetary expenditures) had a discernible effect
on unemployment and wage levels.

Let us look more closely at how public sector wage policy emerged in the Russian institutional context during the transition period. The framework for budget development was very complicated and offered many embedded implicit and explicit
veto points. The procedure was long, was not quite transparent, and at almost any
stage tended to inflate major spending items. The Ministry of Finance was responsible for drafting the annual budget proposal, which was then approved in
draft by the government. Once approved, the draft was forwarded to Parliament,
where it was discussed and reviewed by all major committees dealing with fiscal
and other economic issues. It was then subject to approval by the lower house
(State Duma) in four readings. After that, it was considered by the upper house (the
Federation Council), and if approved, it was signed by the president.

According to the Russian Constitution, the government was not generally accountable to the Parliament but almost exclusively to the president. The Parliament was in general very limited in its powers, having little direct influence on
the government but enjoying the rights of budget approval and law-making. Legislators were more likely than the government to oppose austerity measures and
take an expansionist stance. Haggard, summing up both theoretical arguments

and empirical evidence, notes that "legislators with limited influence over policy are likely to distance themselves from the chief executives, particularly during times of economic distress; this is especially true in presidential systems and where parties are weak."[6] All the points mentioned in this quotation, though they are based on many country cases, apply directly to recent Russian experience. The expansionist stance of Russian legislators was further strengthened by ideological polarisation and partisanship within the lower chamber, which was dominated by the left-wing and nationalist opposition represented by Communists, Agrarians, and Zhirinovsky's party. Independent representatives made up a significant proportion of the lower chamber and also became prone to vote in favour of short-term solutions. Facing re-election every few years, they found it difficult to support measures that were currently unpopular but that could lead to potential long-term economic gains.

In its opposition to downsizing general government, the lower chamber was explicitly and implicitly supported by the upper chamber, representing regional interests. Parliament consistently raised expenditure, in particular, increasing salaries, wages, pensions, and benefits. One reason for this was the incentive for Parliament to approve the budget without significant delays. Failure to approve a budget would have permitted the government to set its future spending based on the level of the actual (usually sequestrated) spending for the previous year. This would not only have increased monitoring costs for the Parliament and its bodies while potentially leaving the Ministry of Finance with more discretionary power, but would also have resulted in very low levels of federal expenditures. Politically, the Parliament had a strong motivation to avoid this outcome.

The incentives for the government to set an austere budget dominated but were not without dispute. All Chernomyrdin's cabinets from 1992 to 1998 were actually divided governments with strong elements lobbying for particular sectoral interests. However, the fiscal portfolios were usually controlled or influenced by more "liberal" members of the government. They were motivated by pressure from the international financial institutions, which insisted on limiting budget deficits and having budgets approved in time as a condition for external financial bailout—a point that helped to give them extra clout.

The political and economic importance attached by the government and Parliament to getting the budget passed in a timely fashion pushed both sides to compromises that raised expenditures. While draft budgets were typically tailored to limit expenditures, austere budgets could not pass in the legislature. They were sent to conference committees for conciliation, where projected spending was usually inflated. Even pro-government deputies often lobbied for particular regional or industrial groups. The conflict between the government and Parliament was, therefore, an institutional given.

The limited capacity of the government to raise revenues and collect taxes expanded the gap between feasible spending levels and the actual budget allocations.[7] In practice, the inflated budgetary allocations were often not fully

disbursed due to insufficient revenues. Revenue shortfalls led directly to payment arrears, including unpaid wages.

Political Business Cycles

Presidential and parliamentary elections also affected wage claims on the government. Between 1993 and 1996, four electoral campaigns took place, which
generated wage promises that appeared to be politically motivated. Policy
swings associated with electoral cycles are known as "political business cycles." Nordhaus formalised the hypotheses and key facts about such fluctuations in his seminal paper.[8] Although most observers have believed for decades
that incumbent politicians try to manipulate the macroeconomy before elections to increase the likelihood of re-election, the empirical evidence of this
behaviour is generally very fragmentary. In developed market economies,
well-institutionalised politics and fiscal transparency leave politicians with
limited room for such policy swings.

Russia was clearly quite different: transparency of fiscal policy was lacking
and politicians enjoyed considerable room to manoeuvre on the eve of elections.
This increased the likelihood of politically induced cycles in the Russian economy. Treisman and Gimpelson found that politically motivated manipulation of
policy in Russia was associated with significant escalation of wage spending in
the periods leading up to elections.[9] Correspondingly, the political and economic
costs of these upswings were shifted to the periods after the elections.

Table 7.1 provides statistical evidence highlighting significant pre-election
shifts in the rates of change for selected parameters for which monthly data are
available. For example, the rate of change in the minimum wage showed consistent upward shifts in all of the selected pre-electoral periods. It made sense for
politicians to focus on the minimum wage, because average wages were harder
for voters to monitor directly. Average wage data were available to voters only
with a time lag, whereas the legislatively set minimum wage was known to most
voters. Over the period 1992–1997, the minimum wage was raised eleven times,
of which seven (or 64 percent) fell in pre-election periods.[10]

Though the minimum wage was too low to affect most workers directly, the
impact of its adjustment was not purely symbolic. Public sector wages were based
on the uniform tariff scale (UTS), which was indirectly linked to the official minimum wage. In addition, all social allowances and family benefits were calculated
with reference to it, contributing to increases in total social expenditures. Minimum wage adjustments also appeared to influence wage setting outside the public sector. Real wages grew more rapidly during three of the four selected election periods than in any other spells of equal duration.[11] Only in the period prior
to the 1996 presidential elections was there a lag in real wage growth.

Did policy-makers miss the opportunity to influence the 1996 elections by adjusting wages? This would have been surprising, considering that prior to that

Table 7.1 Signs of Opportunistic Political Business Cycles (OPBC) in Russia (Change in Election Periods Relative to Mean Change in Other Similar Periods, Selected Financial and Economic Variables)

	Referendum: March–April 1993 (1 month)	Parliamentary Election: October–December 1993 (2 months)	Parliamentary Election: August–December 1995 (4 months)	Presidential Election: January–June 1996 (5 months)
ECONOMIC AND FINANCIAL POLICY INSTRUMENTS				
Change in real minimum wage (%)	2.01	2.23	.31	.29
Change in real minimum pension (%)	–.93	2.27	–.11	2.73
Change in real federal spending on health, education and social policy (Dec. 1995 roubles, billions)	n.a.	n.a.	4.14	.19
Change in real federal spending on transfers to regions (Dec. 1995 roubles, billions)	n.a.	n.a.	.03	1.10
Change in rate of growth of real monetary base (% points)	.60	.87	1.24	–.35
Change in volume of GKO's and OFZ's outstanding (Dec. 1995 roubles, billions)	n.a.	.12	.44	2.36

Table 7.1 Signs of Opportunistic Political Business Cycles (OPBC) in Russia (Change in Election Periods Relative to Mean Change in Other Similar Periods, Selected Financial and Economic Variables) (Continued)

	Referendum: March–April 1993 (1 month)	Parliamentary Election: October–December 1993 (2 months)	Parliamentary Election: August–December 1995 (4 months)	Presidential Election: January–June 1996 (5 months)
ECONOMIC OUTCOMES				
Change in survey unemployment (ILO definition, % points)	–.82	1.43	–.26	–.83
Change in real average wage (%)	2.76	.53	.15	–.57
Change in rate of increase of real wage arrears (% Dec. 1995 arrears total)	–.04	–.19	.20	–.74
Change in percent of population in poverty (% points)	–2.20	–1.46	.00	.32
Increase in inflation rate (% points)	.16	–1.18	–1.89	–.21
Increase in inflation rate in third and fourth months after the vote (% points)	3.80	.16	.22	.77

Source: This table is from Daniel Treisman and Vladimir Gimpelson, "Political Business Cycles and Russian Elections, or the Manipulations of 'Chudar,'" Discussion Paper CIRGJE-F-39, Faculty of Economics, University of Tokyo, February 1999, 12.
Note: Each figure is the mean value for the pre-vote period expressed in standard deviations above or below the mean for all equal-length periods. Figures in italics are on the side of the mean predicted by OPBC theory. All series seasonally adjusted and detrended.

election politicians had a longer time interval for inflating the wage trend than they had in previous cases, and the electoral stakes were very high. It appears that an alternative mechanism was used to adjust wages. Public sector wages were selectively raised. In the science sector, for example, the year-on-year growth in the real wages due to be paid was 12 percent. When the 1996 elections were over, the rate of wage growth in the sector fell from 15–16 percent in Q2–Q3 (compared with the same period one year before) to 3 percent in 1997 Q1.[12]

Where policy led to promises that were greater than the economy was able to deliver, wage arrears accumulated. Variables indicating the change in the rate of increase of real wage arrears are shown in table 7.1. In three out of four cases, the results are in line with the opportunistic political business cycles theory (i.e., they have significant and negative values). However, 1995 marks an exception, with a positive and modest increase in the rate of change. Real wage arrears in the pre-election period grew that year at about the same rate before and after the event. A possible explanation for this may be found in the influences of other variables. First, a drastic devaluation of the rouble between late 1994 and early 1995 significantly discounted real wage arrears and made them politically less costly. Then, in the first half of 1995, the government gave top priority to disinflation and containment of the costs of inflation, rather than limiting real wage arrears. Concurrently, the government made repeated promises to pay wage debts as soon as possible in order to create a positive background against which it could ignore the mounting stock of arrears.

Unemployment makes another interesting case in the political business cycle story. The survey unemployment rate is difficult to affect within short periods; bringing it down takes time and serious effort. Furthermore, in Russia it was expected to go up, in part due to the impact of various deflationary measures. However, in three of the four pre-election periods shown in table 7.1 the rate of increase in unemployment actually slowed. While changes in the unemployment rate are influenced by a variety of factors, it is likely that wage arrears were one contributing factor, particularly in 1995 and 1996 when they began to rise substantially in real terms and as a percentage of GDP. To the extent wage arrears reduced pressure to layoff surplus labour, they also helped to reduce the growth in unemployment. Also, nonpayment of wages was one reason for the declines in employer contributions to the Employment Fund. Shortfalls in this fund led to unemployment benefit arrears and may have increased worker resistance to lay-offs and unemployment while contributing to increased tolerance of deteriorating conditions at their jobs. Thus, the strange logic of labour market adjustment may have operated as follows: tighter monetary policy and stabilisation (or limited growth) in real wages did not lead to rapid rises in open unemployment. Instead, in some cases the rate of increase in unemployment actually fell but was combined with massive wage arrears.

Once both general elections were over, the electoral campaign shifted to the regions. Since autumn 1996, almost all Russian regions have undergone elections of governors and regional and local legislatures. These campaigns were very expensive for regional budgets, and while no special studies exist on how regional elections affected economic policy, they probably led to increases in the public wage bill as well.

Regional Governments and Redistributive Politics

Variation and change in public employment in Russian regions were associated with a number of factors. As noted previously, the various interest groups had a strong but uneven influence on adjustment policies, sometimes blocking or distorting them. Regional bureaucracies were among the strongest groups, with their own vested interests and mixed goals. Since regional governments sought to remain in office, they were afraid of growing unemployment and wage arrears that could threaten social stability. Likewise, they favoured wage increases in their regions and increased public employment (in some cases, acting as employers of last resort). Regions remained big employers and had responsibility for most of the educational and health-care facilities, as well as some housing, among other activities.

Interestingly, against the background of general contraction, some parts of the public sector actually succeeded in increasing employment in the 1990s, even in absolute terms. This clearly happened in public administration, education, and health. Although the latter two sectors had relatively low wages, their total wage bill expanded as a result of the employment growth.[13] In addition, the direction of change and the relative share of this employment varied greatly across regions. Some regions experienced a decrease in the share of public employment in the total, while most of the regions succeeded in increasing it. Most of this employment expansion happened at the regional level of government and had to be financed from regional budgets.

Most of the regional budgets were heavily dependent on financial flows from the federal government, but the rules for allocating financial transfers to regions were flexible or unclear and subject to permanent bargaining between regional and central governments.[14] In their tug of war with federal authorities, regional officials sometimes even misallocated funds earmarked for public wages and then requested new funds from the centre. This largess was also unevenly allocated.

In order to assess the nature of variation in public employment across Russia's regions, Gimpelson and Monousova considered the association of this variation with potential factors of influence during the period 1995 to 1997.[15] They ran regressions to consider whether: (i) the size of public sector employment was associated with GDP level, following the famous "Wagner's Law," whereby richer regions might be expected to have larger public sectors;[16] (ii) the regional public sector might be considered "an employer of last resort," whereby high unemployment in one period might lead to increased public employment in the next; or (iii) higher transfers from Moscow were associated with higher levels of public employment (given that the wage bill accounted for a major portion of the regional budgets).

The results are presented in table 7.2, providing robust evidence that larger transfers were likely to be associated with higher public employment. A modest inverse association also developed with regional GDP, indicating that richer regions did not tend to have larger public sectors. Subsidy-dependent and poor regions tended to employ relatively more people in the selected sectors (health care, education, and public administration). Moreover, checks on causality seem to support the assumption that the public employment was dependent, while per capita transfers were on the right-hand side of the equation. Higher unemployment was not clearly associated with higher public employment. Apparently,

Table 7.2 OLS Regression of Public Employment (PE), Cross-Sections for 1995–1997 (Standard Errors Estimated as Robust White-Corrected)

	Dependent variables		
Independent variables	*PE95*	*PE96*	*PE97*
pe92	.6225***	30.405*	26.167**
	(7.845)	(1.937)	(2.44)
Unempl	.000854	.1340	.1058
	(0.890)	(1.126)	(1.038)
Gdp	−3.25e-06	.0001887**	.0001368***
	(−1.404)	(−2.106)	(−3.734)
Transfer	.000296***	.04289*	2.7646**
	(3.225)	(1.763)	(2.196)
Capital	.0097	−3.1900	1.3751
	(0.812)	(−1.599)	(0.543)
Ethnic	.0111**	1.5202	.5738
	(2.076)	(1.656)	(0.805)
age 0–15	−.00223	−.1217	.1043
	(−1.281)	(−0.345)	(0.329)
Age ov55	−.0019	−.2355	−.2258
	(−1.565)	(−1.364)	(−1.641)
Urbaniz	−.00012	−.0451	−.0450
	(−0.486)	(−1.197)	(−1.262)
Constant	.2051**	27.803**	23.28*
R-squared	0.78	0.62	0.71
F	44.47	9.54	15.47
N	78	77	77

Notes: All independent variables are lagged by one year relative to the dependents.
*denotes significance at 10% level, ** – 5%, and *** is for 1% level. T-values are given in parentheses.
Source: Vladimir Gimpelson and Galina Monusova, "Public Employment and Redistributive Politics in Russian Regions" (paper presented at the Slavic Research Center Workshop, University of Hokkaido, Sapporo, Japan, July 21–22, 1999).

evidence of the association between public employment and financial assistance to regions did not mean that transfers were used directly to finance public employment as an employer of last resort. Among the main recipients of federal money were other sectors and, above all, the housing sector (where utilities were still heavily subsidised), which received the largest share of these subsidies.[17]

The EBRD's *Transition Report* noted that "the system of intergovernmental transfers generated numerous possibilities for ad hoc bargaining and created incentives for regional governments to keep their spending high and their revenue low. A mathematical formula introduced in 1994 to calculate regional transfer needs created perverse incentives for regions to run wage arrears as a way of extracting transfers from the federal level."[18] Such incentives led to a mass concealment of potential tax base by the regions, which was made possible by the lack of transparency in regional public finance. Instead of seeking to boost tax collection, many regional administrations were more interested in finding ways of squeezing more transfers from Moscow. Some studies provide evidence that federal subsidies to the regions were used for political appeasement in the bargaining between Moscow and regions.[19] Others like McAuley or Hanson argue that allocation of transfers had an equalising effect with respect to social need across regions.[20]

General government was the largest single wage debtor, and the relationship between public sector employment and wage arrears across regions is significant and positive. Health care and education were persistently underfunded and ran huge stocks of wage debts. Funds earmarked for wages in these sectors were reportedly channelled to other needs. The bulk of the wage bill in these sectors was to be financed from regional budgets. However, regional and local authorities often gave priority to paying wages to those working in the central administration over other budget-funded activities. Thus, administrative employees gained relative to workers in the education and health sectors, not only with respect to employment and wages owed, but also in terms of wages actually paid out to them.

The existence of overstaffed but underpaid public employment in education and health care aggravated many difficulties. The loss of skills due to employee quits and the decline in prestige and motivation contributed to lowering the quality of services. Wage arrears coupled with low basic salaries led to growing political and social tensions. Since employees in these sectors were relatively well organised and easily mobilised, they became major contributors to labour unrest, to some extent destabilising the country at large and increasing pressure on public finances (adding leverage to regional claims for more transfers). This situation eroded the middle class, as teachers, doctors, and scientists were often part of its core. It also helped to inhibit public sector reform and probably was correlated with nontransparency and corruption, all of which further undermined the credibility of the government. A vicious circle was created: increased public employment in some sectors and regions was associated with low pay and late pay due to budget constraints. Regions justified claims for more funds with large and in some cases growing public sectors, which generated more arrears. The growing stock of wage arrears was politically explosive and gave strength to regional demands for more subsidies.

Although the public sector was directly responsible for a substantial portion of the wage arrears stock, it was not the worst offender. Its share of the total fluctuated over the mid-1990s in the range of 15 to 25 percent. However, its role was much more significant than this share might suggest. The fact that government (whether federal or regional) was not committed to meeting its obligations set a pattern that became rooted as a social norm. Private sector managers were given an additional incentive to do the same. On the one hand, the Russian government lost moral authority to punish private employers. On the other hand, weak state institutions were unable to enforce labour contracts, even if they wanted to. By making incomplete and late payments, the government decreased the reservation wage for the whole economy. Instead of cutting nominal wages or using large scale lay-offs, managers reduced the real value of labour compensation, delivering it late or only partially.

WHY DID PRIVATE AND SEMIPRIVATE EMPLOYERS TEND TO SET WAGES THAT THEY COULD NOT PAY?

There are numerous reasons why private and semiprivate employers followed the government in an unsustainable wage race. First, the tariff scale designed primarily for the public sector was used by many private employers as a pay guideline. To some extent, the upward shift in the UTS indirectly translated into higher nominal nonpublic sector wage levels. Especially during the first years of transition, this occurred in large privatised firms, where managers continued to utilise traditional wage-setting approaches. Second, employers relying on wrong signals may have overestimated future cash resources. The "virtual," barter-based economy led to price confusion; widespread use of barter left firms short of cash and complicated cash flow management. Moreover, as discussed earlier, many privatised firms sold goods or services to budgetary institutions that, in turn, were often late in settling their accounts, leading to long chains of arrears. Third, the coordination between firms in wage-setting was poor, and many firms attempted to retain and motivate skilled labour by paying an efficiency wage.[21] This generated "leapfrogging" by workers seeking higher wages, as can happen when wages are settled in a decentralised way.

Delayed wage payments also reflected "the relative power of managers in relation to workers, which the standard view suggests [was] greater in Russia than in Central and Eastern Europe."[22] As Alfandari and Schaffer note, this reflected the fact that Russian managers placed much lower priority on paying workers than, for example, Polish managers did.[23] This relative power of managers had its source not only in the weakness of trade unions but even more in the inability of the state to facilitate contract enforcement and to punish violations of labour law. As Earle and Sabirianova point out, "The more general the practice, the easier it may be to persuade workers that it is somehow legitimate, or at least not the management's fault. The costs of using arrears are inversely related to their prevalence due to a decreasing probability of punishment."[24]

Small private firms did not generally hire labour from the pool of unemployed. Instead, they pulled the best workers from state or privatised firms by offering much higher labour remuneration. Their offers were often based on the assumption of low nonwage labour costs, an approach that was facilitated by evasion of taxes and social contributions. This competition between different types of employers resulted in upward pressure on nominal wages in state and privatised firms and probably helped to raise the average nominal wage level in the economy.

Finally, where the government and large employers delayed payment of legally contracted wages, and this violation of laws was not punished, it created clear incentives for all other employers to follow the practice. The result was an epidemic of wage arrears across all sectors and types of firms, including those that were profitable and faced no liquidity constraints (indeed, those firms with cash made hefty profits by investing their wage arrears in debt instruments such as the short-term state treasury bills known as GKOs). Nonpayment became a new social norm among employers and shifted the whole system to this new equilibrium. Paying "in time and completely" became a collective good and exiting from the arrears trap would have required the implementation of politically costly selective incentives (like enforced bankruptcy of large firms or punitive fines for delaying payments).

WHY DO WORKERS ACCEPT WAGE DELAYS?

While one might posit reasons for employers' behaviour with respect to wage arrears, this leaves open the question of why workers accepted such ongoing cheating in the form of late and truncated pay. To use Hirschman's famous expression, were there issues of "exit and voice" for workers? In other words, what kind of incentives and alternatives did workers have? What role did trade unions play?

One might expect that in a situation where millions of employees were not paid for months, mass social unrest would ensue. Given that the cheated workers were still at their jobs and heavily unionised, it would seem an easy task to mobilise them for industrial action. In fact, although arrears contributed to growing social tensions and protests, little of what might be called mass social unrest materialized. In view of the scale of wage delays and nonpayments, this is surprising. Wage arrears did actually cause some "wild cat" strikes and individual actions by completely discouraged people. Russian newspapers reported numerous cases of hunger strikes, blocking of strategic roads, even suicides caused by extreme de-

spair. Yet such actions appeared to contribute less to instability than did other social and political ills, such as constitutional stalemates between the executive and
legislative branches, "wars" between various Kremlin clans, and permanent in-
trigue among the Moscow political elites.

Table 7.3 reports the dynamics of strike activity in the Russian Federation since
1991. The first peak came in 1992 when the toughest stabilisation measures were
introduced. A second and stronger wave of disputes arose in 1995 and was linked
to growing wage arrears. But even this strike movement involved a smaller scale
of industrial dispute than is registered in most affluent OECD countries in a typical year.[25] Reporting these data, Goskomstat observes that the changes in the
propensity to strike closely approximate the changes in the incidence of wage arrears. According to the statistics, 99 percent of all collective actions in the economy were directly induced by nonpayments. The trend continued in 1997–1998,
with miners and teachers becoming more and more militant. May 1998 was
marked by a new surge of miners' protests over unpaid wages, which resulted in
the blocking of strategic railroads and freight traffic. Although the protests remained sectorally and geographically quite localised, they increased the pressure
on government and raised doubts about the capacity of the authorities to resist
growing fiscal pressures and wage demands.

A breakdown of the data on strikes by sectors shows that the bulk of industrial
disputes appeared in the coal and educational sectors, followed by the health-care
sector. Clearly, these sectors faced the most severe wage backlogs, though the difference in militancy between them and other sectors could hardly be attributable
to wage arrears alone.

On the whole, however, workers accepted arrears with surprising tolerance. A
number of reasons probably account for this. First, as Connor wrote, "Labour, in

Table 7.3   Strikes in Russia, 1991–1998

Year	Number of enterprises where strikes were registered	Number of employees involved in strikes, thousands	Number of participants in strikes, per enterprise, individuals	Person-days lost per employee days
1990	260	99.5	383	2.1
1991	1,755	237.7	135	9.7
1992	6,273	357.6	57	5.3
1993	264	120.2	455	2.0
1994	514	155.3	302	4.9
1995	8,856	489.4	55	2.8
1996	8,278	663.9	80	6.0
1997	18,675	836.9	45	6.5
1998	12,456	530.7	43	5.4

Source: Goskomstat.

Russia, is weak—a taker of prices, not a maker, and largely unable to exert strong influence over its environment."[26] Second, employees feared the possibility of losing their jobs and being pushed into unemployment. Third, public labour market institutions did not seem to offer much help in coping with joblessness. Thus, workers may have considered alternatives like underemployment and underpayment to be lesser evils. Each of these dimensions merits a closer look.

Weak Voice

The low level of union voice and mobilisation capacity in Russia under transition derived in part from structural changes within the labour force. Here, one could mention the growth in the non-unionised private sector and the growing heterogeneity and segmentation within the formally unionised workforce. Although trade union membership remained substantial, amounting to roughly three-quarters of the labour force, organised labour failed to exert a corresponding influence on labour market outcomes. As Connor noted at the time, "Russian trade unions are too weak to dictate terms in a turbulent transition economy. Management has the upper hand in labour disputes."[27] As in other transition economies, trade unions in Russia were divided into "old" successors of the Communist unions and "new" ones with "grass roots" support that emerged in the beginning of the democratic transformation.[28]

The Federation of Independent Trade Unions of Russia (FNPR) represented the former type of union and dominated the trade union scene. Being dependent on employers and—to some extent—the government, FNPR sought to avoid confrontation with them. In the dispute over back wages, FNPR representatives "confined themselves primarily to political lobbying in collaboration with the employers on behalf of their particular branch of the economy."[29] The new, independent trade unions emerged in late 1980s as a part of the growing democratic movement. They had limited institutional and financial resources and were confined to certain sectors or firms. Having limited mobilisation capacity, they adopted a strategy of pursuing individual employers through the judicial system, of providing legal advice and representing small groups of workers in courts.[30] Although they won in a number of cases, this could hardly change the general trend.

The more competitive employees did have both exit and voice options at their disposal and exhibited a propensity for mobility to other jobs, particularly with respect to jobs in the new private sector (as discussed in chapters 2 and 4). Even where they stayed on with their current employer, their stronger bargaining power and louder political voice enabled them to engage management directly, either individually or within small groups, and to settle disputes without intervention by the trade unions. This decreased incentives for solidarity with other workers.

Less competitive employees had a weak voice and even fewer options for exit. Underemployment weakened even further those who continued to stay on at ailing or nonpaying establishments, since those with bargaining power and voice were likely to quit. The stayers, having nowhere to go, became dependent on managers' discretion. Acceptance of wage arrears seemed the least costly option to many of them. Many believed that they could at least save their jobs, with the prospect of eventually getting their back wages and with the option of moonlighting to survive. Underemployment increased the share of social costs imposed on them, but in many cases it weakened the threat of lay-off.

The losers in the economic transition often became locked into jobs with state-run firms and firms with monopoly power. They concentrated in industries such as those related to infrastructure (e.g., railways or public transportation) or in sectors such as public education and health—all of which tended to be more centralised and/or heavily unionised than the rest of the economy. Such a situation brings to mind Freeman's warning that "Unions limited to losing groups in the public sector, as in the marketizing economies, can endanger reforms."[31] And, as Nelson wrote, "Unions in strategic sectors may exercise tremendous economic and political leverage, even if the labour movement for the nation as whole is not strong."[32] Given the high militancy of miners' and teachers' trade unions and the background of generally impotent trade unions at large, a potential for such leverage may have existed in Russia as well.

Threat of Open Unemployment

The actual or perceived threat of job loss also contributed to the acceptance of underpayment. Fear of unemployment led to reductions in workers' demands and made workers more tolerant of deteriorating terms of employment. No open unemployment had occurred in Russia prior to the start of the transition. Since reforms were expected to cause mass dislocation of labour, it was generally presumed that transition would involve very high unemployment. Warnings came from proponents of reforms as well as from opponents, though their political reasons and arguments differed.

Many political players had some stake in pushing up forecasts. Proponents of reforms wanted to demonstrate the depth of the needed transformation and the scale of existing distortions. Social sector ministries referring to these forecasts lobbied for more resources and more power in economic policy-making. Opponents of reforms manipulated figures in an attempt to stress the potential for a "national catastrophe" resulting from shock therapy. Pessimistic claims were supported by some ILO experts who favoured state-led, piecemeal, and socially oriented reforms over more macro-oriented and orthodox IMF/WB prescriptions.[33] Nearly all of the predictions overestimated the actual trend in unemployment rates (as discussed earlier). Being widely reported by the mass media, these forecasts increased public fears. Thus, even before the reforms really got off the ground, the general public expected mass unemployment and, as the popular saying goes, "fear has big eyes."

In 1989, when hardly a hint of radical economic changes was in the air, public opinion already perceived unemployment as a major problem. Half of those surveyed were afraid of losing their jobs. After 1992, roughly 70 to 80 percent of respondents were likely to admit to having such fears. These figures were fairly stable and showed little change over time (see table 7.4), despite the relatively modest levels of open unemployment.

Poland and Hungary presented a significant contrast to the Russian situation. It is probably fair to say that at the beginning of the reform process in these countries, high unemployment was generally considered to be unavoidable and an important step in the transition to a restructured market-oriented economy. Hungary began to introduce some elements of unemployment protection legislation in the late 1980s, preparing itself for forthcoming joblessness. It was commonly understood that existing labour hoarding would soon turn into rapidly growing unemployment. In Poland, the Balcerowicz government capitalised on the period of "extraordinary politics" to implement harsh and far-reaching economic measures without seeking a corresponding and simultaneous extension of the social safety net.

Table 7.4   Perception of Unemployment in Public Opinion (Percentages of Positive Responses)

	"People became more afraid of losing jobs"	*"There are unemployed among my relatives and friends"*	*"There is a threat of mass lay-offs in my enterprise"*	*"I am likely to lose my job due to enterprise closure or employment cuts"*
November 1989	49	—	—	—
November 1992	70	—	—	—
April 1993	80	41	46	37
August 1993	80	43	47	41
December 1993	—	—	—	37
January 1994	82	51	48	—
May 1994	83	60	43	46
September 1994	—	—	—	38
November 1994	77	64	34	37
March 1995	81	66	35	43
January 1996	70	70	27	36
January 1997	—	—	37	50
September 1997	—	—	29	35

Sources: Lyudmila Khakhulina, "Povedenie rabotnikov na rynke truda v usloviyakh perekhoda k rynochnoy ekonomike" (Employees' Behaviour in the Situation of Economic Transition), in *Sotsialnaya politika v period perekhoda k rynku; problemy i resheniya* (Social Policy in the Transition Period), ed. Anders Aslund and Michail Dmitriev (Moscow: Moscow Carnegie Center, 1996), 17; Informatsionny bulleten, VCIOM, no. 6. (1997).

In Russia, as noted earlier, fear of mass dislocation and soaring unemployment became an additional factor pushing people to accept deteriorating employment conditions, including wage arrears. Clarke was probably right in saying that "in this case, the problem with Russian reform is not that unemployment has not risen sufficiently high to drive wages down to a level attractive to private investors, but that the threat of unemployment has driven wages down so low that enterprises have little incentive to rationalise production and raise productivity, preferring instead to put their energies and resources into realising profits through marketing and financial speculation."[34]

Labour Market and Welfare Institutions

An efficient and effective public employment service can help the unemployed to survive periods of joblessness. The existence of such support can help to reduce resistance to restructuring and associated unemployment. Although a more detailed account of the performance of the State Employment Service (SES) is given in chapter 6, it is important to recall here that the meagre unemployment benefits were also in arrears in many regions. In some cases, the delay in benefits even exceeded the average delay in wages. The prospects of getting a new job through the SES were limited as well, since most employers did not report vacancies or were reluctant to hire the unemployed. All of this provided the less competitive workers with additional incentives to stay with their jobs.

Also, in contrast to the fear of unemployment, keeping an "old" job could provide at least some in-kind compensation. Enterprise-related social benefits added about 5 percent to total labour costs in general, but larger firms, which were most likely to be in arrears, provided most of such benefits. This portion of compensation tended to be less flexible than cash wages and was often paid even when cash was scarce. The larger the benefit portion of compensation was, the stronger the incentives for workers to tolerate backlogs in wages. This institutional feature of the Russian labour market distorted price signals to employees and so contributed to employees' acceptance of nonpayment. In turn, by accepting wage arrears, workers sent a message to employers to keep social assets intact and to take liberties in generating new wage arrears.

POLITICAL OUTCOMES OF LABOUR MARKET ADJUSTMENT

This section discusses the political pay-offs of the chosen adjustment path. Does adjustment through underemployment and nonpayments help to manage politically workers' tolerance of reforms? Or, on the contrary, does it amplify tensions? While history only informs us of the actual path taken, one may consider what otherwise might have happened; one can examine more closely key relationships between labour market indicators and such political outcomes as labour militancy and electoral support for reformers.

The existing literature on the political economy of reforms in other countries deals almost exclusively with unemployment in its open and explicit form. Rising unemployment is often considered an outcome that can topple governments and derail reforms. In the introduction to a special issue of *Comparative Political Studies* on patterns of economic voting in Poland, Peru, and Mexico, Stokes wrote that "[R]ising unemployment generated pessimism about the future and opposition to the government and reforms in all three countries. . . . Apparently, unemployment is such a catastrophic event that when people think the probability of losing their job is high, they interpret this unambiguously as bad news and hold the government accountable."[35] Przeworsky linked this argument to the post-Communist reality: "There are good reasons why unemployment should turn people against reforms. Whatever else one may think about the communist economy, it did provide full employment. Moreover, full employment was the principal mechanism of income insurance. Hence, when unemployment appeared and began to climb, people found themselves not only without jobs but also without incomes and other services that were traditionally provided by places of work. . . . Hence the prospects of unemployment are frightening."[36]

Attributing substantial weight to unemployment, Przeworsky argued (in an earlier article) that the mounting unemployment was heavily responsible for changes in political support to reforms. He wrote that "whereas they [Poles] are willing to believe that unemployment indicates that reforms are working, losing jobs is a price they are not willing to pay. The prospect of unemployment erodes support for the reform program."[37] On the other hand, exceptionally low unemployment rates observed in the Czech Republic contributed to political and social stability in the early stages of transition. This helped to stabilise Klaus's government and served as an important component in political compromise with trade unions.[38]

Now let us turn back to the Russian case. As discussed earlier, underemployment was considered by the government and public opinion to be a lesser evil than open unemployment. Social and political gains from the chosen strategy were explicitly stressed by Russian sociologist Leonid Gordon, who believed that "the Russian society has groped—partially deliberately, partially spontaneously—for a few rational methods that come with short-time employment, involuntary unpaid leaves, etc. Transition to unemployment goes here gradually, through partial employment, which is tolerated by society clearly easier than a one-time lay-off of many millions of employees. Besides that, underemployment does not always end up with unemployment."[39] This point finds agreement with some Western observers: "Amidst all the gloom, this avoidance of mass unemployment in the face of enormous structural shocks might seem to be the great achievement of the Russian transition."[40] This implies that underemployment offers some political advantages for policy-makers in comparison with open unemployment.

One of the ways to measure the political implications of this adjustment mode is to look at labour militancy; as mentioned earlier, despite the dramatic deterioration in living standards and employment conditions, it remained rather low. Would it have been higher under an alternative solution? It was not likely to be substantially different because of the tendency for "bargaining power and militancy [to] decline in hard times and increase in prosperity."[41] At the same time, the underemployment-underpayment model probably reinforced the passivity of labour; it served to redistribute losses from stronger (more competitive) to weaker (less competitive) workers, thereby segmenting the labour force and further weakening employees' voice.

Chart 7.1 illustrates how unemployment and wage arrears can affect the labour force. Let us assume that the curved line represents the distribution of workers in the Russian economy according to their bargaining power ("weak" versus "strong"). The curve is skewed towards "weak." In the chart, those heavily affected by wage arrears are to the left of the AB line. This line is almost vertical, since it separates the weakest from the strongest in a generally segmented labour market (with respect to wage arrears). The CD line designates those who were affected by unemployment, as indicated by the shaded areas. Since a portion of unemployment was due to use of bankruptcies and lay-offs, it also affected some relatively "stronger" workers. This less selective effect is reflected by the fact that CD crosses AB and is sloping. As one can

Chart 7.1   Effect of Wage Arrears Versus Unemployment on Weaker and Stronger Workers

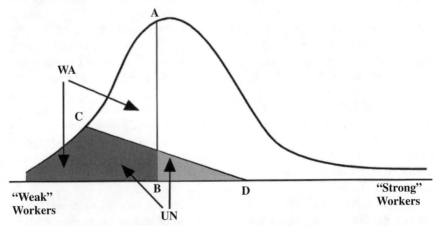

Note: WA refers to those affected by wage arrears. UN refers to those affected by unemployment.
Source: Adapted from Vladimir Gimpelson, "The Politics of Labor Market Adjustment. The Case of Russia," Collegium Budapest, Institute for Advanced Study, Discussion Paper Series, No. 54 (November 1998), 33.

see, in this example, wage arrears affected a larger number of workers than un-employment. Wage arrears also disproportionately affected those who were weaker. While unemployment affected fewer workers, it even touched some of the stronger workers.

If employers turned to lay-offs more often and wage arrears less often, line AB would shift to the left and line CD to the right. Given the nature of wage arrears as spreading partial wage cuts across a large number of workers, it is possible that similar savings might have been reaped through lay-offs, affecting fewer workers (in combination with a better utilisation of the remaining employees). This suggests a political trade-off between the two effects. Although it cannot be said with certainty, it may have been possible for the government to boost its support through a trade-off whereby a moderate increase in unemployment was offset by a larger decrease in those affected by wage arrears, especially if this was coupled with measures to pay unemployment benefits on time and thereby decrease the fear of unemployment.

In reality, however, expanding arrears moved the AB line to the right, pulling in more and more stronger workers and increasing the pool of losers. This correlated with some increase in voice from the "stronger" workers who were hurt, and it expanded the electorate's opposition to the government. Of course, this chart presents a very simplified static picture and it is difficult to assess the precise effects of an alternative policy, as the actual developments would be much more complex, subjective, and dynamic. For example, following years of unkept government promises, a substantial increase in unemployment may have prompted a strong political backlash even where genuine efforts were made to improve social protection for the unemployed.

During the transition period, Russian reforms have passed through a number of electoral tests.[42] The December 1995 parliamentary and the July 1996 presidential elections were the most recent such events in the period considered here. By the end of 1995, underemployment and especially nonpayments had already emerged as very hot public issues, although some observers noted that the major electoral factors went beyond pure economic considerations. Colton, for example, in his study of economic factors in the 1995 parliamentary elections in Russia concluded that "economic causes, it would be fair to say, merit a respectable but unsensational niche in our understanding of how Russian voters have behaved to date."[43] It was argued that political values and preferences in Russia were quite strong and stable and had more influence on electoral outcomes than economic variables. Nevertheless, economic variables did appear to matter, even if only as second order factors.[44]

Among the economic factors considered here with respect to elections, the incidence and duration of wage arrears appeared to be among the most important. They were, for example, strongly and negatively correlated with voting for the incumbent president.[45] Contrary to what one might have expected, given workers' fears, it would probably be fair to say that open unemployment was not a major issue in winning or keeping office. In fact, a positive association existed between the level of unemployment and voting for the incumbent administration, which may at first seem to be counterintuitive. If unemployment in Russia was viewed by the population with fear, then how can it be positively linked with support for incumbents in office? Several considerations help to explain this point. First, unemployment actually affected only a relatively small share of the population directly, and those in work may have given other factors priority in their voting strategies. Indeed, wage arrears touched more people's lives. Second, where increases in unemployment were linked to progress in restructuring, the negative votes of disgruntled unemployed people may have been offset by positive votes by the growing group of winners who supported the incumbents.

The division of society into winners and losers was more complex than a simple split between *nouveau riches* and new poor, including the unemployed. Intermediate groups developed along the continuum from winners to losers. Their positions were rather dynamic and depended on many factors. Inflow into unemployment consisted mostly of people with the least "marketable" skills. Losing a job did not come as a surprise to them; usually, they had some warning such as a period of underemployment or underpayment. Many people knew to expect such an outcome in the near future. Thus, the potential unemployed often considered themselves among the losers even before they had actually lost their jobs. The group of losers included the unemployed as well as those with perceptions that they could not win.[46] In addition, in the Russian case, many underemployed and underpaid were likely to fall into the latter subgroup, even if they were not laid off. Both subgroups had negative perceptions of government policy and showed little support for it, as is documented by various polls. While unemployment in general was comparatively low (and arrears were mounting), its marginal increase changed neither the proportion of losers, nor their attitude to the government.

However, the situation was more complicated with winners. Although restructuring brings more unemployment, it also increases the number of winners. Potential winners were much less aware of their chances of becoming actual winners. Shedding unproductive labour, as well as obsolete facilities and technologies or social assets, may have given a boost to some firms and increased their profitability and competitiveness. Niche-filling opportunities gave an impetus to some limited private sector job creation, which even created some opportunities for unemployed, and so on. These developments brought additional people into—or closer to—the group of winners. The changes concerned those whom Rychard calls "winning losers," eventually expanding the proportion of "winning winners." If the growth of the number of perceived winners had been substantial, it could have had an effect on the electoral outcome, offsetting all or a large part of the losers' impact. However, the poor economic conditions and personal perceptions in Russia were such that this was not the case.

CONCLUSION

This chapter has examined how the unsettled or distorted nature of Russian politics contributed to the pattern of labour market adjustment, in particular as it was characterised by wage arrears. Among the factors tending to push up wage bills to unsustainable levels (while limiting employment reduction) were the country's political institutions, the political business cycle, and the nature of fiscal relations between the centre and regions. Meanwhile, the weak voice for workers, a strong fear of unemployment, and a particular configuration of labour market institutions and social protection allowed employers to discount the actual value of inflated wage contracts.

The avoidance of high unemployment seems initially to have given a positive side to the arrears story. Arrears allowed political elites to cope with the "Great Contraction" in output early in the transition and later to manage a tight monetary policy against a background of poor fiscal performance. This resulted in relative political calm from 1995 to 1997, with the most extreme forms of workers' dissatisfaction kept at bay.

The negative side of the policy relates to the postponement of institutional and structural reforms, which increased pressures on public finance and on enterprise cash balances in the longer term. This contributed to a further deterioration in the fiscal performance of the economy and raised new questions about the sustainability of macroeconomic stabilisation in general. A new burst of wage arrears in the first half of 1998, as a result of an acute fiscal crisis, posed a real threat to Russia's fragile political and social stability. It increased the militancy of the most cohesive segments of the labour force and intensified political pressure on the government. Since the government had already taken unemployment into account, it was dealt a much stronger blow by the underpaid than by the unemployed. All of these factors contributed to the full-blown financial and political crisis in August 1998, which put an end to a more than two-year period of relative macroeconomic stability.

Might the crisis become a catalyst for the long-awaited structural reforms? And if these reforms are implemented, will there still be room for "the Russian way" of labour market adjustment? Answers to these questions are still to emerge.

NOTES

1. By the mid-1990s, it was an open question whether there was really a risk of inflationary demand on the part of consumers in an economy where investment and consumer demand had already collapsed and where much of the wealth of consumers had been eroded through the waves of inflation following price liberalisation in 1992.

2. Gilles Alfandari and Mark Schaffer, "'Arrears' in the Russian Enterprise Sector," in *Enterprise Restructuring and Economic Policy in Russia,* ed. Simon Commander, Qimiao Fan, and Mark Schaffer (Washington, D.C.: EDI—The World Bank, 1996), 125.

3. Nadezhda Ivanova and Charles Wyplosz, "Arrears: The Tide That Is Drowning Russia," *Russian Economic Trends* 8, no. 1 (Winter 1999): 24–35.

4. Operational issues did play a role as well, in that misallocation of funds and budgetary sequestration aggravated difficulties with paying bills.

5. Stephen Haggard and Robert Kaufman, ed., *The Politics of Economic Adjustment, International Constraints, Distributive Conflicts, and the State* (Princeton, N.J.: Princeton University Press, 1992); Stephen Haggard, "Democratic Institutions, Economic Policy and Development," in *Institutions and Economic Development. Growth and Governance in Less-Developed and Post-Socialist Countries,* ed. Christopher Clague (Baltimore and London: Johns Hopkins University Press, 1997), 121–149.

6. Stephen Haggard, "Democratic Institutions, Economic Policy and Development," 143.

7. As summed up in *OECD Economic Surveys: The Russian Federation 1997* (Paris: OECD, 1997), 6, "The regular non-fulfilment by the Federal Government of its own budgeted allocations, due in part to unrealistic budgets that echo political confrontations between the Government and the Duma, has added fuel to the fire of escalating non-payment problems in the economy, also implicitly undermining overall efforts to promote the law and contract enforcement."

8. William Nordhaus, "The Political Business Cycle," *Review of Economic Studies* 42 (1975): 169–190.

9. Daniel Treisman and Vladimir Gimpelson, *Political Business Cycles and Russian Elections, or the Manipulations of "Chudar,"* Discussion Paper no. CIRJE-F- 39, Faculty of Economics, University of Tokyo, 1999.

10. One increase came a month prior to the April 1993 referendum, one fell two months before the December 1993 elections, three within August–December 1995, and, finally, two increases in January–July 1996.

11. Real wages are a rather crude indicator, since the government could only directly influence wages in the public sector. However, both wage indicators seem to correlate.

12. *Russian Economic Trends* 6, no. 3 (1997): 52.

13. According to the authors' estimates, the total wage bill in health care, education, and public administration made up about 12 percent of total general government expenditures during the period from 1993 to 1995, but jumped to 17 percent in 1996. It accounted for 15 percent in 1997.

14. For more on fiscal federalism and transfers, see *OECD Economic Surveys: The Russian Federation 1997,* Annex III.

15. Vladimir Gimpelson and Galina Monousova, *Public Employment and Redistributive Politics in Russian Regions* (paper presented at the Slavic Research Center Workshop, University of Hokkaido, Sapporo, Japan, July 21–22). The dependent variable was public employment in a given year (1995, 1996, or 1997). The independent variables were public employment in 1992 (to take inertia in public employment into account), plus variables for GDP and transfers per capita, and unemployment. Controls were added for age profile, urbanisation, capitals, and ethnic regions. All independent variables with the index (t-1) were lagged by one year relative to the dependent variable, since one might assume that any visible effect on public employment of changes in GDP, unemployment, or transfers was likely to come with a lag. Thus, the equation to be estimated was the following: $PE(t) = b0 + b1PE(92) + b2GDP(t-1) + b3UNEMPL(t-1) + b4TRANS(t-1) + b5AGE0\_15(t-1) + b6AGEov55(t-1) + b7URBANIZ + b8CAPITALS + b9ETHNIC$

16. Adolph Wagner postulated in the 1880s that growth in the government share of GNP was a result of economic progress.

17. Lev Freinkman and Michel Haney, *What Affects the Russian Regional Governments' Propensity to Subsidize?* World Bank, Policy Research Working Paper no. 1818, August 1997. Although largely privatised, the housing sector also had a public component.

18. *Transition Report 1998* (London: EBRD, 1998), 15.

19. Daniel Treisman, "Deciphering Russia's Federal Finance: Fiscal Appeasement in 1995 and 1996," *Europe-Asia Studies* 50, no. 5 (July 1998): 893–906.

20. Alistair McAuley, "The Determinants of Russian Federal-Regional Fiscal Relations: Equity or Political Influence?" *Europe-Asia Studies* 49, no. 3 (May 1997): 431–444.

21. See Vladimir Gimpelson and Douglas Lippoldt, *Labour Restructuring in Russian Enterprises: A Case Study* (Paris: OECD, 1996), and "Labour Turnover in the Russian Economy," in *Labour Market Dynamics in the Russian Federation,* ed. Douglas Lippoldt (Paris: OECD, 1997), 17–55.

22. Alfandari and Schaffer, "'Arrears' in the Russian Enterprise Sector," 133.

23. Alfandari and Schaffer, "'Arrears' in the Russian Enterprise Sector," 128.

24. John Earle and Klara Sabirianova, "Wage Arrears in Russia: An Exploration of Causes and Consequences" (Stockholm: SITE, unpublished paper, 1998), 18.

25. However, some transition countries (e.g., Croatia, Hungary, Slovakia, and Slovenia) had even lower levels of strike activity.

26. Walter Connor, "Labor in the New Russia: Four Years on," *Problems of Post-Communism,* no. 2 (March–April 1995): 11.

27. Connor, "Labor in the New Russia: Four Years On," 8.

28. For more information on Russian trade unions, see, for example, the works of Simon Clarke, Walter Connor, and Linda Cook (all in English), and Leonid Gordon and Eduard Klopov (in Russian).

29. Simon Clarke, "Trade Unions and the Non-Payment of Wages in Russia" (University of Warwick, UK, 1997), 2.

30. Clarke, "Trade Unions and the Non-Payment of Wages in Russia."

31. Richard Freeman, "What Direction for Labor Market Institutions in Eastern and Central Europe?" in *The Transition in Eastern Europe,* vol. 2, ed. Olivier Blanchard, Kenneth A. Froot, and Jeffrey Sachs (Chicago and London: NBER Project Report, University of Chicago Press, 1994), 24.

32. Joan Nelson, "Organized Labor, Politics, and Labor Market Flexibility in Developing Countries," in *Labor Markets in an Era of Adjustment,* ed. Susan Horton, Ravi Kanbur, and Dipak Mazumdar (Washington, D.C.: World Bank/EDI, 1995), 356.

33. See, e.g., Guy Standing, *Russian Unemployment and Enterprise Restructuring: Reviving Dead Souls* (London and Geneva: Macmillan and ILO Study Series, 1996).

34. Simon Clarke, "Structural Adjustment without Mass Unemployment?" in *Structural Adjustment without Mass Unemployment? Lessons from Russia,* ed. Simon Clarke (Cheltenham, UK: Edward Elgar Publishing, 1998), 53.

35. Susan Stokes, "Public Opinion and Market Reforms: The Limits of Economic Voting," *Comparative Political Studies* 29, no. 5 (October 1996): 514.

36. Adam Przeworsky, "Public Support for Economic Reforms in Poland," *Comparative Political Studies* 29, no. 5 (October 1996): 535.

37. Adam Przeworsky, "Economic Reforms, Public Opinion, and Political Institutions: Poland in Eastern European Perspective," in Luiz Carlos Bresser Perreira, Jose Maria

Maravall, and Adam Przeworsky, *Economic Reform in New Democracies: A Social-Democratic Approach* (Cambridge: Cambridge University Press, 1993), 166.

38. David Stark and Laszlo Bruszt, *Postsocialist Pathways: Transforming Politics and Property in East Central Europe* (Cambridge: Cambridge University Press, 1998), 205 and 211.

39. Leonid Gordon, "Polozheniye naemnykh rabotnikov v Rossii 90–kh godov," *Sotcialno-trudovye issledovaniya,* VII (Moscow: IMEMO, 1997), 70.

40. Clarke, "Structural Adjustment without Mass Unemployment?" 42.

41. Nelson, "Organized Labor, Politics, and Labor Market Flexibility in Developing Countries," 363.

42. An assessment as to whether they were really democratic is outside the scope of this chapter.

43. Timothy Colton, "Economics and Voting in Russia," *Post-Soviet Affairs* 12, no. 4 (1996): 289–317.

44. Vladimir Mau and M. Gasparyan, "Ekonomika i vybory: opyt kolitchestvennogo analyza," *Voprosy economiki* 4 (April 1997): 111–129.

45. John Earle and Klara Sabirianova, "Wage Arrears in Russia: An Exploration of Causes and Consequences."

46. Andrzey Rychard, "In Search Of 'Winning Losers,'" *Social Research* 63, no. 2 (Summer 1996): 465–486.

8

Conclusions: Transition *and* Turmoil

The antitotalitarian revolution brought in its wake a new labor culture based on private property for production assets, and even more importantly, on the individual's real ownership of his or her labor force, including the freedom to dispose of it as he or she sees fit. Vladimir Magun, "Labor Culture," in *Russian Culture at the Crossroads: Paradoxes of Postcommunist Consciousness*.

THE FIRST STAGE OF TRANSITION IN RUSSIA

The implementation of reforms during the period between 1992 and the second quarter of 1998 marked a sort of maturation in a process that had begun through experimentation in the 1980s. During Gorbachev's tenure in particular, various innovations were put in place, involving the introduction of new incentives and some economic flexibility (e.g., the formation of cooperatives, the use of new compensation schemes at some plants, and Glasnost and increased openness in public debate). With the launching of more far-reaching reforms in 1992, the centre of gravity shifted from attempts to salvage the system of central planning toward implementation of a new market-oriented and democratic system. This involved a fundamental change in the mechanisms governing economic, political, and social relations and even a change in national status for Russia. Labour market participants were to be freed to act in their own best economic interests within the framework of a well-regulated market economy.

By mid-1998, the transition was still not complete with respect to basic aspects of the new system. There remained many market distortions and impediments to change. A key indicator of malaise in the labour market was the low rate of job creation. It reflected the hostile environment faced by businesses and, in particular, the uncertainty and risk associated with creation of employment in the formal sector. To create or expand a business meant confronting the lack of clear and transparent administrative regulations (including especially tax rules), exposure to criminality, and vulnerability to payment arrears, among many other difficulties.

In the absence of substantial job creation, unemployment levels gradually crept up in a process whereby many of the less competitive workers were gradually squeezed out of employment. Reallocation of labour proceeded on a slow track, eventually reaching significant proportions but not achieving the kinds of shifts seen in transition countries farther west. Although some restructuring did occur, much still remained to be done as the initial period of economic transition came to a close.

As the unemployment rate drifted into double digits, any move toward deep restructuring would have meant further displacement and extremely high mass unemployment. Political decisions that may have led to even more unemployment in the short term were avoided (e.g., enforcement of bankruptcy provisions). The risk was that if unemployment rose to involve, say, one in five workers (instead of one in ten) the political fall-out could have become explosive. As it was, with roughly nine in ten workers still employed, political pressure increasingly focused on wage arrears among the employed majority.

A broad group of formal sector losers emerged over these years, including those who saw themselves as *potential* losers. Because burdens were shared through negative wage flexibility and arrears, many workers actually lost some economic ground. This was tolerated in part because many had alternative sources of income from informal activities or placed a high value on near-term job security. For a variety of economic—and, in some cases, social or political— reasons, employers tended to prefer to adjust to demand shocks by decreasing the price of labour and the volume of hours rather than the number of employees. Thus, employment declined gradually. Employment conditions deteriorated, while restructuring lagged. Labour mobility grew for many "movers," albeit with much churning, and a large group of stayers were left behind.

THE CRISIS OF 1998

The story told in this book is focused on the period leading up to the events of 1998, but it is not a story to be told in isolation. Rather, it is part of a continuum and with strong influences that linger to the present day.

The Asian financial crisis in late 1997 stimulated capital outflow from many emerging country markets and prompted heightened investor concerns vis-à-vis the transition countries. Pressures mounted through mid-1998, when international financial turbulence served as a catalyst for a serious crisis in Russia with economic, political, and social dimensions. Already in the period leading up to the crisis, falls in commodity prices led to deterioration in the current account balance and further increased borrowing needs. Revenue shortfalls continued to plague state budget implementation, highlighting the need for fiscal adjustment and reform. Such reforms, however, remained politically unfeasible. This situation was accompanied by increasing pressures on the rouble and capital outflow. Foreign investors became increasingly unsettled. These economic difficulties were paralleled by increased tensions across the whole political landscape, particularly targeting the president and government. Politicians of the left and centre united in an offensive. Rumours circulated about a possible coup d'etat, a huge devaluation of the ruble, or a debt default, among other possibilities. Work stoppages increased, with most linked to complaints concerning wage arrears.

On August 17, the government (headed by Sergey Kirienko) and the Central Bank announced a partial default on the domestic debt (GKOs). The ruble was permitted to float and subsequently fell substantially. These developments sent shock waves across the economy. Many banks and insurance companies, which had heavily invested in short-term securities, became insolvent overnight and the payment system was paralysed. Inflation accelerated. Between August and December 1998 consumer prices rose by about 70 percent. In all, real GDP fell about 5 percent in 1998 and the decline in industrial output was slightly larger.

The growth in unemployment accelerated only modestly after the crisis. By the end of the year, the unemployment rate had increased by about 2 percentage points to 13.3 percent. In most sectors, neither mass enterprise closures nor lay-offs became a reality. Certain service sector enterprises were hard hit, particularly in finance. However, these firms were largely concentrated in a few of the most urban regions. And, since these sectors employed many workers on extremely flexible terms of formal and informal secondary employment, the effects of downsizing in these firms did not show up fully in the standard labour statistics. Many of those who lost such jobs simply returned to their main formal jobs. Others working in these sectors lost in terms of wages, but their human capital helped them to keep their jobs or find new ones. In sum, employment and unemployment exhibited only a moderate reaction to the August shock.

While the quantity side of the labour market showed limited sensitivity to the macroeconomic developments, the price side continued to be marked by high flexibility. Real wages fell by about 30 percent through the end of 1998. The proportion of the population with income below the official subsistence level rose by early 1999 to exceed more than a third. Also, the value of pensions was greatly eroded as the state failed to adjust them to compensate for inflation.

The events of the second half of 1998 launched an avalanche of grim predictions. Many analysts foresaw a meltdown of the economy, mass lay-offs, enterprise closures, soaring unemployment, social unrest, and disarray in the government and state administration. This scenario was apparently based on standard expectations that firms facing an extreme credit crunch, collapse in demand, and general uncertainty, would downsize drastically. At the same time, it seemed to some that major economic indicators were tending to move in this direction.

At the time of writing these conclusions in early 2000, one and a half years had passed since the crisis of August 1998 and, although the ultimate outcome was still far from certain, some of the dust had already settled. Already by early 1999, developments began to deviate from the worst case scenario. The year 1999 witnessed a return to growth in output, with GDP rising by about 3 percent. Admittedly, this was partly a reflection of the poor performance of the preceding year, but by the end of the year output nevertheless managed to exceed the pre-crisis level (i.e., the average for 1997). Industrial production registered a more substantial increase of 8 percent and rose to exceed the pre-crisis level by more than 2 percent. Early in 1999, employment also began to grow, eventually yielding a net increase of nearly two million during the course of the year (attaining a level not seen since 1997). And, during the second half of the year, unemployment dropped back to about 12 percent of the labour force. Real wages remained stable, even rising somewhat in the last quarter of the year. Wage arrears fell over the course of 1999, as the government cut its stock of wage arrears in half and key commercial sectors of the economy (industry, construction, transport, and agriculture) cut their stock of wage arrears by 40 percent.

In sum, the developments in 1998 and 1999 illustrated a similarity to the trend observed in the earlier transition period. As in 1992 and 1994, the brunt of the adjustment to the macroeconomic shock was borne by the price side of the labour market. However, the latest crisis was also followed by nonnegligible shifts in employment, as well as a partial recovery in output stimulated by favourable exchange rate movements and some easing of the enterprise-held debt burden (e.g., the value of the stock of wage arrears was reduced through inflation), among other factors.

ADVANCING THE TRANSITION

During the first years of transition and turmoil, the Russian approach to labour market adjustment was characterised by such features as: segmentation in the labour market with high mobility for certain groups; steady but gradual redeployment of labour resources; low levels of job creation; use of quite substantial wage flexibility as a tool for adapting to changing economic conditions— especially downward wage flexibility (including arrears) for the less mobile groups during downturns; quite gradual growth in open unemployment; very modest and often inadequate social protection provided by the state for those pushed into unemployment; a dependence on marginal employment in inefficient enterprises as a sort of social safety net; and substantial levels of secondary employment and informal sector activity.

Was the particular Russian pattern adjustment ultimately useful in facilitating transition? Or, did it needlessly delay the transition and result in missed opportunities and turmoil? Was this approach to labour market adjustment appropriate in view of the situation?

In the early years of the transition, a piecemeal and gradual approach may have helped to maintain social cohesion and buffer the macroeconomic shocks. At a time when the population had limited familiarity with market mechanisms and key labour market institutions were not yet in place, this may have had some short-term beneficial effects in sustaining support for reform as privatisation and reductions in direct subsidies were carried out. Some genuine, but limited, labour market adjustment did occur as enterprises acted gradually to reduce overstaffing. Moreover, some narrow institutional development in a positive direction occurred (as exemplified by the SES or the new labour statistical systems), even if under the circumstances of the Russian transition these institutions remained under-utilised or under-resourced.

On the other hand, the continuing dependence on this adjustment approach hampered the functioning of markets and slowed the much-needed reallocation of labour. The negative wage flexibility brought sharp declines in earnings that weakened consumer demand and compounded the plight of Russian producers. Wage arrears and unpaid leaves persisted by virtue of new and informal rules and poor law enforcement; with time, such practises became institutionalised as a new social norm. This use of flexibility appears to have contributed to a sort of inertia in many older enterprises; it acted as a kind of shock absorber, enabling firms to delay action on restructuring and shielding some workers from displacement even as their employment conditions worsened. This occurred while the society and economy continued to face uncertain times and turmoil from periodic shocks and inconsistent policies.

Was an alternative approach possible and what would it have entailed? For example, what if limited steps had been taken to enforce labour law, collect arrears, and strengthen bankruptcy provisions? For one thing, wages would have been less flexible and employment more flexible. Underemployment would have been translated into open unemployment. Although the Russian state took action to develop a framework for social protection, the SES system was fragile and may have been overwhelmed by such a huge increase in unemployment. As for employers, such an approach would have forced the closure of many indebted firms. Here again, the social safety net for enterprises—in the form of the bankruptcy system—may have been overwhelmed, if for no other reason than the limited capacity of the courts and the lack of capable trustees. On balance, it seems that a such a tough approach with enterprises and workers by itself was not the solution—or at least, it was not sufficient. A more comprehensive approach was required, one that would not only attack the problems of unmet obligations, but one that would also create positive incentives for efficient enterprises.

What lessons can be drawn from this? One might begin by considering a key symptom of the malaise: the low rate of job creation. Improved performance in this area could play a key role in facilitating the redeployment of laid-off workers released as inefficient enterprises close or restructure. Such an environment would provide improved opportunities and, coupled with a better-targeted safety net, could help to overcome some of the resistance to more far-reaching reform and restructuring. In Russia, any sustained increase in job creation will probably be a clear indication that an appropriate market-oriented policy is being effectively implemented and that an environment conducive to increased output is in place. Thus, one might begin by considering what might be needed in order to promote job creation.

First of all, experience from a range of market-oriented countries has shown that macroeconomic policy does play an important role in promotion of employment. An appropriate macro framework includes sound public finances, price stability, and aggregate demand managed to promote growth while minimising inflationary pressures.[1] On these counts Russia scored some success, although greater consistency was needed.

Second, the operation of markets and sustained job creation depend partly on the development of appropriate institutions. A good macroeconomic economic policy by itself cannot guarantee a healthy economy, particularly under conditions of economic transition. Institutions can provide participants with a degree of security and a framework that facilitates the functioning of the market. In this regard, a key element of policy went wrong in Russia. Policy-makers failed to support fully the development of institutions. Indeed, in some ways the Russian labour market experienced deinstitutionalisation, as trade unions weakened and workers failed to gain a voice as enterprise stakeholders; as informal sector or grey market activity expanded at the expense of the formal sector; and as law enforcement (including contract enforcement) and administration weakened. The extreme wage flexibility, for example, was partly rooted in such deinstitutionalisation.[2] One of its manifestations, the accumulation of wage arrears, represented a breakdown in the institutions governing the relationships between workers and employers, work and reward, and legal injury and due recourse.

The establishment of an appropriate legal framework constitutes an important element of institutional development. Such a framework can help to encourage job creation, for example, by fostering a certain amount of predictability and transparency for labour market participants and investors, by protecting legal rights and due process for enterprises and shareholders, and by assuring a minimum, but adequate, level of social protection for those at risk of displacement due to restructuring (stayers) or those who take risks by moving (movers). In Russia, the need for improvement of the legal framework extended beyond the basic means to combat criminality to include all of these dimensions and more.

A further dimension in building institutions is the development of the administrative capacity and effectiveness of the public agencies. This is obviously a critical element of policy implementation in areas ranging from tax collection to social protection. Here again, Russia made insufficient headway despite some improvements. For example, the State Employment Service succeeded in establishing a nation-wide network of employment offices and improving the qualifications of a portion of its staff. However, the effectiveness of the SES remained hampered by a number of issues such as extreme funding constraints, continuing staff training shortfalls, and problems with the relevant laws (e.g., which poorly structured and targeted benefits).

With respect to corporate governance, policy in many transition countries has had to address issues related to insider control and enfranchising workers and outside stakeholders. Russia faced similar challenges but did not move sufficiently to address them. The lack of transparency in decision making and the limited participation of outside stakeholders in decision making may have deprived some enterprises of an important check on the power of managers. They may have also decreased the positive incentives for managers to take strategic action in the medium or long-term interest of the firm. Moreover, the lack of a constructive trade union presence and of genuine collective bargaining may have deprived some enterprises of what could be potentially a positive force for consensual change.

Third, the effective promotion of large-scale, sustainable job creation generally requires a coherent and positive policy environment at all levels of government. In Russia, the state continued to distort the operation of the market through poorly structured taxes and inappropriate administration. As highlighted in a recent report by McKinsey Global Institute, there remained considerable distortions linked to wrong-headed government intervention, causing unequal circumstances for competing businesses.[3] For example, differences arose in effective tax rates or energy prices for companies in a given sector. Some enterprises received preferential treatment in terms of access to land, procurement opportunities, permits and licenses, or infrastructure. Small and medium enterprises (SMEs) in the private sector, in particular, faced disadvantages in relations with the state administration in such areas as tax-related disincentives, insufficient protection from crime, and unequal access to information and services.[4] These and other distortions hampered the profitability of the most productive firms and cushioned pressures on inefficient firms to restructure.

Despite the various problems discussed in this book, it is notable that even under the difficult conditions of the first phase of transition in Russia, the private sector grew through privatisation and new business start-ups to account for perhaps one-third or more of formal sector jobs. Even in recently privatised firms, some adjustment often resulted. Freed from inappropriate constraints and granted a stable and supportive environment, there is reason to hope that the private sector would respond and contribute even more substantially to employment growth and economic expansion.

Failure to act to address the problems and promote job creation in the future may result in increased informalisation of the economy, lagging growth, and a further closure of options. One consequence may be a continuation of the gradual erosion of economic capacity. It is notable that in 1997, after five years of transition and turmoil, the average Russian employee produced the equivalent of only 16 percent of the output of the average U.S. employee (even when output is converted using purchasing power parities).[5] In the same year, an average worker in the Czech Republic, Hungary, and Poland produced roughly twice as much as the average Russian worker. On one hand, given the relatively high literacy and numeracy in Russia, this is an indication of the potential under the right conditions for the Russian worker to make rapid gains in output. On the other, it is an indication that if Russia is to begin to catch up and improve living standards, it must increase its lagging productivity, and it must ensure that the market signals reach participants and provide them with incentives to do so.

In the first phase of transition, many Russian workers and enterprises have exhibited a dynamism and willingness to adapt. Their behaviour has generally constituted a rational response to an uncertain and distorted environment. This responsiveness is a healthy sign. It provides an indication that, given the proper incentives, it is likely that Russian labour market participants would use their recently acquired economic freedoms and developing market skills not only as they see fit, but in a way that on a collective basis would work to promote improved living standards for the nation as a whole.

NOTES

1. *The OECD Jobs Study: Facts, Analysis, Strategies* (Paris: OECD, 1994).

2. Many foreign observers and analysts also failed to recognise the lack of appropriate institutional development in the early stages of the reform. At the time, the so-called "Washington consensus" among international financial institutions called for priority emphasis in the transition countries to be placed on such macro-issues as combating inflation, attacking fiscal imbalances, and instituting rapid privatisation. This position has now been modified in response to calls for a broader approach that also takes into account issues such as enhancement of social policy (needed to maintain the consensus for reform), environmental sustainability, and institutional development (required for improvement of corporate governance and public administration), among other issues. See Douglas North, *The Contribution of the New Institutional Economics to an Understanding of the Transition Problem,* WIDER Annual Lectures 1 (Helsinki: WIDER/The United Nations University, March 1997), and Joseph Stiglitz, *More Instruments and Broader Goals: Moving toward the Post-Washington Consensus,* WIDER Annual Lectures 2 (Helsinki: WIDER/The United Nations University, January 1998), for discussion of these dimensions.

3. McKinsey Global Institute, *Unlocking Economic Growth in Russia* (prepared with assistance from Bob Solow, Olivier Blanchard, Dick Cooper, and Ted Hall), McKinsey and Company, Moscow, October 1999.

4. Despite the constraints, it is notable that SMEs exhibited a capacity to create new jobs, often paying better and more timely wages than older, larger firms. To some extent, the SMEs thereby generated "winners" interested in further reform.

5. These figures are from the authors' own calculations, drawing on output data from the World Bank, International Comparison Programme database, and employment data from the OECD Labour Force Statistics database, except for data on Russian employment, which were drawn from *Russian Economic Trends,* 11 February 2000.

Data Sources Annex

The main goal of this annex is to help the reader to better understand the main sources of data used in this book, including a bit about their origin and design, representativeness, and comparative advantages and disadvantages. However, it is not intended here to provide a comprehensive evaluation of Russian labour market statistics. Broader and more detailed reviews of these statistics are available from a number of specialised studies.[1]

LABOUR MARKET DATA IN THE RUSSIAN FEDERATION

The principle institutions providing labour market data used in this book were the State Committee of the Russian Federation on Statistics (Goskomstat) and the State Employment Service (SES). During the transition period, Goskomstat regularly published data on employment (full-time and part-time), unemployment, inactivity, wages, wage arrears, labour turnover, and other indicators. These data were drawn either from administrative reporting of firms or from specially designed sample surveys of households (e.g., the periodic labour force surveys). The SES was responsible for active and passive labour market programs. As such, it generated administrative data on a number of variables related to the interaction of job-seekers or employers with its local offices. It issued periodic reports with indicators of some of its main activities, including unemployment registrations and ₋employment benefits, among others. Thus, Goskomstat and the SES each published quite a lot of labour market information, sometimes on a cooperative basis.[2]

Some of the key labour market indicators used in this volume can be found in the *Russian Economic Trends* (RET) publications. These quarterly and monthly reviews of major trends and developments in the Russian economy were prepared by teams of Russian (from the "Working Centre for Economic Reform" of the government of the Russian Federation) and West European economists (including experts from the Centre for Economic Performance of the London School of Economics and the Stockholm Institute of Transition Economics and East European Economies).[3] Aggregate indicators published in the RET were based on official Goskomstat data but adjusted for consistency over time and international comparability.

Despite improvements over time, the official labour market data in Russia remained very fragmented and incomplete in the period covered by this volume. Officially published indicators shed some light on major trends but only in fairly aggregate terms. To get a more nuanced and differentiated picture of the actual developments, the authors drew on various supplementary data sources as a complement. These alternative sources varied from case studies at a few firms to mass surveys covering rather large samples households or firms. Thus, while the analyses presented often begin with official aggregate data, they are often confirmed and expanded using various alternative data sets.

Among the main supplementary data sources cited in the present text are: the Russian Longitudinal Monitoring Survey (RLMS) developed by the University of North Carolina and various Russian partners; a special enterprise survey undertaken by the World Bank in 1994; the Russian Labour Market Flexibility Surveys (enterprise surveys) of the International Labour Office; the Russian Economic Barometer (REB, enterprise surveys) of the Russian Academy of Sciences' Institute of World Economy and International Relations; public opinion polls and surveys conducted by the Russian Centre for Public Opinion Research (VCIOM); case studies of the Institute for Comparative Labour Relations Research (Moscow); the All-Russian Labour Monitoring Survey of the Ministry of Labour (an enterprise survey conducted in the mid-1990s); and the New Russia Barometer household surveys of the Centre for the Study of Public Policy (University of Strathclyde). These institutions provide detailed descriptions of their statistical instruments through their publications and Internet sites.

The following sections describe in more detail the main groups of data collection instruments used here: household surveys, administrative data of the SES, employer surveys, administrative data from Goskomstat, and case studies.

Household Surveys

1. The Russian Labour Force Survey—A labour force survey (LFS) is a household survey that provides a view, at a given point in time, of employment, unemployment, and the inactive population (i.e., those who remain outside of the labour force). In Soviet times, the LFS was not conducted in Russia. While the economy was state-run and full employment was the norm, administrative sources—especially enterprise reporting—could capture most economic activity and could satisfy official statistical needs. However, the transition to a market system made the introduction of the LFS very important in order to capture information on areas of the labour market that were only poorly covered by ad-

ministrative reporting, such as small businesses, private sector firms, and the inactive population.

The first LFS in Russia was conducted by Goskomstat in October 1992, with follow-up iterations in October 1993, October 1994, March and October 1995, March 1996, October 1997, and October 1998. Budget problems prevented Goskomstat from realising its plans to conduct the survey more frequently. Originally, Goskomstat surveyed a sample of 0.6 percent of the working-age population (in Russia, this is the population aged 15 to 72 years).[4] Cost considerations later forced Goskomstat to reduce the sample size and shorten the original questionnaire. Basic aggregate results of the surveys were routinely published in various Goskomstat publications, including *Current Statistical Survey*.

Although the LFS is the preferred tool for monitoring unemployment developments in most OECD countries, it has both advantages and disadvantages. With respect to the Russian labour force survey, several of the most important ones are listed as follows:[5]

Principal Advantages

- Generally, the LFS definitions conformed to international standards for comparability (e.g., it was not necessary to be registered as unemployed with an employment service to be counted as unemployed).
- The LFS was based on a representative sample and therefore captured information on the whole population of the unemployed, including those who were not seeking the placement assistance of the employment service.
- The LFS provided for fairly good comparability of measures over time, despite some adjustments to the sample size and procedures during the period.
- The LFS provided background information on the household situation and was flexible enough to accommodate supplementary questionnaires that permitted collection of additional information for special studies.
- The LFS was carried out independently and was a new statistical instrument that did not suffer from the same problems of adaptation to market circumstances that the older statistical systems faced.

Principal Disadvantages

- Although the LFS initially had a very large sample intended to be representative at the regional level, the sample was reduced in the mid-1990s; in any event, as with any sample survey, this instrument was subject to sampling error, particularly where the sample was disaggregated to consider smaller groups.
- Due to budget problems, the LFS was conducted relatively infrequently and the period for the sample in 1996 differed from the other years.

- Given the long intervals between iterations, the LFS was not well-suited for tracking flows, although it did provide some information on changes in status between iterations.

2. The TACIS LFS supplement—Researchers interested in labour market developments in Russia during the early transition period faced two serious logistical problems when working with the LFS data. First, the questionnaire lacked some important variables. Second, for technical reasons, micro-data from the LFS were usually not available to outside researchers; the data were stored on outdated mainframe machines in nonstandard formats.[6] To overcome these problems, a special TACIS-ACE project on "Regional Labour Market Types in the Russian Federation" was launched in 1996. As part of this project, a special supplementary questionnaire was attached to the March 1996 LFS in five regions.[7] Chapter 4 of the book heavily relies on the data from this supplement.

The regions covered by the TACIS LFS supplement were selected to highlight the significant regional variation across the Russian Federation (figure A.1), each representing a different geographical and economic macroregion that can be considered by applying a variation of Hanson's typology of Russian regions.[8] Using this approach, one might say that Chelyabinsk and the Chuvash Republic fell in the "ordinary" category. However, they each had interesting features: Chelyabinsk for its concentration of defence industries and the Chuvash Republic for its significant agricultural sector. Krasnoyarsk Krai was one of the natural resource regions. Moscow city and Moscow Oblast both experienced relatively high-tech modes of regional development, but with significant variations: Moscow city belonged to the group of commercial hub/gateway regions, whereas Moscow Oblast represented a regional economy with a large share of older industrial enterprises in need of restructuring.

Table A.1 presents the regional samples and table A.2 quantifies certain aspects of the variation across these regions with respect to the labour market and living standards. The latter table illustrates the magnitude of economic and social differentiation. This was manifested by variation in the urbanisation level, unemployment, key income indicators, and small and medium-size enterprise development. This differentiation in basic characteristics confirms that the selection of regions represented a range of labour market experience.

3. The Russian Longitudinal Monitoring Survey (RLMS)—This survey was another important source of microdata on households. The RLMS was a periodic, nationally representative household survey with eight iterations conducted between 1992 and 1998; it focused on health and economic topics and was carried out by a team led by scholars from the Carolina Population Center of the University of North Carolina in cooperation with the Institute of Sociology (Moscow) and other Russian institutions, with partial financial support from USAID. This is the only ongoing longitudinal survey in Russia.

Table A.1 Regional LFS Sample Structure, March 1996 (Persons)

	Chelyabinsk Oblast	Chuvash Republic	Krasnoyarsk Krai	Moscow City	Moscow Oblast
Total Sample, of which:	3,683	1,488	3,449	10,043	7,080
Employed	1,936	816	1,992	5,804	4,216
Employed as a 59.5% Share of All Respondents	52.6%	54.8%	57.8%	57.8%	

Table A.2 Selected Indicators of Regional Differentiation, 1995 (Percentages, Except as Otherwise Noted)

Indicator	Russia	Chelyabinsk Oblast	Chuvash Republic	Krasnoyarsk Krai	Moscow City	Moscow Oblast
Urban population[1]	73.1	81.3	60.6	73.9	100.0	79.7
Unemployment[2]	8.7	8.3	9.6	9.1	5.2	9.5
Income, thousand roubles[3]	532.9	433.4	285.4	598.9	1707.8	368.5
Average monthly wage, thousand roubles[4]	531.6	529.7	285.6	830.1	726.7	481.5
Top income earners[5]	10.5	4.6	0.1	15.0	40.1	1.1
Change in total employment[6]	–3.1	–2.9	–4.0	–0.9	–3.5	–3.4
SME employment[7]	13.3	11.2	12.1	11.1	26.6	11.2
Large enterprise employment[8]	76.5	85.3	87.9	85.5	58.5	73.5

Notes: (1) The share of urban population in the total. (2) Unemployment as a percentage of the labour force. (3) Monetary monthly income, per capita. (4) In Moscow, this figure is lower than income, probably because of a higher incidence of underreported wages. (5) The share of population with monthly income over 1 million rubles. (6) Percent employment change for the year, large and medium firms. (7) SME share in employment by official estimates, percent. (8) Large firm share in employment, percent.
Source: Calculations based on data from *Rossiysky statistichesky ezhegodnik* (Russian Statistical Yearbook) (Moscow: Goskomstat, 1996).

Chapters 2, 5, and 7 include references to the RLMS sixth and to the seventh rounds of interviews, which were carried out during the period of October to December in both 1995 and 1996. In total, about 9,000 individuals were interviewed in each round, including over 4,000 employed. The survey questionnaire included a number of basic variables relating to the individual (e.g., sex, age, education, wages actually paid, and wage arrears), as well as to his/her employer (e.g., firm size, age, and ownership). As a national household survey, the RLMS provided fairly consistent coverage, irrespective of such factors as the size, sector, or age of the firm that employed the individual (i.e., not subject to certain of the limitations of the enterprise-based data collection).[9]

ADMINISTRATIVE DATA OF THE SES

These data provided information on the registered unemployed (including unemployment benefit recipients), other registered job-seekers, and vacancies listed by employers. For the purposes of this present analysis, these data served as a complement to the data from the main Goskomstat surveys. The administrative data had some advantages, in that they reflected a complete count from the various registers and could provide detailed information (e.g., on regions or small groups) with none of the sampling error associated with surveys. In addition, the data could be used to track stocks, flows, and durations for many variables. This information was useful in assessing the demand for SES services and labour market programme take-up. Some limitations existed, however. During the early years considered here, the SES data systems were just being developed and probably suffered from some inconsistencies as procedures were worked out, automated systems were put in place, and staff were trained. As with all administrative data, the SES data were not necessarily reflective of the overall situation in the labour market but rather tracked the interaction of employers and job-seekers with the SES. The data also suffered from several breaks in series, particularly as a consequence of changes in the Employment Law in 1996 (which, for example, reduced the incentives to register for unemployment benefits by increasing the qualifying period from twelve to twenty-six weeks).

EMPLOYER SURVEYS AND ADMINISTRATIVE DATA FROM GOSKOMSTAT

1. Administrative data on establishments (1-T form)—With respect to employers, many OECD Member countries use the enterprise as the unit of observation, meaning generally the operating enterprise as opposed to the legal or owning enterprise. In other OECD Member countries, the establishment is used; this is essentially a separate locational unit under common ownership, generally producing related products. As the establishment is a sub-unit of the enterprise, it provides more disaggregated job turnover data.

In the Russian context, however, the reporting unit reflected the needs and origins of the statistical system, which, in the case of enterprise data during the period considered here, drew heavily on the pre-transition administrative systems. In most cases the reporting units were enterprises or organisations, but in certain situations the reporting units were large establishments reporting on various associated facilities or a central facility (e.g., a hospital) that reported on a number of related entities (e.g., various clinics in nearby areas) that may or may not have been formally attached to it. The emphasis was on a practical collection of data that was meaningful at the aggregate level rather than at the local or regional-level.

Most of the labour market information from enterprises or large establishments was collected through the statistical "1-T" form (T refers to *trud,* the Russian word for "labour"). This form was submitted by the reporting units on a quarterly basis and included various indicators of employment, part-time employment, hirings, and separations, among others. Filing the form was mandatory for all large and medium-sized firms and organisations, which covered some 75 percent of the total employment. In most sectors, this included firms with over two hundred employees. However, smaller firms were included as well, in part reflecting continued reporting by declining enterprises or units divested from large parent firms and in part based on a sampling approach. The data set covered all types of ownership, including all state-owned enterprises as well as those newly privatised and a sample of *de-novo* private firms.

The Russian employer data should be used with care. They were distorted to a certain extent by changes due to the very economic restructuring that is analysed in this volume. In some cases, privatisation resulted in discontinuity in employers' economic activities or reporting practices. Break-ups of large or medium enterprises caused further distortions, including the loss of some units from the reporting system, where break-ups left some of the minor component units below the reporting thresholds (and they opted to stop reporting) or the reattribution of component units to different sectors (e.g., in some cases large manufacturing enterprises spun off their social assets). Thus, except where it was possible to control for such changes, it was not possible to make tight distinctions at the enterprise level or even for narrow sectors. Nevertheless, the aggregate figures for regions or broader sectors still provided a useful indication of general trends, as a large majority of reporting units continued to be captured by the administrative statistical system.

A number of additional data issues concern the administrative statistics on employers. First, the coverage of firms was not complete and many published series excluded small enterprises. The incomplete coverage of small firms left out a portion of a very dynamic part of the economy. This also reduced the ability of the system to monitor the private sector, as up to 90 percent of small firms were privately run. Second, the published data did not distinguish between continuing enterprises, start-ups, and closures, making it difficult to follow important aspects of enterprise developments. Third, despite collecting relatively detailed information on enterprise characteristics, Goskomstat did not routinely process all the data collected. Thus, some series were generally not available for analytical purposes.

2. The TACIS "Labour and Job Turnover in the Russian Economy" project— In order to overcome some of these drawbacks and to get a deeper insight into

labour market dynamics developments, a TACIS-ACE project was designed (No. T95-4099-R) in cooperation with Goskomstat to produce a detailed database drawing on the administrative data from the T-1 form.[10] The resulting database covered four regions (Moscow, Krasnoyarsk Kray, Chelyabinsk Oblast, and the Chuvash Republic), providing employment and financial data at the firm level for two years. The combined data set for 1996 included 6,335 enterprises, representing the main types of ownership and including a census of state-owned and newly privatised enterprises as well as a sample of *de-novo* private firms. The regions covered are the same ones as for the TACIS LFS supplement described earlier and included high (Krasnoyarsk, Chelyabinsk) as well as low (the Chuvash Republic) turnover regions. The sample covered high (trade and construction) and medium (industry) turnover sectors. However, some limitations remained. For the data set used here, small firms were not adequately covered.[11] And, important employee characteristics were not covered by the data set (e.g., skill level, gender, age, or tenure of those hired or separated).[12]

3. Other enterprise surveys—The analysis of enterprise behaviour and labour market developments was facilitated by the availability of data from several independent surveys. Two sources of supplementary information included the Russian Economic Barometer and the All-Russian Labour Monitoring Survey, which were especially helpful in filling gaps concerning larger enterprises.

CASE STUDIES

This volume draws not only on representative survey data (usually considered "hard") but also on "soft data" produced by case studies. The case study approach was helpful in providing information for the development of hypotheses and survey questionnaires, confirming the findings from more representative approaches and filling certain gaps in the data. The case study methodology has several attributes that made it a particularly useful tool in gaining insights on labour market developments in the Russian context.[13] First, case studies could be used to gather data—admittedly not representative, but possibly indicative—which were not yet fully available through administrative or survey sources (e.g., information on the composition of personnel by firm). Second, case studies allowed more careful targeting of questions and the collection of detailed information not routinely collected from staff in enterprises (e.g., questions were put not only to directors, but also to personnel managers or union leaders). Third, the case study approach helped to provide detailed information on institutional and environmental factors that in the post-Soviet era continued to influence the behaviour of enterprises (e.g., on the interaction between managers and public agencies). Given that enterprises are rather complex and, to a certain degree, heterogeneous entities, such features do not always come to light through other approaches.

Chapter 3, in particular, draws on a case study looking at the labour market changes within four medium-to-large size enterprises located in two regions. The names of these firms were changed in our discussion in order respect their confidentiality. The enterprise-specific information was collected in the field during May–August 1995 and supplementary national level data was collected in the period since. As noted in the chapter, two of the firms were located in Kaluga, a medium-sized city some 180 kilometres west of Moscow. The other two were located in the big Siberian city of Krasnoyarsk. These two cities were chosen, in part because they offered a contrast in conditions faced (e.g., geographic location, economic base, and population size) and in part because they were the administrative centres of two regions targeted by the OECD for technical cooperation activities, thus affording greater data accessibility. The firms studied represented machine building and light industry. They were privatised under various schemes during 1991–1994. Naturally, this sample cannot be representative, but it did provide an indication of the situation facing certain enterprises in this group.

Key data on employment, wages, separations, and hirings were obtained from the enterprises' administrative records. Qualitative information was collected through interviews with managers, professionals, workers, and trade union activists. At each firm, ten to fifteen employees with different statuses were interviewed. Further qualitative information of a more general nature was collected from interviews with regional and local officials.

Case studies were also used to collect information on the operation of labour market programmes. Field visits were conducted in a number of regions, including Astrakhan, Kaluga, Krasnoyarsk, Moscow, Novosibirsk, Samara, St. Petersburg, and Tomsk. These visits involved interviews with various local, regional, and national officials (e.g., in the offices of the state administration, Goskomstat or the SES), as well as with various users of government services. This information (and the local statistical information that was collected) supported the research for various segments of this volume, particularly chapter 6.

STATISTICS ON EMPLOYMENT IN SMEs

Official data on employment in small and medium-size enterprises (SMEs)[14] were based on a special administrative reporting procedure covering these firms. During the period covered here, Goskomstat compiled SME statistics by aggregating data from annual reports submitted by all SMEs and adjusted these data using tax collection data and some other data sources. However, the methodology of adjustment was never made public and the reliability of these data remains unclear. Nevertheless, SME indicators based on these series might be considered as providing rough lower-bound estimates.

A variety of factors played a role in distorting the statistics for SMEs, generally biasing them downward. Irrespective of their origin, small businesses were reluctant to advertise their activity and, according to some estimates, only one-third to one-half of all small firms fully reported their activity to local statistical offices. Many of these firms also sought to avoid reporting to the tax authorities.[15] Generally poor law enforcement made this possible on a large scale. Other distortions were the result of re-registration of SMEs as "entrepreneurs without legal entity" (meaning a change in statistical category) and stronger fiscal pressure due to tightening of monetary policy in 1995–1996.

Between 1992 and 1996, the data definitions for SMEs changed twice, which prevents proper comparisons over time. The governmental decree of May 11, 1993, (N446) "On Priority Measures in Development and State Support of Small Entrepreneurship in the Russian Federation," considered as SMEs, start-up firms as well as those already functioning and having employment under certain limits. These were differentiated by sector and varied from 200 for industry and construction, 100 for research and development (R&D), to 15 for retail trade and catering.

The federal law "On the State Support of Small Entrepreneurship in the Russian Federation," adopted in June 1995, decreased the maximum limit to 100 employees. Accordingly, small businesses in industry, construction, and transportation were considered to employ up to 100 employees, in agriculture and research and development up to 60, in wholesale trade up to 50, and in retail trade and personal services up to 30. For other sectors or business activities, the upper limit was established as 50 employees per firm. This law became effective with respect to statistics in 1996, and contributed to the decreases in the number of SME firms, the total employment in SMEs, and the correlation of SMEs with private sector. Many new private businesses surpassed the employment limits established for small businesses; for example, private banks and large trade or construction companies were often above the limits. On the other hand, some small (in terms of employment size) firms filed the same reports as large do.

The pool of firms covered by the SME data included those with various forms of ownership, but private ownership dominated, accounting for roughly 90 percent of the total in 1995. However, private firms varied in their origin and, as noted earlier, they included *de-novo* firms as well as old privatised ones or spin-offs.

Table A.3 presents the aggregate data, keeping in mind the previously mentioned breaks in series and caveats. According to the official statistics, the peak for SMEs in the economy was in 1994, with declines in the following years. In 1995 and 1996, the total number of SMEs in the economy decreased compared to the 1994 level. The 1996 data, in part reflecting the definitional changes, show a decline in employment, whereby the number of full-time employees dropped by 33 percent within just three quarters with respect to the 1995 average. In 1997, the data show SME employment rising slightly from the 1996 level, but still well below the levels reported for 1994 and 1995. Then in 1998, partly a result of the financial crisis, SME employment fell further.

Table A.3 Small and Medium Enterprises in the Russian Economy

	1993	1994	1995	1996	1997	1998
Number of SMEs, Thousands Firms	865.0	896.9	877.3	841.7	861.1	868.0
SMEs Employment, Thousands Individuals	6,830	8,479	89,45	6,269	6515	6,208
SMEs: Share in Total Employment, Percent*	9.6	12.0	13.1	9.5	10.1	9.8

Source: Goskomstat.
*—authors' calculations

Selected Russian Regions

NOTES

1. See, for example, *Labour Statistics for a Market Economy. Challenges and Solutions in the Transition Countries and Eastern Europe and the Former Soviet Union,* ed. Igor Chernyshev (Budapest: CEU Press, 1995), or *Labour Market Dynamics in the Russian Federation,* ed. Douglas Lippoldt (Paris: OECD, 1997).

2. With respect to the analyses in this volume, the most important of these were the Goskomstat sources, such as the annual *Rossiysky statistichesky ezhegodnik* (Russian Statistical Yearbook), *Trud i zanyatost v Rossii* (Labour and Employment in Russia), *Sotsialnoye polozheniye i uroven zhizni naseleniya Rossii* (Social Situation and Living Standards); and the monthly *Sotcialno-economicheskoye polozheniye Rossii* (Socio-Economic Situation in Russia), among others. The State Employment Service issued a variety of publications, but we drew in particular on its annual employment programmes and semiannual bulletins with main indicators.

3. More details on the RET can be found on the Internet at: http://www.hhs.se/site/ret/ret.htm.

4. The LFS sample design is discussed succinctly in Tatyana Gorbacheva, "The Guidelines for the Transition of Russian Federation Statistics for the Study of Employment and Unemployment Through Labour Force Surveys," in *Labour Statistics for a Market Economy*, 143–152.

5. This section draws on Douglas Lippoldt and Sunder Magun, *Enhanced Labour Market Monitoring: Unemployment in the Russian Federation* (Paris: OECD, 1994).

6. Beginning in 1997, Goskomstat shifted to use a standard approach to coding and storing the data.

7. The TACIS-ACE project (no. T94-1073-R) was also supported by the OECD. Details concerning the regional LFS supplement are referenced in Hartmut Lehmann, Jonathan Wadsworth, and Alessandro Acquisti, "Grime and Punishment: Job Insecurity and Wage Arrears in the Russian Federation" (Bonn, IZA Discussion Paper no.65, October 1999), 3–4. The project was coordinated by H. Lehmann and team members included Ye. Gontmakher, I. Leiprecht, V. Starodubrovsky, J. Wadsworth, and R. Yemtsov and, on behalf of the OECD, D. Lippoldt.

8. For details on the typology, see Philip Hanson, "How Many Russias? Russia's Regions and Their Adjustment to Economic Change," *The International Spectator* 32, no. 1 (January–March 1997): 43–44. Note also that in figure 1 (below), due to space constraints, Moscow City and Moscow Oblast are simply shown as "Moscow." For additional information about the selection of the regions covered by the TACIS supplement, see Viktor Starodubrovsky, "Typology of Regional Labor Markets in the Russian Federation" (unpublished paper, Moscow, December 1996).

9. More detailed information on the survey is available on the Internet at: http://www.cpc.unc.edu/projects/rlms/rlms_home.html.

10. The project was coordinated by H. Lehmann and the team included A. Acquisti, V. Gimpelson, J. Konings, D. Lippoldt, and M. Schaffer.

11. A subsequent wave of data collection under the project yielded a more complete coverage in this regard for a later year.

12. This may be important if, as is likely, these factors contributed significantly to mismatch and thereby had an impact on labour turnover. See Vladimir Gimpelson and Douglas Lippoldt, "Labour Turnover in the Russian Economy," in *Labour Market Dynamics in the Russian Federation*, 17–55.

13. See, e.g., *The Russian Enterprise in Transition: Case Studies*, edited by Simon Clarke (Cheltanham: Edward Elgar, 1996), for a further example of the application of a case study approach in the study of Russian enterprises.

14. In Russian statistical publications, these firms are simply labelled as small enterprises.

15. See M. Gordon, "The Russian Economy: Notes from the Underground," *New York Times*, May 18, 1997.

References

Aghion, Philip, and Olivier Blanchard. "On the Speed of Transition in Central Europe." In *NBER Macroeconomics Annual 1994*, edited by Stanley Fischer and Julio Rotemberg, 283–320. Cambridge: MIT Press, 1994.

Alfandari, Gilles, and Mark Schaffer. "'Arrears' in the Russian Enterprise Sector." In *Enterprise Restructuring and Economic Policy in Russia*, edited by Simon Commander, Quimiao Fan, and Mark Schaffer, 87–139. Washington, D.C.: World Bank, 1996.

Aslund, Anders. "Social Problems and Policy in Postcommunist Russia." In *Sustaining the Transition: The Social Safety Net in Postcommunist Europe*, edited by Ethan Kapstein and Michael Mandelbaum, 124–46. New York: Council on Foreign Relations, 1997.

Aukutsionek, Sergey, and Rostislav Kapeliushnikov, "Rossiyskiye promyshlenniye predpriyatiya na rynke truda" (Russian Industrial Enterprises on the Labor Market). *Voprosy ekonomiki* 6 (1995): 48–56.

Bilsen, Valentijn, and Jozef Konings. "Job Creation, Job Destruction, and Growth of Newly Established, Privatized, and State-Owned Enterprises in Transition Economies: Survey Evidence from Bulgaria, Hungary, and Romania." *Journal of Comparative Economics* 26, no. 3 (September 1998): 429–445.

Boeri, Tito. "Unemployment Outflows and the Scope of Labour Market Policies in Central and Eastern Europe." In *Lessons from Labour Market Policies in the Transition Countries*, edited by Salvatore Zecchini, 445–47. Paris: OECD, 1996.

Boeri, Tito, Michael Burda, and Janos Kollo. *Mediating the Transition: Labour Markets in Central and Eastern Europe*. London–New York: CEPR-Institute for East-West Studies, 1998.

Boycko, Maxim, Andrey Shleifer, and Robert Vishny. *Privatizing Russia*. Cambridge, Mass., and London: MIT Press, 1995.

Brainerd, Elizabeth. "Winners and Losers in Russia's Transition." *American Economic Review* 88, no. 5 (December 1995): 1094–1116.

Chernyshev, Igor, ed. *Labour Statistics for a Market Economy*. Budapest: Central European University Press, 1994.

Clarke, Simon. "Structural Adjustment without Mass Unemployment?" In *Structural Adjustment without Mass Unemployment? Lessons from Russia*, edited by Simon Clarke, 9–86. Cheltenham: Edward Elgar Publishing, 1998.

——— . *The Formation of a Labour Market in Russia.* Cheltenham: Edward Elgar Publishing, 1999.

Clarke, Simon, and Veronika Kabalina. "The New Private Sector in the Russian Labour Market." *Europe-Asia Studies* 52, no. 1 (January 2000): 7–32.

Commander, Simon, and Fabrizio Coricelli, eds. *Unemployment, Restructuring and the Labour Market in Eastern Europe and Russia.* Washington, D.C.: World Bank, 1995.

Commander, Simon, Sumana Dhar, and Ruslan Yemtsov. "How Russian Firms Make Their Wage and Employment Decisions." In *Enterprise Restructuring and Economic Policy in Russia,* ed. Simon Commander, Qimiao Fan, and Mark Schaffer, 15–51. Washington, D.C.: World Bank, 1996.

Commander, Simon, Qimiao Fan, and Mark Schaffer, eds. *Enterprise Restructuring and Economic Policy in Russia.* Washington, D.C.: World Bank, 1996.

Commander, Simon, Une Lee, and Andrey Tolstopiatenko. "Social Benefits and the Russian Industrial Firm." In *Enterprise Restructuring and Economic Policy in Russia,* edited by Simon Commander, Qimiao Fan, and Mark Schaffer, 52–83. Washington, D.C.: World Bank, 1996.

Commander, Simon, John McHale, and Ruslan Yemtsov. "Russia." In *Unemployment, Restructuring, and the Labor Market in Eastern Europe and Russia,* edited by Simon Commander and Fabrizio Coricelli, 147–92. Washington, D.C.: World Bank, 1995.

Commander, Simon, and Mark Schankerman. "Enterprise Restructuring and the Efficient Provision of Social Benefits." In *The Changing Social Benefits in Russian Enterprises,* edited by Douglas Lippoldt, 115–30. Paris: OECD, 1996.

Commander, Simon, and Andrey Tolstopiatenko. "Unemployment, Restructuring and the Pace of the Transition." In *Lessons from the Economic Transition: Central and Eastern Europe in the 1990s,* edited by Salvatore Zecchini. 331–50. Paris, OECD, and Kluwer Academic Publishers, Dordrecht, Netherlands, 1997.

Cook, Linda. *Labour and Liberalisation: Trade Unions in the New Russia.* Twentieth Century Fund Press, 1997.

De Melo, Martha, Cevdet Denizer, Alan Gelb, and Stoyan Tenev. *Circumstance and Choice: The Role of Initial Conditions and Policies in Transition Economies.* Policy Research Working Paper no. 1866, Washington, D.C.: World Bank, December 1997.

Desai, Padma, and Todd Idson. "The Wage Arrears Crisis in Russia." Unpublished paper, Columbia University, 1997.

Doeringer, Peter, and Michael Piore. *Manpower Analysis and Internal Labor Markets.* Lexington, Mass.: Lexington Books, 1971.

Earle, John, Saul Estrin, and Larisa Leschenko. "Ownership Structures, Patterns of Control, and Enterprise Behavior in Russia." In *Enterprise Restructuring and Economic Policy in Russia,* edited by Simon Commander, Qimiao Fan, and Mark Schaffer, 205–52. Washington, D.C.: World Bank, 1996.

Earle, John, and Klara Sabirianova. "Wage Arrears in Russia: An Exploration of Causes and Consequences." Unpublished paper, Stockholm, SITE, 1998.

Employment and Unemployment in Economies in Transition: Conceptual and Measurement Issues. Paris: OECD, 1993.

Employment Outlook. Paris: OECD, various years.

Freeman, Richard. "What Direction for Labor Market Institutions in Eastern and Central Europe?" In *The Transition in Eastern Europe,* edited by Olivier Blanchard, Kenneth A.

Froot, and Jeffrey Sachs, 1–29. Chicago and London: University of Chicago Press, National Bureau of Economic Research Project Report, vol. 2, 1994.

Gaddy, Clifford, and Barri Ickes. "Russia's Virtual Economy." *Foreign Affairs* 77, no. 5 (September/October 1998): 53–67.

Gimpelson, Vladimir. *The Politics of Labour Market Adjustment: The Case of Russia.* Budapest: Collegium Budapest, Discussion Paper Series, no. 54, November 1998.

Gimpelson, Vladimir, and Douglas Lippoldt. *Labour Restructuring in Russian Enterprises: A Case Study.* Paris: OECD, 1996.

——— . "Labour Turnover in the Russian Economy." In *Labour Market Dynamics in the Russian Federation,* edited by Douglas Lippoldt, 17–55. Paris: OECD, 1997.

——— . "Labour Turnover in Russia: Evidence from the Administrative Reporting of Enterprises in Four Regions." Vienna: Institute for Advanced Studies, *Transition Economic Series,* no. 4, 1998.

——— . "Private Sector Employment in Russia: Scale, Composition and Performance (Evidence from the Russian Labour Force Survey)." *The Economics of Transition* 7, no. 2 (1999): 505–533.

Gordon, Leonid. "Polozheniye naemnykh rabotnikov v Rossii 90-kh godov" (Situation of Wage-Earners in Russia in 90s). *Sotcialno-trudovye issledovaniya,* no. 7, Moscow: IMEMO, 1997.

Grogan, Louise, and Van den Berg, Gerard. "The Duration of Unemployment in Russia." Discussion Paper no. TI 99-011/3, Amsterdam: Tinbergen Institute, January 1999.

Grosfeld, Irene, Cladia Senik-Leygonie, Thierry Verdier, Stanislav Kolenikov, Elena Paltseva. "Dynamism and Inertia on the Russian Labour Market. A Segmentation Model." Document no.1999–03. Paris: DELTA, April 1999.

Hirschman, Albert O. *Exit, Voice and Loyalty.* Cambridge: Harvard University Press, 1970.

Informatsionny bulleten VCIOM (VCIOM Information Bulleten. Economic and Social Change: Public Opinion Monitoring). Various issues, Moscow, 1992–2000.

Jackman, Richard, and Catalin Pauna. "Labour Market Policy and the Reallocation of Labour Across Sectors." In *Lessons from the Economic Transition: Central and Eastern Europe in the 1990s,* edited by Salvatore Zecchini, 373–92. Paris: OECD and Kluwer Academic Publishers, 1997.

Kapeliushnikov, Rostislav. "Job Turnover in a Transitional Economy: The Behaviour and Expectations of Russian Industrial Enterprises." In *Labour Market Dynamics in the Russian Federation,* edited by Douglas Lippoldt, 57–86. Paris: OECD, 1997.

——— . "Chto skryvaetsya za 'skrytoy bezrabotitsey'?" (What Is Hidden behind "Hidden" Unemployment?). In *Gosudarstvennaya i korporativnaya politika zanyatosti* (State and Corporative Employment Policy), edited by Tatyana Maleva, 75–111. Moscow: Moscow Carnegie Center, 1998.

——— . "Russian Labour Market: Adjustment without Restructuring." In *Issues on Theory of the Transition,* edited by Vladlen Martynov et al., 85–161. Moscow: IMEMO, 1999.

Konnings, Josef, Hartmut Lehmann, and Mark Schaffer. "Job Creation and Job Destruction in a Transition Economy: Ownership, Firm Size, and Gross Job Flows in Polish Manufacturing, 1988–91." *Labour Economics* 3, no. 3 (September 1996): 299–317.

Kornai, Janos. *The Socialist System: The Political Economy of Communism.* Princeton, N.J.: Princeton University Press, 1992.

————. "Transformational Recession: The Main Causes." *Journal of Comparative Economics* 19, no. 1 (August 1994): 39–63.

Layard Richard, Stephen Nickell, and Richard Jackman. *The Unemployment Crisis.* Oxford: Oxford University Press, 1994.

Layard, Richard, and Andrea Richter. "Labour Market Adjustment in Russia." *Russian Economic Trends* 3, no. 2 (1994): 85–103.

Lehmann, Hartmut, Jonathan Wadsworth, and Alessandro Acquisti. "Grime and Punishment: Job Insecurity and Wage Arrears in the Russian Federation." Bonn, IZA Discussion Paper no. 65, October 1999.

Lehmann, Hartmut, and Jonathan Wadsworth. "Tenures That Shook the World: Worker Turnout in Russia, Poland and Britain." Bonn, IZA Discussion Paper no. 90, December 1999.

Lindbeck, Assar, and Dennis Snower. *The Insider-Outsider Theory of Employment and Unemployment.* Cambridge: The MIT Press, 1998.

Lippoldt, Douglas, ed. *The Changing Social Benefits in Russian Enterprises.* Paris: OECD, 1996.

————. *Labour Market Dynamics in the Russian Federation.* Paris: OECD, 1997.

Magun, Vladimir. "Labor Culture." In *Russian Culture at the Crossroads: Paradoxes of Postcommunist Consciousness,* edited by Dmitry N. Shalin, 279–97. Boulder, Colo.: Westview Press, 1997.

Maleva, Tatyiana, ed. *Gosudarstvennaya i korporativnaya politika zanyatosti* (Moscow: Moscow Carnegie Center, 1998).

Mikhalev, Vladimir, and Nils Bjorgsten. *Wage Formation during the Period of Economic Restructuring in the Russian Federation.* Paris: OECD, 1995.

Milanovich, Branko. *Income, Inequality, and Poverty during the Transition from Planned to Market Economy.* Washington, D.C.: World Bank, 1998.

Nelson, Joan. "Organized Labor, Politics, and Labor Market Flexibility in Developing Countries." In *Labor Markets in an Era of Adjustment,* edited by Susan Horton, Ravi Kanbur, and Dipak Mazumdar, 347–75. Washington, D.C.: World Bank, 1995.

North, Douglas C. *The Contribution of the New Institutional Economics to an Understanding of the Transition Problem.* WIDER Annual Lectures 1, Helsinki, WIDER/UNU, March 1997.

Obzor ekonomitcheskoy politiki v Rossii za 1998 god (Survey of the Economic Policy of Russia in 1998). Moscow: Bureau of Economic Analysis, 1999.

OECD Economic Surveys: The Russian Federation 1995. Paris: OECD, 1995.

OECD Economic Surveys: The Russian Federation 1997. Paris: OECD, 1997.

The OECD Jobs Study: Facts, Analysis, Strategies. Paris: OECD, 1994.

The OECD Jobs Study. Part II. Paris: OECD, 1995.

Przeworsky, Adam. "Economic Reforms, Public Opinion, and Political Institutions: Poland in Eastern European Perspective." In Luiz Carlos Bresser Perreira, Jose Maria Maravall, and Adam Przeworsky, 132–98. *Economic Reform in New Democracies: A Social-Democratic Approach.* Cambridge: Cambridge University Press, 1993.

Radayev, Vadim. "Small Enterprises in Russia: Current Status and Development Policy." Unpublished paper, Paris: OECD, 1996.

Richter, Andrea, and Mark Schaffer. "The Performance of De Novo Private Firms in Russian Manufacturing." In *Enterprise Restructuring and Economic Policy in Russia,* edited by Simon Commander, Qimiao Fan, and Mark Schaffer, 253–74. Washington, D.C.: World Bank, 1996.

Rose, Richard. "Evaluating Workplace Benefits: The Views of Russian Employees." In *The Changing Social Benefits in Russian Enterprises,* edited by Douglas Lippoldt, 39–60. Paris: OECD, 1995.

———. *Getting Things Done in an Anti-Modern Society: Social Capital Networks in Russia.* Studies in Public Policy, no. 304, Centre for the Study of Public Policy, University of Strathclyde, Glasgow, Scotland, 1998.

Rossiya v tsifrakh (Russia in Figures). Moscow: Goskomstat, various years.

Rossiyskiy statisticheskiy ezhegodnik (Russian Statistical Yearbook). Moscow: Goskomstat, various years.

Russian Economic Trends. Working Centre for Economic Reform and RECEP, various monthly and quarterly editions, 1992–2000.

Sabirianova, Klara. "Makroekonomichesky analyz dynamicheskikh izmenenyi na rossiyskom rynke truda" (Microeconomic Analysis of Labor Market Dynamics in Russia). *Voprosy ekonomiki,* no. 1 (January 1998): 42–58.

Shleifer, Andrei, and Daniel Treisman. *Without a Map. Political Tactics and Economic Reform in Russia.* Cambridge: The MIT Press, 2000.

Sotsialno-economitcheskoye polozhenie Possii (Social-Economic Situation of Russia). Moscow: Goskomstat, various years and issues.

Sotcialno-trudovye issledovanya (Social-Labour Studies). Moscow: IMEMO, various issues, 1994–1998.

Standing, Guy. "Why Measured Unemployment in Russia Is So Low: The Net with Many Holes." *Journal of European Social Policy* 4, no. 1 (1994): 35–49.

———. *The "Shake-Out" in Russian Factories: The RLFS Fifth Round.* Geneva, ILO, Labour Market Papers, no. 14, 1995.

———. *Russian Unemployment and Enterprise Restructuring. Reviving Dead Souls.* London: Macmillan Press, 1996.

Stiglitz, Joseph E. *More Instruments and Broader Goals: Moving toward the Post-Washington Consensus.* WIDER Annual Lectures 2, Helsinki, WIDER/UNU, January 1998.

A Study of the Soviet Economy, vol. 2. Paris: IMF/WB/OECD/EBRD, 1991.

Transition Report 1997. London: EBRD, 1997.

Transition Report 1998. London: EBRD, 1998.

Trud i zanyatost v Rossii (Labour and Employment in Russia). Moscow: Goskomstat, various years.

Vaughan-Whitehead, Daniel, ed. *Paying the Price. The Wage Crisis in Central and Eastern Europe.* London: Macmillan Press, 1998.

World Development Report 1996. Washington, D.C.: World Bank, 1996.

Zecchini, Salvatore, ed. *Lessons from the Economic Transition: Central and Eastern Europe in the 1990s.* Paris: OECD and Kluwer Academic Publishers, 1997.

Index

active labour market programs, 146, 150, 153, 154, 201

administrative leaves (unpaid leaves), 18–19, 43, 48, *50*, 51, 71, 81, 91, 108, 111

Alfandari, Gilles, 123n40, 167, 177

Alesina, Alberto, 7

arrears, xiii, 6–7, 9, *50*, 52, 90, 123n40, 130, 132–33, 160, 162, 170, 194; inter-enterprise, 132, 167; tax–, xiii, 86, 132; budget–, 5, 128, 133; wage-, 5–7, 10, 20, 71, 74, 80–81, 84, 93, 108, 113–14, *115*, 119, 125, 129, 131–38, 140–42, 143n19, 165–67, 173–74, 176–80, 183, 185–88, 194–96

Aslund, Anders, 130

Aukutsionek, Sergey, 42, 56

bankruptcy, xiii, 66, 90, 113, 185, 194

barter, 5, 6, 9, 52, 177

Blanchard, Oliver, 2

Boeri, Tito, 32

Brainerd, Elisabeth, 130, 137

budget constraints, 2, 9, 66, 89–90, 93, 128, 136, 141, 165

case study, 16, 65, 67–68, 86, 93n1, 202, 208–9

Charap, Joshua, 101

churning, 6, 10, 28, 42, 58, 148, 194

Clarke, Simon, 96n33, 183, 212n13

collective agreement, 78, 84, 129

collective bargaining, 12–13, 20, 84–85, 129, 199

Colton, Timothy, 186

Commander, Simon, 17, 37, 47, 85, 105, 121n18, 148, 158, 163n3

Connor, Walter, 180

Constitution of the Russian Federation (1993), 7, 168

Cook, Linda, 96n33

corporate governance, 65–66, 90, 199

corruption, 6, 176

CPI, 4, 96n24, 136. *See also* inflation

De Melo, Martha, 4

deskilling, 73, 94n9

discouraged workers, 33

Earle, John, 101, 134, 178

economically active population (EAP), 6, 32–33, 103. *See also* labor force participation

education, 8, 17, 22n32, 38–39, 57–58, 108, 115, 117–18, 137

elections, 127, 167, 170, 173, 186

employment: informal, 10, 103, 126, 195; part-time, 105, 111, 113, 119, 122n38, 201, 207; private sector, 99–101, *102*, 104; to population ratio, 14, 18; in public sector, 38–39, *102*, 174, 175, 176; secondary, 10, 105, 112, 126, 195–96; short-time, 8, 105; in SME, 103; subsidised, *153*, 155; temporary, 150

About the Authors

Vladimir Gimpelson, Ph.D., is a senior research associate with the Institute of World Economy and International Relations, the Russian Academy of Sciences, in Moscow. He is also a research fellow at the Institute of Sociology, Moscow, Russia, and at the Institute for the Study of Labour (IZA), Bonn, Germany. During the mid-1990s, he worked as a consultant in a number of OECD projects and, later, as a senior fellow at the Collegium Budapest. In 1998-1999, he taught as a visiting professor at the University of Tokyo, Japan. Since the early 1990s, he has specialised in the Russian economic transition, with particular emphasis on labour market and political economy issues. He has published about 100 papers in journals and collective volumes.

Douglas Lippoldt is an international economist at the Organisation for Economic Co-Operation and Development in Paris (1992-present). He works as a contributing author for the annual *Employment Outlook* publication and as a member of teams conducting national labour market policy reviews. Previously, he was an international economist in the U.S. Department of Labor and the U.S. Bureau of Labor Statistics. During the 1990s, he managed a range of technical cooperation projects in transition countries, focusing particularly on the Russian Federation. He is author/editor of a substantial number of papers and several books on labour market developments in transition and OECD countries. He co-authored the present volume in a personal capacity.

V. Gimpelson (left), D. Lippoldt (right)